W9-CHZ-693

GUY FIERI FAMILY FOOD

Guy Fieri Family Food

125 REAL-DEAL RECIPES

Kitchen Tested, Home Approved

GUY FIERI

With Marah Stets

wm

WILLIAM MORROW

An Imprint of HarperCollins*Publishers*

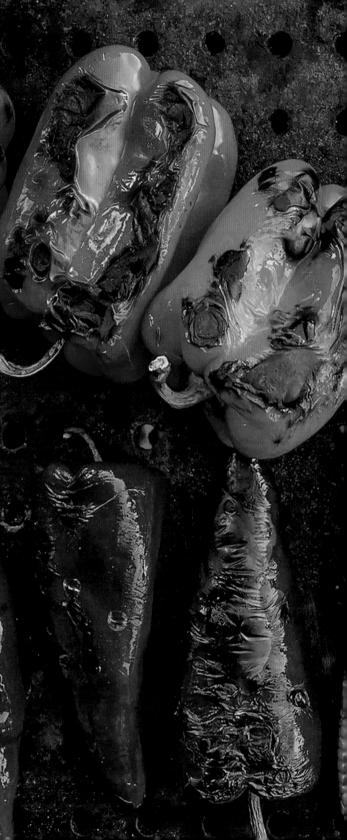

***NEW YORK TIMES* Bestsellers by Guy Fieri**

GUY ON FIRE

GUY FIERI FOOD

DINERS, DRIVE-INS AND DIVES:
The Funky Finds in Flavortown

MORE DINERS, DRIVE-INS AND DIVES:
A Drop-Top Culinary Cruise Through America's Finest and Funkiest Joints

DINERS, DRIVE-INS AND DIVES:
An All-American Road Trip . . . with Recipes!

HarperCollins books may be purchased for educational, business, or sales promotional use. For information please e-mail the Special Markets Department at SPsales @harpercollins.com.

FIRST EDITION

Illustrations by Joe Leonard
Photographs by Aubrie Pick, except pages xiii, 15, 17, 93, 98, 131, 187, and 218: courtesy of the Fieri family; page 19 (Guy and Jimmy John) and 189: courtesy of Food Network; page 25 (trophy) by Cassie Jones

Library of Congress Cataloging-in-Publication Data has been applied for.

ISBN 978-0-06-224473-4 (hardcover)
ISBN 978-0-06-265306-2 (B&N signed edition)
ISBN 978-0-06-266245-3 (BAM signed edition)
ISBN 978-0-06-266836-3 (FNS signed edition)

16 17 18 19 20 INDD/QDG 10 9 8 7 6 5 4 3 2 1

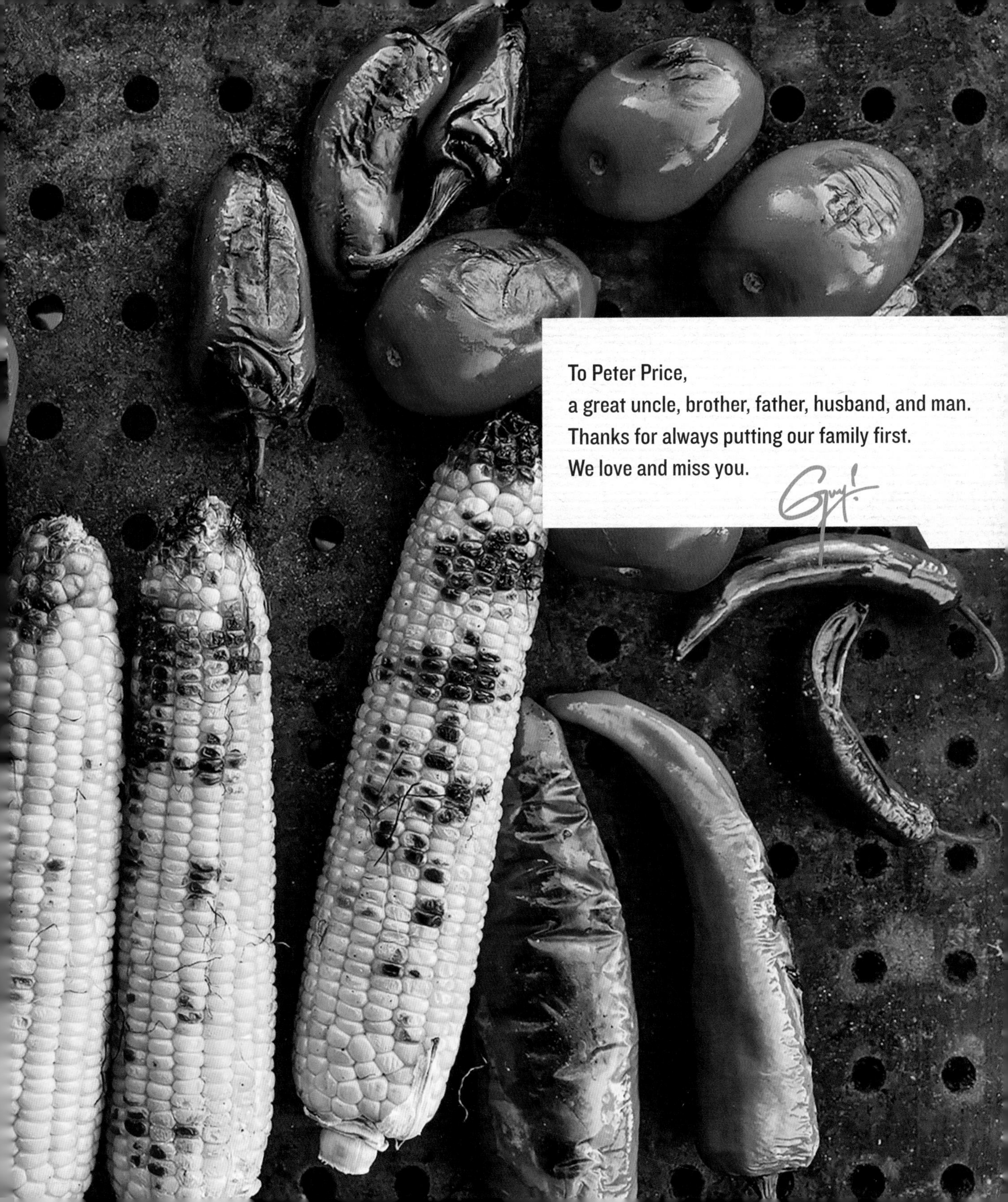

To Peter Price,
a great uncle, brother, father, husband, and man.
Thanks for always putting our family first.
We love and miss you.
Guy!

Buffalo Chicken Soup (page 138)

Contents

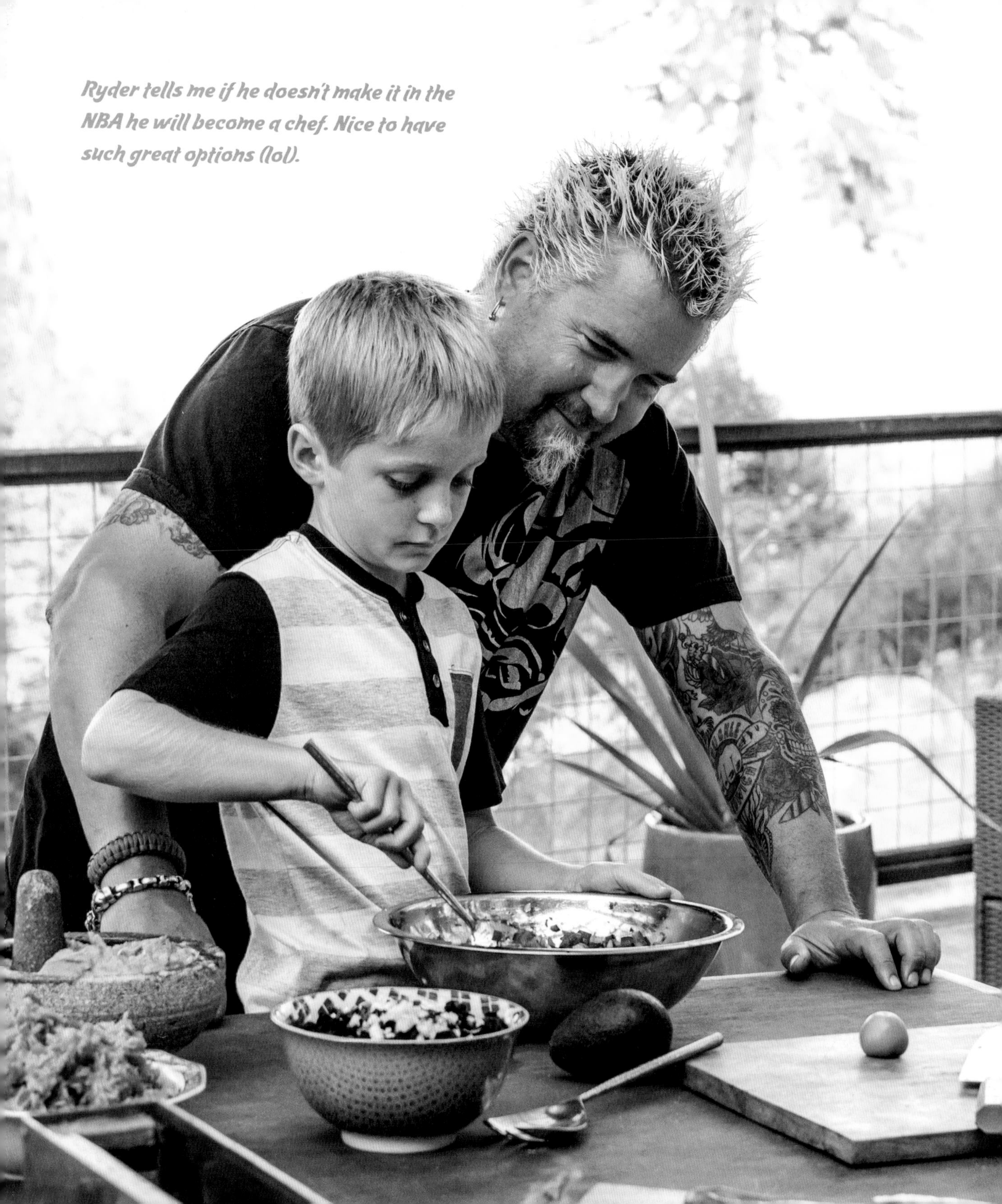

Ryder tells me if he doesn't make it in the NBA he will become a chef. Nice to have such great options (lol).

Foreword

A Few Words from Guy's Dad, Jim

When our kids were young, my wife, Penny, and I closed up our saddle shop in Ferndale, California, every evening by five thirty and headed home to cook dinner. Almost every night Guy and his younger sister, Morgan, were home at six to set the table and eat dinner. We were lucky to live in a town with a one-block-long Main Street that had everything from a bank to a grocery store, so we could stop on the way home to pick up whatever provisions we needed and still have dinner on the table before the sun set.

By the time he was in middle school, Guy was making dinner at least a couple of nights a week. This was less because of a blossoming passion for cooking than because of a household rule that excused whoever made dinner from washing the dishes afterward. A rule that did not exist, by the way, until Penny and I noticed that every evening at the same time our son suddenly had an urgent need to see a man about a horse, if you know what I mean. These bathroom visits would last just long enough for the final pot to be dried and put away.

Now, I know that if Guy were writing this, he'd say that making dinner himself was the only way he could get an alternative to his parents' forays into macrobiotic and vegetarian cooking, and that learning to cook was the result of a finely tuned survival instinct. I'm here to set the record straight: Guy Fieri learned to cook when he was a kid because we wouldn't let him get out of doing the damn dishes every night.

Guy is not the first in our family to learn to cook out of "necessity," no matter how broadly that term is defined. The traditions of Guy's two grandfathers reverberate every day in the life that he and Lori have built for themselves and their boys. My father, Louis Angelo Ferry (it was he who Anglicized "Fieri," our original surname, in the 1930s), was effectively orphaned at the age of two when his mother died. This was at a time when widowed fathers didn't typically take up the mantle and raise their kids alone, so Louis bounced around among various family members for a while, and eventually landed with his uncle, Zio Amelio (*zio* is Italian for "uncle").

It was no soft landing by today's standards. For a while he traveled and worked with Amelio, then with a cook for an Ohio road crew. Louis left school after finishing the sixth grade—not so unusual in 1920s Appalachia—and he and Amelio became coal miners. By the time he was a young man, Dad was making his living as a traveling salesman. I guess being on the move was second nature to him by then. When he was home on weekends he'd cook enough to get him through several days out on the road.

On the other side of the family, Penny's dad, Henry Price, also grew up poor. He put himself through law school at Emory University by working in food prep and made his living thereafter as a lawyer. For decades, his method of making dinner went something like this:

6:00 P.M.: Think about fixing dinner.
7:00 P.M.: Go to store for ingredients for dinner.
8:00 P.M.: Return to store to pick up ingredients forgotten during first trip to the store.
9:30 P.M.: Wake the kids—it's time to eat!

It reminds me just a little of a guy I know well, although our Guy's timing is more civilized . . . at least on most nights. And when he knows travel is coming that's going to keep him away from home, the sight of Guy cooking up a storm to keep Lori and the kids going for a few nights without him is like going back through time and catching a glimpse of my dad preparing enough food to keep him sustained during a busy week on the road.

So Guy didn't fall far from the family tree when it comes to habits or timing, but neither did he miss the lessons Penny and I tried to impart, I'm happy to say. In spite of his well-known affectionate ribbing about the "krazy" healthy food we allegedly forced our kids to eat, today he has a profound respect for all kinds of food, a deep understanding of food systems, and an innate sense of how crucial it is to treat food and eating with respect, so that we can foster the social interactions that are the lifeblood of family and friendships.

People often ask Penny and me, "Aren't you proud of what Guy has done?" If they're asking about his material success, I don't think he ever explicitly strove for that part. The truth is that when Guy was a kid he never fully realized how little money we had, or that there were things we couldn't do because we were being frugal and saving. I don't think our children noticed because we were privileged to live in a small town where everyone seemed to know and look out for everyone else, and there was always a helping hand for a person in need. It was the kind of place where being home to eat dinner with your family every night instead of going out to eat all the time or spending your money on big trips was simply what people did.

That nightly ritual of family dinner allowed Penny and me to really know our children, and them to really know us. The kids heard a lot from us about love, respect, humility . . . and the lasting benefits of compounding interest. The connection between these might not seem obvious at first, but I firmly believe in imparting to kids a healthy respect for the money they can earn and an understanding of what they can do with it. If you treat your money wisely and well, then someday you might be able to help someone out who really needs it, and that's really the crux of it all, isn't it?

For his part, Guy has let his insatiable interest in food and cooking and his instinctive generosity lead him in a direction that actually benefits other people. He was doing this from the time he opened his very first restaurant, when Penny and I used to think he spent as much time coaching and counseling employees who came to him with personal concerns as he did managing them at their jobs. But those humble beginnings put him on his current path, where among other things he is able to shine an extraordinarily large spotlight on a lot of mom-and-pop restaurants across the country, giving many of them a chance at a level of success they wouldn't otherwise have.

So, ask me whether I'm proud of all that Guy has done to use his hard-earned platform day and night to help people, and I'll say yeah, I'm phenomenally proud of my son—not just for that, but because he's never lost sight of what's most important in life: family, friends, and the art of eventually getting dinner on the table. That's a legacy any father would be proud of.

Introduction

People often assume that because of my crazy travel and work schedule, when I'm at home the very last thing I want to do is cook. Man, that could not be further from the truth. When I'm at home, especially after I've been away for a while, I feel a genuine obligation to gear up and get cooking . . . for my family. Of course there are some times when I, just like anybody else, feel exhausted from the demands of the outside world. But even when I'm tired, cooking is one of the things that I do best. A family is like a village—it runs optimally when everyone does their job. My job? Make great food.

But there's something more, something beyond the practical when-Dad's-here-he-makes-dinner level. It's that **cooking is the finest way I know to celebrate and honor my family.** It's kinda like I'm putting my arms around all of them and telling them how thankful I am to—and for—them. I'm saying thanks for being here, thanks for holding down the fort while I was away, I love you guys. . . . Here's some Bacon-Roasted Turkey with Scalloped Potatoes and Caramelized Balsamic Brussels Sprouts (page 101). Forget greeting cards and flowers—*this* is the way to go.

On nights when I'm home, it's my greatest joy to cook for and then sit down with the whole crew—my wife, our kids, my parents (they live right next door!), and the kids' cousins when they're around—and eat together. Even better is when I can get some of them in on the preparation action, which is when we whip out dishes like the ones in the All Hands on Deck chapter (page 158). But even when it's mostly just me doing the cooking, knowing that it means that we'll all be sitting down together is the greatest gift I can give *and receive.* That's the origin of this book. It's the food I like to feed my family to engage them, to show how much I appreciate them, to bring them together—and also because they're hungry.

I've gotta take a moment here to say that I think that in a world where the distractions for kids and adults alike just get more and more enticing, we owe it to ourselves and our families to shut all that down for a little while and just be together at the dinner table. This time is critical to talk about our experiences, decompress from outside stresses, and recharge. When I was a kid, there was no acceptable excuse for my sister and me not to be at the table at six every night. Granted, for our kids today it's more like seven thirty and it's not quite every night—what with practices, work, and twenty-first-century life—but the idea is the same. Come together, talk about your day, be accountable to the other people in the house (this is *so* important as they grow into teenagers, believe me), and, crucially, *enjoy each other.* This isn't about one dinner, man, it's about our whole society!

Okay, off my soapbox. The point is that I've tried to pull together here a collection of my most legit cooking, creative recipes, and outside-the-box ideas, in the hopes that I can reinforce strong family bonds for all of us. I will consider this book a success if it inspires you and your family not only to cook some real-deal food but also to spend time together.

Maybe you'll look at the All Hands on Deck chapter with your kids and they'll say, "Let's make tamales and kebabs together!" Or The Brick Burger (page 26) in the Sandwiches & Burgers chapter will make your kids' mouths water. Or the Grains & Greens chapter will move you to include more of these crazy-good—and crazy-good-for-you—foods into your regular dinner rotation. Or the off-da-hook recipes in Guy Outta Bounds will make all of you say, "Yeah! That looks like a good time!"

You know, another question people ask me all the time is where's my favorite place to eat. I hope this book will help make your answer the same as mine: where my family is, right at home.

Hunter's high school graduation, 2015.

The Equipment Guy'd

A band can't play a concert without its instruments, a racecar driver won't win any races without a car, and no one is going to enjoy preparing dinner without the right tools for the job. You definitely don't need a zillion-dollar culinary arsenal, but you'll be a lot more excited to roll up your sleeves and get cooking if you have a few key pieces of equipment. So here's what I want with me if I'm ever stranded on a desert island.

Wait. Desert islands have kitchens, right?

Knives. The most important tools in the kitchen are good knives. You don't need dozens, but at a minimum get yourself the best chef's, paring, and serrated bread knives you can. The thing to know about good knives is that the structure of the blade is strong, but the sharp edge is delicate. So treat your knives well. Sharpen them regularly—you can do it at home or take them to a reputable knife sharpener from time to time—and use a sharpening steel often to keep the blade honed. Don't store knives in a drawer unless their blades are protected, because repeatedly bumping into other tools will dull them more quickly. And when you scrape chopped ingredients off a cutting board, use the back side of the knife rather than the blade side.

Tongs. If a good knife is first, tongs are the second most important kitchen implement by a very thin margin. (Now, if I could just figure out a way to get tongs with a *blade,* it'd be my ideal version of a Swiss army knife. . . .) Tongs are like an extension of your hand, so it's crucial that they be reliable. They've gotta be comfortable to hold, have good spring, and be firm and strong enough that you can move around a hot pan with them. There are all different kinds—long handled, short handled, with straighter heads for grasping or cupped heads for tossing ingredients, and with heads made of poly or silicone so they can be safely used in nonstick pans. There's pretty much a set of tongs for every kind of job—the key is to make sure you don't waste your money on poorly made ones!

Pots and pans. You absolutely don't need a huge collection of pots and pans to make great food. The bare-bones basics are one small and one large saucepan, a sturdy skillet, and a wide, straight-sided sauté pan with a lid—all made from good-quality stainless steel is fine. Beyond those, a handful of other pots and pans are fundamental to a well-stocked kitchen.

Eight-inch nonstick skillet. When all you want is a quick-and-easy omelet but all you've got is a 12-inch stainless steel skillet, you're less likely to cook and more likely to order takeout. Don't balk at the nonstick—it's not what it was thirty years ago when we were all terrified that the surfaces would chip and we'd be eating chemicals. Today's nonstick pans are made of safe, strong materials. They're very forgiving if you want to cook with just a little oil, and it's a breeze to clean them.

Twelve-inch cast-iron skillet. These timeless pans are ridiculously affordable and incredibly resilient, much more so than most of the fancy-nancy pans on the market. I know people who are using the very same skillet their grandmother cooked on. This is the perfect pan for searing steak and making hash, and it's the only pan that is as useful in a regular kitchen as it is on an outdoor fire pit.

Enameled cast-iron Dutch oven. For long-simmered Sunday gravy, big batches of beans, beef stew, Super Bowl chili, chowder for a crowd—or you name it—a 5- to 7-quart heavy-lidded Dutch oven is on point.

Stockpot with a tight-fitting lid. These come in sizes from 8 to 20 quarts and beyond, and the lid helps to intensify the heat in the pot and expedite the cooking process. If you think the stockpot you have is the right size, get one that's 4 quarts bigger. Once you get into the habit of making stocks and big pots of stew, you'll find that you can always find a reason to make more.

Pressure cooker. I love this pot so much I wrote a whole chapter about it (see Under Pressure, page 202). I won't say anything more here—don't want to steal my own thunder, ya know?—except that this is the most efficient kitchen tool there is.

Sturdy baking sheets. The most ideal type is sturdy, rimmed, and measures around 18 x 13 inches—it's called a half sheet pan.

It's good for everything from baking cookies and roasting meat and vegetables to all sorts of prep work like draining fried food and quickly cooling cooked grains. They're workhorses; it's worth having a few of these.

Thermometers. I hate to think about people spending lots of time and money carefully choosing and preparing great ingredients and then missing out on the best possible results because of one intangible—almost invisible—but incredibly important element: temperature. We can't see it, so it's easy to think it doesn't matter, but when we're baking, the oven temperature is critical; when we're frying, the temperature of the oil is critical; and when we're roasting a chicken, its internal temperature is critical. Ya picking up on a theme here? You need thermometers!

First, get yourself a good oven thermometer—two, if possible. The temperature you "set" your oven to is not always the actual temperature inside. Plus, conventional ovens have hotter and cooler areas, so a couple of thermometers will let you see where these "zones" are. (Convection ovens mitigate hot and cold zones somewhat with a blowing fan that circulates the heat more evenly.)

And for taking the temperature of your roasting or grilling meat, get a great digital instant-read thermometer. There are all sorts of different models—you can get one that you use at the moment you need a temperature reading or you can get one with a probe that remains in the food during cooking and sends the temperature reading to an external source, either via a temperature-safe tether to a small monitor outside the pot or oven or even by Bluetooth to your phone. The only kind I'm not a big fan of is a bimetallic thermometer with a dial display. These need to be calibrated or you just can't trust 'em. That said, it's better than nothing, and I'm definitely not a fan of nothing.

Wooden spoons. I don't have to tell you what these are for, right? I'll just focus on what I recommend you look for in this crucial bit of equipment. You don't need dozens of wooden spoons, but a few nice thick ones of various lengths and shapes are useful, just like with spatulas. You want long handles so that you can reach the very bottom of big pots of food. (A little shout-out here to proper stirring technique: Stir from the bottom of the pot! That is, unless you've forgotten to stir for a while and the bottom is burned. In that case, let that stuff stay down there and stir just above it so that you don't mess up the whole batch with burned bits.)

Silicone or rubber spatulas. In a restaurant kitchen, if we left behind all the stuff that clings to the sides of every jar of tomato paste, sour cream, and mustard, it'd actually add up to enough lost money to affect our bottom line. This is the kind of thing that got me obsessed with making sure I always have a selection of really good silicone or rubber spatulas on hand. At home you don't need quite the arsenal of a restaurant kitchen, of course, but it's good to have at least a few heat-resistant spatulas of various sizes and shapes. They're good not only for scraping clean every jar, can, or bowl you use, but also for stirring, mixing, and folding ingredients. Make sure you have at least one with a long handle for cooking—it keeps your stirring hand safe from the heat.

Metal spatula. A high-quality regular metal spatula is good to have, for sure, but my true preference for most jobs is a nice long metal fish spatula. With its thin, oversized head, it's good for flipping all sorts of foods, not just fish. You want one that's sturdy enough to hold a substantial burger but not so stiff that it doesn't have any give; a little flexibility and a thin blade make it easier to get it under the food that needs flipping.

Cutting boards. I love beautiful wood cutting boards, but to be honest, they're not the most practical choice. In my opinion, you'll get the most bang for your buck with a good poly board. Not ceramic, not glass, not anything with a hard surface that's going to dull your knives. I recommend having somewhere between three and five boards that are the biggest size you can get that'll still fit in your sink, dishwasher, and the cabinet where they're stored. The color-coded ones are great to help ensure that you don't put the salad ingredients on the board you just used to cut the raw chicken.

Mandoline. Nothing beats this tool for cutting vegetables into perfectly even, thin slices. I talk more about it (with pictures!) on page 126.

Pizza cutter. When you eat as much delicious pizza as my family does, you've gotta have a good, sharp rolling pizza cutter. If you need a reason to buy one, check out the recipes beginning on page 187.

Pepper grinder. Nothing compares to the flavor and aroma of freshly ground pepper—store-bought pre-ground black pepper isn't even in the same league. If you're still buying it, do yourself a big favor and go out (or online) right now and get a good pepper grinder—I love Turkish grinders—and whole peppercorns instead. You'll never go back to that sawdust-in-a-bag again.

I'll mention here that for grinding more than a tablespoon or two of pepper or for any other spice, an electric spice grinder is the way to go (see page 80).

Citrus press. It bums me out when someone juices lemons, limes, or other citrus with anything other than a serious citrus press. All I can think about is what's being left behind and wasted. There's some family lore around oranges that I think makes me particularly sensitive to this. My gramps Henry Price grew up dirt poor. And I mean that literally—they had dirt floors in their house in Georgia. One year Gramps (long before anyone called him that) scraped together what little money he had to buy a case of oranges, and he gave an orange to each of his (seventeen!) brothers and sisters for Christmas. When I think about how precious the gift of a single orange was to them, it makes me determined never to waste a single drop. A good citrus press will literally turn the peel inside out, so there's no question you've gotten every bit of juice. Gramps would appreciate that.

Microblade zester/grater. I probably reach for one of these every time I cook, to add a bit of citrus zest to a dressing, to grate a little ginger for a sauté, to shred a carrot so that it melts into a sauce, or to top a bowl of pasta with a light dusting of Parmesan cheese. Ideally you'll have two or three rasp graters with grating surfaces ranging from fine to coarse. It's important to store them with their guards on to keep the blades from getting bent (and to keep everyone's fingers safe—those buggers are sharp!).

(One quick note about grated cheese in the recipes: Most cheese is listed in the ingredients by weight, because that's generally how it's bought, followed by a grated volume. For hard cheeses such as Parmesan, the grated volume given is based on what is essentially ground cheese, like what you get if you buy it from the cheese counter at the grocery store. If you use a microblade or fine rasp grater at home to grate hard cheese, the volume will be greater than what you buy pre-grated in the store.)

Vegetable peeler. A sharp peeler that is comfortable for you to hold is a must-have for quickly and easily peeling the skin off many fruits and vegetables. This tool is also good for shaving thin strips of hard cheeses such as Parmesan or ricotta salata and slicing vegetables like carrots into long ribbons.

Colanders and strainers. One big colander is a necessity for everything from draining cooked pasta and vegetables to steaming tamales (see page 163). It's even better to have a couple of them; collapsible colanders are great if you have limited storage. Mesh strainers are good for rinsing and draining smaller amounts of food such as canned beans as well as straining stock and rinsing grains. A medium-mesh strainer is a general-purpose workhorse. It's nice to also have one with fine mesh for straining things like sauces, although in a pinch you can line a medium-mesh strainer with a coffee filter.

Salad spinner. I can't stand wet greens. If they're in a salad, dressing runs off the lettuce and pools uselessly at the bottom of the bowl. If they're in a sauté, the extra moisture causes the hot oil to spit and spatter. Greens that are to be cooked should have water clinging to them when they go into the pot only if the recipe says so; otherwise, you want well-dried greens to begin. And the best way to get a few extra days of storage on fresh herbs is to rinse them well, dry them completely, and keep them in an airtight container in the refrigerator. A good salad spinner doesn't cost much; it'll save you from using bunches of paper towels; and it helps keep fresh greens contained, lessening the risk that they'll come in contact with raw meats or other cross contaminants.

High-powered blender. It might appear from the outside that all blenders are created equal, but they most definitely are not, and the difference between one style and all the others leads me in this instance to suggest a single tool that might, admittedly, cost the equivalent of a down payment on a car. But just because a car has four wheels and a windshield doesn't mean it can race Le Mans, and just because a blender has a blade and motor doesn't mean it can go the distance in the kitchen. There's nothing more irritating than having a blender full of stuff that your machine can't blend. It's a mess. There's only one blender on the consumer retail market that really gets the job done, and it's the Vitamix (I'm *not* getting paid for this!). Take it from me: it's worth every penny.

Immersion or stick blender. Now, here's a seriously useful tool that doesn't get anywhere near the respect it should. With just a few presses of a button, an immersion blender can turn lumpy gravy silky smooth or create creamy texture in a soup right in the pot (check it: Lentil Dal Chowder with Grilled Garlic Naan, page 150). They're lightweight, dishwasher safe, and inexpensive. Many even come with attachments that transform them into mini food processors or electric whisks.

SANDWICHES
& BURGERS

The Ultimate Guy'd to the Ultimate Food

Some people think of sandwiches only as a convenience food—the sort of quickie meal that you prepare when you're on the run. Not me. Sandwiches and burgers are my sweet spot, whether we're in one of my restaurants, where they sell like crazy, or in my house, where Hunter and Ryder eat them like crazy. As you'll see from the "101s" and recipes in this chapter, **I probably have more to say about sandwiches and burgers than the average person.** Sure, I agree that we as a nation should probably eat less bread and meat. And yes, it's true that I will sometimes make sandwiches at lunchtime that threaten to put my family into a food coma. But the key word there is *sometimes*. The point is that my philosophy is *always* that sandwiches don't have to be ordinary, throwaway meals. Do them right and treat them with some respect, and **they will be righteous!**

The Origins of an Obsession

Mom and Dad say we only lived without a fully working fridge for a few months, not a full year. I say when they write their book, they can tell their version.

I can't say for sure, but my sandwich obsession might have its roots in that crazy period of my childhood (by which I mean the whole thing) when we didn't really have a lot of deli meat at home. My periodically vegetarian parents didn't believe that deli meats were "good" for us, so they didn't buy them for us. Truth is, we didn't even have a working fridge for a whole year, so we wouldn't have had anywhere to store them anyway. When it broke, as refrigerators sometimes do, Dad didn't repair it, as people sometimes do—at least not in the traditional way that people repair things. He "fixed" that fridge by cutting a hole in the bottom of it and in the floor below it. He secured a screen in there to keep the mice out, and then he just let the basement air come up to cool the box! (Freaked me out!)

Now, they also had a saddle shop uptown in my original hometown of Ferndale, California. There they had a perfectly good refrigerator that had no hole in its bottom and used regular electricity to stay nice and cold. And you know what else was in that fridge? Salami, ham, mayonnaise, mustard, great bread—all sorts of amazing fixings for fabulous sandwiches. See, Mom and Dad knew that if they provided delicious lunches for their employees, they would happily eat at work and stay on the floor during the lunch hour, when everyone else in town came out of work to do their shopping. Clever, right?

I'm also clever. And such a junkie for sandwiches that I left school at lunch every day and rode my bike uptown to the store so that I could raid their cold refrigerator for the ingredients for my lunch. I skipped recess for years just so I could get a killer deli sandwich! You know, now that I think about it, maybe Mom and Dad knew exactly what they were doing with that whole "broken" fridge thing . . . hmmm?

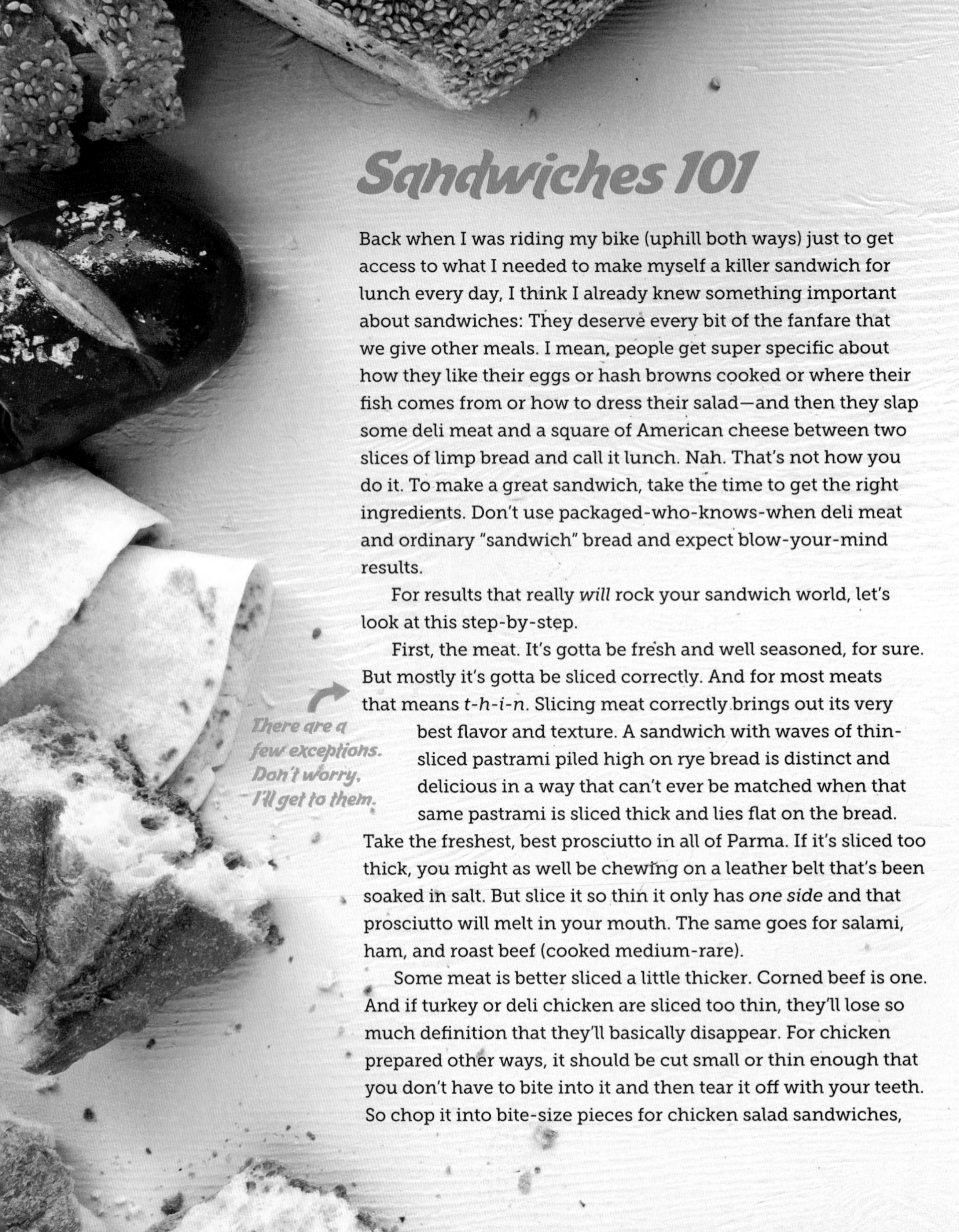

Sandwiches 101

Back when I was riding my bike (uphill both ways) just to get access to what I needed to make myself a killer sandwich for lunch every day, I think I already knew something important about sandwiches: They deserve every bit of the fanfare that we give other meals. I mean, people get super specific about how they like their eggs or hash browns cooked or where their fish comes from or how to dress their salad—and then they slap some deli meat and a square of American cheese between two slices of limp bread and call it lunch. Nah. That's not how you do it. To make a great sandwich, take the time to get the right ingredients. Don't use packaged-who-knows-when deli meat and ordinary "sandwich" bread and expect blow-your-mind results.

For results that really *will* rock your sandwich world, let's look at this step-by-step.

First, the meat. It's gotta be fresh and well seasoned, for sure. But mostly it's gotta be sliced correctly. And for most meats that means *t-h-i-n*. Slicing meat correctly brings out its very best flavor and texture. A sandwich with waves of thin-sliced pastrami piled high on rye bread is distinct and delicious in a way that can't ever be matched when that same pastrami is sliced thick and lies flat on the bread. Take the freshest, best prosciutto in all of Parma. If it's sliced too thick, you might as well be chewing on a leather belt that's been soaked in salt. But slice it so thin it only has *one side* and that prosciutto will melt in your mouth. The same goes for salami, ham, and roast beef (cooked medium-rare).

There are a few exceptions. Don't worry, I'll get to them.

Some meat is better sliced a little thicker. Corned beef is one. And if turkey or deli chicken are sliced too thin, they'll lose so much definition that they'll basically disappear. For chicken prepared other ways, it should be cut small or thin enough that you don't have to bite into it and then tear it off with your teeth. So chop it into bite-size pieces for chicken salad sandwiches,

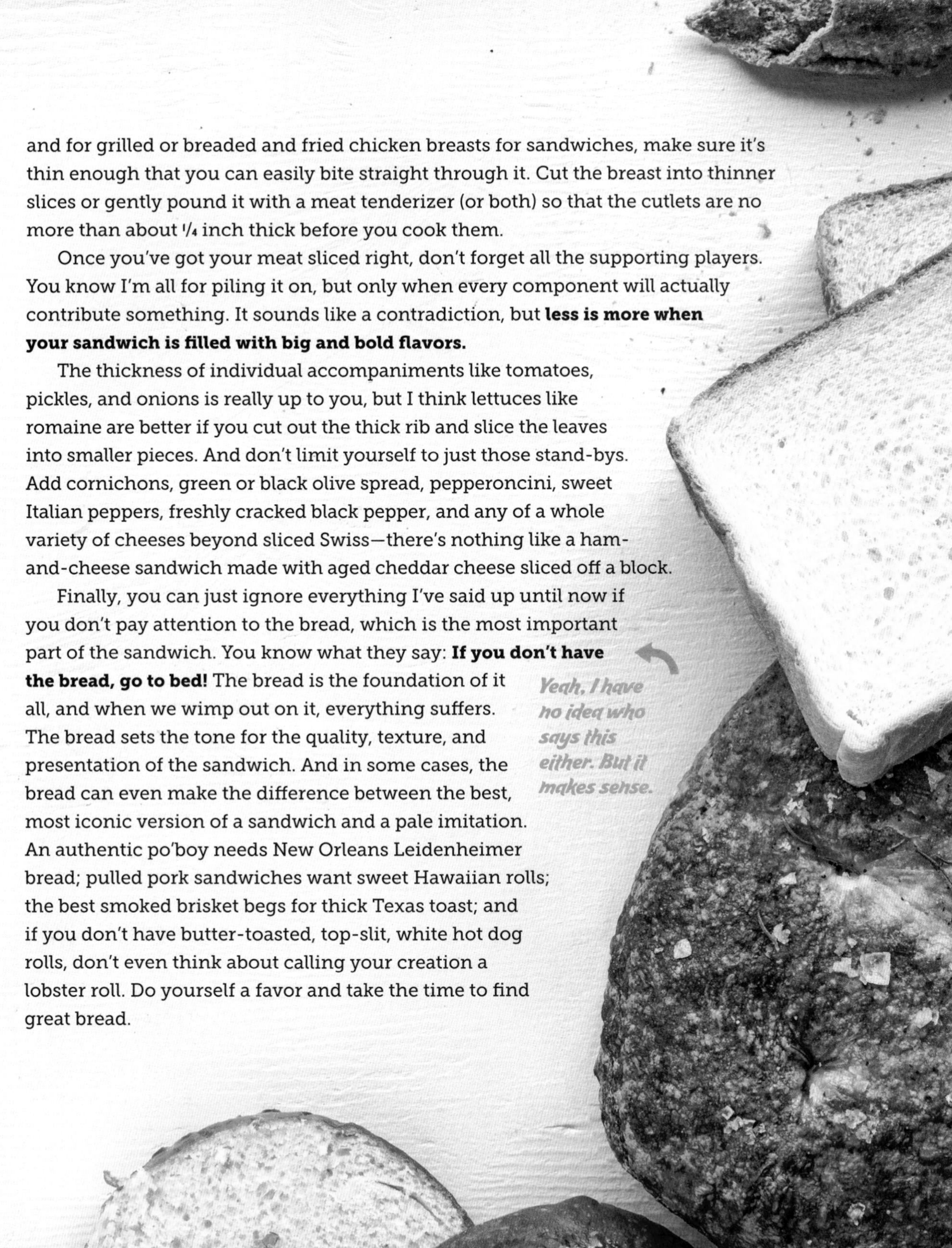

and for grilled or breaded and fried chicken breasts for sandwiches, make sure it's thin enough that you can easily bite straight through it. Cut the breast into thinner slices or gently pound it with a meat tenderizer (or both) so that the cutlets are no more than about ¼ inch thick before you cook them.

Once you've got your meat sliced right, don't forget all the supporting players. You know I'm all for piling it on, but only when every component will actually contribute something. It sounds like a contradiction, but **less is more when your sandwich is filled with big and bold flavors.**

The thickness of individual accompaniments like tomatoes, pickles, and onions is really up to you, but I think lettuces like romaine are better if you cut out the thick rib and slice the leaves into smaller pieces. And don't limit yourself to just those stand-bys. Add cornichons, green or black olive spread, pepperoncini, sweet Italian peppers, freshly cracked black pepper, and any of a whole variety of cheeses beyond sliced Swiss—there's nothing like a ham-and-cheese sandwich made with aged cheddar cheese sliced off a block.

Finally, you can just ignore everything I've said up until now if you don't pay attention to the bread, which is the most important part of the sandwich. You know what they say: **If you don't have the bread, go to bed!** The bread is the foundation of it all, and when we wimp out on it, everything suffers. The bread sets the tone for the quality, texture, and presentation of the sandwich. And in some cases, the bread can even make the difference between the best, most iconic version of a sandwich and a pale imitation. An authentic po'boy needs New Orleans Leidenheimer bread; pulled pork sandwiches want sweet Hawaiian rolls; the best smoked brisket begs for thick Texas toast; and if you don't have butter-toasted, top-slit, white hot dog rolls, don't even think about calling your creation a lobster roll. Do yourself a favor and take the time to find great bread.

Yeah, I have no idea who says this either. But it makes sense.

It's okay to drool!

Crispy Cornflake-Crusted Chicken Sandwich

There was a time when you could say "cornflake crust" and everyone in earshot knew exactly what kind of crisp-'n'-cracklin', outta-this-world crunch you meant. I don't know if you're old enough to remember what I'm talkin' about, but if not, you're about to find out, because this cornflake-crusted chicken sandwich has it in spades. The key is the double dredging, first in seasoned flour and then in panko and cornflakes. The smaller, fluffier panko lightens it all up and keeps the crust from getting too dark.

MAKES **4 servings** • ***TIME*** **1½ hours**

Sriracha ranch

1½ cups Ranch Dressing (page 292)

2 tablespoons sriracha sauce

Crispy cabbage slaw

2 cups thinly sliced green cabbage

1 cup thinly sliced red cabbage

Juice of 1 lemon

¼ cup apple cider vinegar

1 teaspoon celery seeds

2 teaspoons sugar

1 teaspoon kosher salt

Cornflake-crusted chicken

Four 6-ounce boneless, skinless chicken breast halves

2 cups buttermilk

¼ cup dill pickle juice (from the jar)

2 teaspoons granulated garlic

2 teaspoons onion powder

1 To make the sriracha ranch, combine all the ingredients in a small bowl and whisk well to blend. Cover and refrigerate until needed.

2 To make the slaw, combine all the ingredients in a large bowl. Mix well. Cover and refrigerate for about 30 minutes.

3 To make the cornflake-crusted chicken, place the chicken breasts on a cutting board. With a sharp knife, make small crosshatch cuts on both sides, just gently piercing the surface and not cutting too deep into the fillet. (This helps the chicken spread evenly without tearing when pounded.) Cover the chicken with plastic wrap and use the flat side of a meat mallet to gently pound the chicken breasts to ¼ inch thick, shaping the fillet to suit your bun.

4 In a large bowl, combine the buttermilk, pickle juice, 1 teaspoon each of the granulated garlic, onion powder, and salt, ½ teaspoon of the black pepper, and the cayenne. Mix well to combine, then place the chicken fillets in the buttermilk brine and press down to cover completely. Cover and refrigerate for at least 30 minutes and up to 1 hour.

RECIPE CONTINUES →

RECIPE CONTINUED FROM PREVIOUS PAGE

2 teaspoons kosher salt

1 teaspoon freshly ground black pepper

¼ teaspoon cayenne pepper

3 cups cornflakes

1 cup panko bread crumbs

1 cup all-purpose flour

4 hoagie rolls

4 tablespoons Roasted Garlic Butter (page 298) or unsalted butter, melted

¼ sweet onion, finely sliced

2 large kosher dill pickles, finely sliced

1 large heirloom tomato, thinly sliced

5 Place the cornflakes in a food processor and pulse 7 or 8 times, until they are broken down to the size of large bread crumbs. Transfer to a medium bowl and set aside. Place the panko in the food processor and pulse until it is broken down to half its size, 30 to 40 seconds; this will ensure more even coverage as the smaller pieces fill the gaps. Add the panko to the crushed cornflakes and mix to combine. Transfer to a large rimmed dish and set aside.

6 In a medium bowl, combine the flour, the remaining 1 teaspoon each granulated garlic, onion powder, and salt, and remaining ½ teaspoon black pepper. Have ready a wire rack placed over a baking sheet lined with paper towels.

7 Remove the chicken fillets from the buttermilk brine (reserving the brine) and pat them dry with paper towels. Dredge one chicken breast in the seasoned flour. Transfer it back to the buttermilk brine, shake off any excess, and then place it in the panko-cornflake mixture. Gently press the crumbs into the chicken to ensure an even coating and place it on the wire rack. Repeat with the remaining chicken. Let the breaded chicken rest, uncovered, in the fridge for about 20 minutes so the breading can set and holds firm.

8 Preheat the oven to 375°F and set a wire rack on a rimmed baking sheet. Transfer the chicken pieces to the wire rack, spreading them out evenly. Bake for 35 to 40 minutes, until the chicken is firm and cooked through. Leave the oven on.

9 To assemble the sandwiches, brush the cut sides of the rolls with the melted garlic butter and toast them in the oven on a rimmed baking sheet until golden brown (watch them carefully). Smear the cut sides of the rolls with sriracha ranch (about 2 tablespoons per sandwich). Place some sliced onions and sliced pickles on the bottom roll halves, and then top each with a chicken breast. Top each with 2 tomato slices and a heaping spoonful of slaw. Place the top roll halves on top and serve.

'68 Cajun Sandwich
(Named after the '68 Camaro on DDD)

What do you get when you cross a po'boy with jambalaya? This kick-ass open-faced sandwich, that's what. Scooping out the center of the bread and melting cheese in there is **da bomb . . .** Do not, I repeat, do not skip this step. There's a reason these fly right outta the kitchen at the restaurants. You'll have some creole remoulade left over. It's an awesome dipping sauce with barbecued shrimp, or served on hamburgers or Andouille sausage.

MAKES **4 servings** • ***TIME*** **1 hour**

Creole remoulade

1¼ cups mayonnaise

Juice and grated zest of 1 lemon

¼ cup minced drained dill pickles

2 tablespoons dill pickle juice (from the jar)

2 tablespoons prepared horseradish

2 tablespoons Creole mustard

2 tablespoons drained capers, minced

1 tablespoon minced chives

1 tablespoon Worcestershire sauce

3 or 4 dashes of Louisiana hot sauce

Slaw

1 cup finely sliced red cabbage

1 cup finely sliced green cabbage

1 cup julienned carrots

3 tablespoons red wine vinegar

1 tablespoon sugar

Blackening spice

1 tablespoon granulated garlic

1 tablespoon freshly ground black pepper

1 To prepare the remoulade, combine all the ingredients in a medium bowl and whisk well to combine. Cover and refrigerate until needed or store in an airtight container in the refrigerator for 5 to 7 days.

2 To make the slaw, combine all the ingredients in a medium bowl. Mix well and set aside in the fridge for 10 to 15 minutes to let the cabbage soften.

3 To prepare the blackening spice, combine all the ingredients in a small bowl.

4 To make the sandwiches, liberally season the chicken all over with the blackening spice and set aside. Heat 1 tablespoon of the olive oil in a large cast-iron pan over medium-high heat. Add the sausage and sauté until well browned, 4 to 5 minutes. Transfer the sausage to a plate and set aside. Add the chicken to the pan and cook until well blackened all over, 6 to 8 minutes. Transfer the chicken to the plate with the sausage.

5 Heat the remaining 1 tablespoon olive oil in the pan over medium-high heat. Add the garlic, bell peppers, onion, salt, and black pepper and sauté until the vegetables are well charred around the edges, 6 to 8 minutes. Reduce the heat to medium and return the sausage and chicken to the pan. Toss to combine and heat through. Remove the pan from the heat and set it aside, keeping it warm.

RECIPE CONTINUES →

RECIPE CONTINUED FROM PREVIOUS PAGE

1½ teaspoons kosher salt
2 teaspoons ground cumin
2 teaspoons granulated onion
1 teaspoon cayenne pepper
1 teaspoon Italian seasoning
1 teaspoon paprika
½ teaspoon chili powder

Cajun sandwiches

½ pound boneless, skinless chicken thighs, cut into ½-inch cubes
½ pound boneless, skinless chicken breasts, cut into ½-inch cubes
2 tablespoons extra-virgin olive oil
½ pound Andouille sausage, cut on the bias into ¼-inch slices
4 garlic cloves, minced
1 red bell pepper, seeded and finely sliced
1 green bell pepper, seeded and finely sliced
1 medium sweet onion, thinly sliced
1 teaspoon kosher salt
3 or 4 turns freshly ground black pepper
4 torpedo rolls
8 slices cheddar cheese
½ cup minced chives, for garnish

6 Preheat the oven to 350°F. To assemble the sandwiches, use a serrated knife to cut a large "V" channel lengthwise out of the top of each torpedo roll; discard the excess bread. Place 2 slices of cheese in each of the "V" cuts and toast in the oven for a few minutes, until the cheese has melted and the bread is slightly crusty. Divide the slaw among the rolls. Top with the sausage and chicken mixture. Drizzle each sandwich with 1 to 2 tablespoons of the Creole remoulade and garnish with chives. Serve.

Guy Fieri BALTIMORE KITCHEN + BAR

I suggest you play a little
Cowboy Mouth while you eat
(www.cowboymouth.com).

I loved how Yogi Bear said "Pic-A-Nic" basket . . . that's where the name came from.

Turkey Pic-A-Nic on a Pretzel Roll

You want a picnic, without having to go outside with all those flies? Start with a soft pretzel roll. Fill it with savory roasted turkey and some sharp Swiss cheese. Add sweet-n-tangy cranberry relish and BBQ-flavored kettle chips. Top it all off with crispy shredded lettuce and radicchio. **This thing is like a pic-a-nic in your mouth!**

MAKES **4 servings** • ***TIME*** **30 minutes**

Cranberry citrus relish

1 tablespoon extra-virgin olive oil

1/2 cup finely sliced red onion

1 pound fresh or frozen cranberries

1 1/4 cups sugar

1/2 cup pineapple juice

Juice and grated zest of 2 oranges

Turkey sandwich

4 pretzel torpedo rolls

1/2 cup Donkey Sauce (page 296)

8 slices Swiss cheese

1 1/2 pounds thinly sliced roast turkey breast

4 ounces BBQ-flavored kettle chips

1/2 head iceberg lettuce, finely shredded

1 small head radicchio, finely shredded

1 To prepare the relish, heat the olive oil in a large sauté pan over medium-high heat. Add the onion and sauté until lightly browned, 4 to 5 minutes. Add the cranberries, sugar, pineapple juice, and orange juice. Bring to a boil, then reduce the heat and simmer until the cranberries begin to break down, 8 to 10 minutes (fresh cranberries may take a few more minutes). Stir in the orange zest. Transfer the cranberry relish to a bowl, cover, and refrigerate until needed.

2 Heat the broiler to high and set a rack 6 inches from the heat.

3 To assemble the sandwiches, cut the pretzel torpedoes in half lengthwise and lightly toast both sides under the broiler (watch them carefully). Smear the bottom bun halves with donkey sauce. Smear the top bun halves with cranberry relish. Shingle the Swiss cheese slices on the bases, then layer with sliced turkey. Top the turkey with a smear of cranberry relish, then layer with kettle chips. Finish with a mound of shredded lettuce and radicchio. Place the top torpedo halves over the radicchio. Slice in half and serve.

Pork Chop Torta

The pork shoulder chop is a piece of meat with a ton of flavor. It needs just a little **GLC*** to really rock. It's a tough cut, but when it's brined, rubbed with spices, and pan-fried, it'll knock your socks off. And there's no better way to show it off than in a torta, an authentic Mexican sandwich served on oblong, crusty sandwich rolls. Rub 'em with garlic butter and crisp 'em up on a hot griddle before piling them high with the chopped spiced pork, pickled red onions, and creamy avo aioli.

MAKES **4 servings** • ***TIME*** **1½ hours**

Pork chops and beer brine

One 12-ounce bottle Mexican beer

¼ cup lightly packed light brown sugar

1 lime, quartered

4 garlic cloves, smashed

1 bay leaf

2 oregano sprigs

¼ teaspoon red chili flakes

1 teaspoon black peppercorns

2 tablespoons kosher salt

2 cups ice cubes

Four 6-ounce bone-in pork shoulder blade chops

Avocado aioli

1 large egg

1 tablespoon Dijon mustard

¼ cup fresh lime juice

½ cup canola oil

2 ripe Hass avocados, pitted, peeled, and diced

1 To brine the pork chops, in a large saucepan, combine the beer, brown sugar, lime, garlic, bay leaf, oregano, chili flakes, peppercorns, and salt. Cook over high heat, stirring, until the salt and sugar have dissolved. Remove from the heat. Stir in the ice cubes and set aside until cool. Pour the brine into a 1-gallon resealable plastic bag and add the pork chops. Seal the bag tightly and refrigerate for about 1 hour.

2 To make the aioli, combine the egg, mustard, and lime juice in a blender and blend on low speed to combine. With the blender running, add the canola oil in a slow, steady stream. Continue to blend until the mixture is completely emulsified, about 2 minutes total. Stop the blender and add the avocado, salt, black pepper, cayenne, cumin, and cilantro. Blend until smooth. If the aioli is too thick, add a little water to loosen it. Transfer to a bowl, cover, and refrigerate until ready to use.

3 To cook the pork, preheat a cast-iron skillet over high heat. In a small bowl, combine the cumin, achiote, chili de árbol, salt, and black pepper and mix well. Remove the pork chops from the brine and pat them dry. Discard the brine. Liberally season them all over with the dry rub. Add the olive oil to the hot pan and sear the pork chops until well browned, 5 to 7 minutes per side. Reduce the heat and transfer the chops to a plate. Set aside until cool enough to handle.

****That's Guido Lovin' Care . . . Ha!***

2 teaspoons kosher salt

4 to 5 turns freshly ground black pepper

¼ teaspoon cayenne pepper

1 teaspoon ground cumin

¼ cup chopped cilantro

Dry rub

2 teaspoons ground cumin

1 teaspoon achiote powder

1 teaspoon chili de árbol powder

1 teaspoon kosher salt

½ teaspoon freshly ground black pepper

Sandwiches

1 tablespoon extra-virgin olive oil

4 torta bread rolls or hoagie rolls

¼ cup Roasted Garlic Butter (page 298) or unsalted butter, melted

½ cup drained Pickled Red Onions (page 294)

¼ pound Cotija cheese, crumbled (about 1 cup)

1 cup finely sliced red cabbage

1 cup finely sliced green cabbage

One 4-ounce package crispy pork rinds, broken into pieces

4 Brush the cut sides of the torta rolls with melted garlic butter and toast them in the hot skillet until golden brown on both sides, about 45 seconds per side.

5 Using a sharp knife, remove and discard the bone from each pork chop. Coarsely chop the pork meat into ¼-inch cubes and return them to the hot cast-iron skillet for 2 to 3 minutes to crisp up. Transfer the pork to a bowl.

6 To assemble the torta, smear the cut sides of the rolls with the avocado aioli. Divide the pork among the bottom roll halves. Top each with some pickled red onions and sprinkle with crumbled Cotija. Add a handful of green and red cabbage and finish with some crushed pork rinds. Place the top roll halves on top and serve.

The picture they'll show at Ryder's NBA draft.

Chicken Tikka Masala Pocket

For this or any other pocket sandwich, do yourself a favor and get the highest-quality pita you can find. Don't mess around with that mass-produced stuff that's as dry and stiff as cardboard. So **when you picka peck of pita pockets, picka da best!**

MAKES **4 servings** • ***TIME*** **45 minutes, plus 1 hour of chicken marinating time**

Chicken tikka masala

Four 6-ounce boneless, skinless chicken breast halves

1 cup plain Greek yogurt

2 tablespoons tomato paste

Juice and grated zest of 1 lime

4 garlic cloves, minced

1 tablespoon grated ginger

2 tablespoons smoked paprika

1 tablespoon ground turmeric

½ teaspoon cayenne pepper

2 teaspoons ground cumin

1 teaspoon ground coriander

½ teaspoon ground cardamom

2 teaspoons kosher salt

½ teaspoon freshly ground black pepper

Carrot raisin slaw

¼ cup golden raisins

1 tablespoon sesame seeds

2 teaspoons cumin seeds

2 carrots, grated

½ small head red cabbage, grated

¼ cup chopped flat-leaf parsley

3 tablespoons extra-virgin olive oil

1 tablespoon sherry vinegar

1 To prepare the chicken tikka masala, place the chicken breasts on a cutting board. With a sharp knife, make small crosshatch cuts on both sides, just gently piercing the surface and not cutting too deeply into the fillet. Cover the chicken with plastic wrap and use the flat side of a meat mallet to gently pound the chicken breasts to ¼ inch thick. Set aside.

This helps the chicken spread evenly without tearing when pounded.

2 In a food processor, process the yogurt, tomato paste, lime juice and zest, garlic, ginger, paprika, turmeric, cayenne, cumin, coriander, cardamom, salt, and black pepper until combined. Transfer the marinade to a shallow dish, add the chicken, and turn to coat completely. Cover and refrigerate for at least 1 hour and up to overnight.

3 To prepare the slaw, place the raisins in a small bowl and add warm water to cover. Set aside to plump, 10 to 12 minutes. Drain and set aside. In a small sauté pan over medium-high heat, toast the sesame and cumin seeds until fragrant, about 1 minute. Transfer the seeds to a medium bowl to cool. Add the raisins, carrots, cabbage, parsley, olive oil, vinegar, lemon juice, salt, and black pepper and mix well to combine. Cover and refrigerate for at least 30 minutes.

4 To prepare the raita, whisk together all the ingredients in a medium bowl to combine. Cover and refrigerate until needed.

5 Preheat a grill to high. Remove the chicken from the marinade and wipe off any excess (discard the marinade). Season the chicken with salt and pepper. Grill the chicken for 6 to 7 minutes per side, until well marked and

Juice of 1 lemon

2 teaspoons kosher salt

5 or 6 turns freshly ground black pepper

Cucumber raita

1 cup plain Greek yogurt

1 cup grated unpeeled seedless cucumber

1 garlic clove, minced

3 tablespoons chopped cilantro

½ teaspoon ground cumin

¼ teaspoon ground coriander

1 teaspoon kosher salt

5 or 6 turns freshly ground black pepper

Pita and garnishes

4 large whole-wheat pitas

2 tablespoons chopped cilantro

½ cup finely diced pineapple

charred so it's nice and smoky. Set the chicken aside to rest for 10 minutes or so.

6 Meanwhile, place the pitas on the grill domed side up and heat until they puff up and warm through. Cover the pitas with a dome or inverted metal mixing bowl to create steam and make them even softer. Set aside.

7 To assemble the pockets, slice the chicken into strips. In a small bowl, combine the cilantro and pineapple. Cut the pitas crosswise in half. Divide the carrot raisin slaw evenly among the 8 pockets. Top each with sliced chicken, drizzle with some cucumber raita, and garnish with the pineapple-cilantro mixture. Serve.

Arguing right before, and after . . . brotherly love.

The Camp Jackpine Fish Sandwich

Thanks to Jimmy John Liautaud, my brutha from anutha mutha and the founding father of Jimmy John's Gourmet Sandwiches, for introducing me to his fried fish sandwich. I wouldn't ask him to give up any trade secrets, so here's my riff on his original.

MAKES **4 servings •** ***TIME*** **1 hour 10 minutes, plus 4 to 5 hours of refrigeration time**

Roasted red bell pepper mayonnaise

1 cup mayonnaise

3/4 cup coarsely chopped fire-roasted red bell peppers (see page 32)

Juice and grated zest of 1 lemon

1 1/2 teaspoons Dijon mustard

1 teaspoon paprika

Pinch of cayenne pepper

Dash of Worcestershire sauce

1 tablespoon chopped flat-leaf parsley

1 teaspoon kosher salt

3 or 4 turns freshly ground black pepper

Tartar slaw

1/2 head green cabbage, finely sliced

3 teaspoons kosher salt

1/2 sweet onion, grated on a box grater

6 large kosher dill pickles, grated on a box grater, plus 3 tablespoons brine from the jar

1/4 red bell pepper, thinly sliced

1 1/2 cups mayonnaise

1 To prepare the mayonnaise, place all the ingredients in a food processor and pulse until well combined. Transfer to a covered container and refrigerate until ready to use.

2 To prepare the slaw, place the cabbage in a colander set in the sink or on a plate. Sprinkle with 2 teaspoons of the salt and let stand for 10 minutes to draw out the moisture. Rinse and drain the cabbage and transfer it to a large bowl. Strain the onion and pickles in a strainer, squeezing out any excess moisture, and add them to the bowl with the cabbage along with the pickle brine, bell pepper, mayonnaise, mustard, and cayenne. Mix well and season with the remaining 1 teaspoon salt and the black pepper. Cover and refrigerate until ready to use.

3 To prepare the fish, place the eggs in a baking dish with some of the salt and pepper and whisk until well beaten. Pulse the crackers to a powder in a food processor and spread them on a plate. Pulse the panko in a food processor to break it up slightly, then spread it out on a separate plate. Season both plates of crumbs with salt and pepper. Set a wire rack on a rimmed baking sheet.

4 Dip one fish fillet in the egg, then into the crackers. Coat evenly. Shake off any excess crumbs and dip the fillet back into the egg mixture. Finish in the panko mixture, coating evenly and pressing gently so the breading sticks well to the fish. Place the breaded fish on the rack and repeat to

2 tablespoons Dijon mustard

Pinch of cayenne pepper

½ teaspoon freshly ground black pepper

Fried fish

6 large eggs

2 teaspoons kosher salt, plus more as needed

5 or 6 turns freshly ground black pepper

2 cups crumbled saltine crackers (about 1 sleeve)

2 cups panko bread crumbs

1½ pounds boneless, skinless white fish fillet, such as walleye, cod, or snapper, cut into eight 3-ounce pieces

Peanut oil, for frying

For serving

4 ciabatta buns

¼ cup Roasted Garlic Butter (page 298), melted

8 slices American cheese

bread the remaining fish. Leaving the fish on the rack, wrap the whole baking sheet tightly in plastic wrap and refrigerate for 4 to 5 hours.

5 In a deep cast-iron skillet, heat 2 to 3 inches of peanut oil to 350°F. Have ready a wire rack set over paper towels.

6 Working in batches, fry the fish until cooked through and golden, about 3 minutes per side. Using a spider or slotted spoon, transfer the fish to the rack to drain. Season with salt.

7 To assemble the sandwiches, preheat the broiler to high and set a rack 6 inches from the heat source. Brush the cut sides of the ciabatta buns with melted garlic butter and toast until golden brown on both sides, about 45 seconds per side. Smear the cut sides of the buns with the roasted red pepper mayonnaise (about 1 heaping tablespoon per sandwich). Place 2 crispy fish fillets on each of the bottom bun halves. Top each with 2 slices of American cheese and a heaping spoonful of tartar slaw. Place the top bun halves on top and serve.

Crispy Artichoke and Arugula on Focaccia

Thanks to my vegetarian sister and super-health-conscious parents, by the time I was an adult I knew everything I needed to about vegetable sandwiches. The intention behind them is good, but too often their texture is limp and kinda soggy, with flavor to match. Who wants to eat all the way through *that*? Sure, grilling the vegetables can help a little, but . . . yawn. Been there, done that. *This* veggie sandwich, on the other hand, with its crisp, meaty artichokes and tangy red onion relish, comes from a very different place . . . **a place by the name of Flavortown, USA.**

MAKES **4 servings** • *TIME* **45 minutes**

Caramelized red onion relish

3 tablespoons extra-virgin olive oil

2 garlic cloves, minced

1 large red onion, thinly sliced

1 teaspoon kosher salt

½ cup julienned fire-roasted red bell pepper (see page 32)

2 Roma tomatoes, cored and cut into ¼-inch dice

2 tablespoons drained capers, chopped

1 tablespoon chopped flat-leaf parsley

1 teaspoon thyme leaves

2 teaspoons red wine vinegar

1 tablespoon honey

5 or 6 turns freshly ground black pepper

Sandwiches

1 large (approximately 20 x 18-inch) whole focaccia loaf

1 tablespoon extra-virgin olive oil

1 To prepare the relish, heat the olive oil in a small sauté pan over medium-high heat. Add the garlic, onion, and salt and sauté until the onion is lightly caramelized, 6 to 8 minutes. Reduce the heat to medium and add the rest of the relish ingredients. Mix well to combine. Cook for 5 to 7 minutes to heat through and let the flavors combine. Remove from the heat. Cover and refrigerate until ready to use.

2 Preheat the oven to 425°F.

3 Drizzle the focaccia with the olive oil and sprinkle with the rosemary needles. Bake until golden brown and crispy, 7 to 8 minutes. Set aside.

4 In a deep cast-iron skillet over medium heat, heat 2 to 3 inches of canola oil to 350°F. Have ready two rimmed baking sheets, one lined with paper towels.

5 While the oil is heating, in a medium bowl, combine the flour, garlic powder, onion powder, salt, and pepper and mix well. Set aside. In another medium bowl, lightly whisk the egg and buttermilk. Place an artichoke heart in the buttermilk-egg mixture, then dredge it in the seasoned flour

RECIPE CONTINUES →

Oh, my sister would be proud!

RECIPE CONTINUED FROM PAGE 20

Needles from 2 rosemary sprigs

Canola oil, for frying

2 cups all-purpose flour

2 teaspoons garlic powder

2 teaspoons onion powder

2 teaspoons kosher salt, plus more for seasoning

½ teaspoon freshly ground black pepper

1 large egg

1 cup buttermilk

16 canned whole medium artichoke hearts (from two 14-ounce cans), rinsed and drained

Toppings

1¾ ounces Parmesan cheese, shaved (about ½ cup)

1 cup chopped drained giardiniera* vegetables

¼ cup pepitas, toasted (at right)

1 cup baby arugula

*These are jarred pickled vegetables. If your grocery store doesn't have them in the pickle aisle, find another store! Seriously, this stuff makes everything it touches rock 'n' roll.

and place it on the unlined baking sheet. Repeat with the remaining artichoke hearts.

6 Working in small batches, fry the artichokes in the hot oil for 5 to 6 minutes, turning to cook on both sides, until golden brown and crispy. Use a spider or slotted spoon to remove them from the oil and place them on the paper towels to drain. Season with salt.

7 To assemble the sandwich, use a serrated knife to cut the focaccia in half horizontally. Spread about 1 cup of the caramelized red onion relish over the cut sides of both halves. Arrange the crispy artichoke hearts over the relish on the bottom half of the bread. Sprinkle the shaved Parmesan over the artichokes and top with the chopped giardiniera, pepitas, and a big handful of baby arugula. Place the top half of the focaccia on top. Cut into individual sandwich portions and serve.

Toasting Pepitas, Pine Nuts, and Sesame Seeds

Toast in a dry skillet over high heat for 3 to 4 minutes, until browned, shaking the pan as they cook so they brown evenly. Remove from the pan and let cool.

Burgers 101

You might be surprised to hear it, but I was never really a burger guy until I had one at Hodad's in San Diego in 2007. Now, *that's* a burger that deserves respect. I knew it the minute I tasted it. But until I partnered with Carnival Cruise Lines and set out to create a kick-ass concept for my Guy's Burger Joints on their ships, I probably never would have known what it takes to make a truly great one. My team and I sat down and broke down from the beginning everything I wanted to see and taste in a burger. We ended up essentially creating a blueprint for what we think is one of the world's best.

It turns out a great burger is like a great movie—every player has a vital role. The trouble with most burgers (and movies) is that they're mushy, lacking texture and creativity. I'm not saying that it has to be over the top to be fantastic. It just has to have texture, acid, and balance. Those simple (but elusive) elements are all it takes to take a burger from forgettable to mind-blowing.

Our blueprint tells us to start on the outside: the bun. It's the stage that holds everything together and props up the star of the show. Plus, it's a major contributor to the texture of the whole thing. The bun's gotta have enough structure that it can handle some crunch, added by buttering and grilling it. It also has to be soft enough to absorb the juices—but not so soft that it falls apart.

Next come the supporting players: the vegetables and condiments. The vegetables are often the most underappreciated and underplayed part, added only for their good looks. And then a lot of people just pick them off without even thinking about what they bring. But the **vegetables are an essential part of the burger.** They contribute texture, sure, but what we really care about are their acid and moisture. The onion (acid), the pickle (acid and brininess), the tomato (sweet acid and moisture), and the lettuce (crunch) are absolutely key. If it's up to me, I never make the veggies optional. Even if someone picks off that onion and pickle, I want them there long enough to contribute some acid and moisture to the party.

So don't skimp. All the vegetables should be fresh and very thinly sliced right before they're used. When the tomato is sliced thin enough, it kind of melts and forms a good barrier between the burger and the bun to keep the bun from getting soggy. As for the lettuce, if you're using it, choose something that's nice and crispy like iceberg or romaine so that there's some moisture and crunch in there. **(If someone ever puts a piece of red-leaf lettuce on my burger, I'll go insane.** Sure, it looks pretty in all those ads where you can see the ruffle on the outside. But in real life, delicate greens make a great salad but a lame addition to a burger.)

Next, the condiments—mustard, ketchup, and mayo—are about moisture, flavor, and acid. But don't forget balance, which is so important here. If you put as much mustard as the average person puts on a burger, it's all out of balance.

And now for the star of the show: the meat. It's a common misconception that for juicy burgers, you have to make the patties thick and cook them to medium-rare. I'm here to tell you that this is not what makes a juicy burger. If you bite into a burger and think, *OMG, that's one juicy burger,* and then check out the pinkness inside, you may or may not find it. The point isn't whether it's pink—it's whether it's dry.

It's not true for steak either, by the way. I've had some killer juicy steaks that are really thin; they're just cooked really fast over very high heat. That's the secret.

The reason so many home-cooked burgers are too dry is that they start out too thick and then they're cooked at too low a temperature for too long. By the time the burger's internal temperature is in the "safe" zone, you might have a nice crust on it, but it's dried out and cooked all to hell.

So here's the trick. Use fresh ground beef (80/20 meat-to-fat ratio) and *season generously*. Don't worry that salting the meat will dry it out. That's not going to happen here. If you skimp on salt, you lose flavor, and we can't have that. So season generously and let that salt sink down into the meat. Then you'll make 'em thin and cook 'em hot and fast over high heat so you build a nice crust on both sides *and* keep it moist and juicy in the middle.

Heat a cast-iron griddle or skillet over high heat for at least 5 minutes (time it! It's longer than you think). Cook in batches if necessary so you don't overcrowd the pan. After you put the burgers in the pan, don't touch them until they've got a nice sear on, and when you flip them, let 'em land on a new part of the pan so it's blazing hot.

After you cover the burgers with cheese, throw a dome or inverted metal mixing bowl over them. Lift one side of the dome quickly and add a couple of tablespoons of water to the pan under the dome. Ya wanna know why? Because water creates steam and steam means a higher temperature inside that dome so that the cheese melts completely. **There's nothing worse than sweaty cheese on a burger.** Plus, all that steam in there keeps the burger moist. Don't worry about soggy burgers . . . when the dome comes off and the liquid has evaporated, those babies'll crust right up again.

One last thing. Before you cool the pan down, butter the cut sides of the buns and put them on the pan to get a good crust **both inside and out.** It only takes a few seconds on each side and it looks cool and adds texture. And most important—when you take the time to get that crunch on the top, **it shows that you care.**

Now we've laid the scene for the best burger ever. The stage—the buttered and crisped bun—is set; the supporting players are ready to contribute acid and moisture to the play; and the star, the well-seasoned, cooked-hot-and-fast burger, is ready to go. It's nothing without a stage or supporting players, right? You combine all this and you've got the balance you need to make a burger that rocks. And *that* deserves respect.

New York City Wine & Food Festival Burger champs!

The Brick Burger

What's that you say? You want the secret to the most unbelievable gooey-cheesy-extra-crusty-juicy burger *ever*? All you need is a *Brick . . . House . . .*

JK, you only need the brick. It presses the burgers like a panini and crisps the bread while letting all the flavors and juices of the burger and toppings *mingle* together. Like at a house party. A brick house party.

MAKES **4 servings •** ***TIME*** **1 hour**

3 tablespoons sweet pickle relish

¼ cup diced drained jarred pimientos

1½ pounds ground beef (80% lean)

1 teaspoon kosher salt

5 or 6 turns freshly ground black pepper

3 tablespoons Roasted Garlic Butter (page 298), melted

¼ cup Donkey Sauce (page 296)

4 sourdough buns

1 large kosher dill pickle, thinly sliced

¼ sweet onion, thinly sliced

8 slices Swiss cheese

½ pound sliced deli ham

1 beefsteak tomato, thinly sliced

Special equipment

Heavy-duty aluminum foil

2 bricks

1 In a small bowl, combine the pickle relish and diced pimientos. Set aside.

2 Preheat a grill to hot. Form the ground beef into four 6-ounce patties, each about 4 inches in diameter. Season the patties on both sides with salt and pepper. Grill the patties for 4 to 5 minutes, until they have a nice char and blood begins to come to the surface. Flip and cook for 3 minutes on the second side. Remove the burgers from the grill and set aside to cool.

3 Lightly brush the cut sides of the buns with the melted garlic butter. Toast the bun halves on the grill until golden and crisp, about 45 seconds per side. Set aside.

4 Reduce the grill heat to medium.

5 To assemble the burgers, lightly smear donkey sauce on the cut side of each bun. Cover the bottom bun with 3 pickle slices and 1 or 2 onion slices. Top with the burger, 1 teaspoon of the relish mixture, 2 slices of Swiss cheese, some sliced ham, and 2 tomato slices. Cover with the top bun halves.

6 To finish the burgers, wrap each burger in heavy-duty aluminum foil, forming a tight packet and sealing around the edges. Place the burgers back on the grill and put a brick on top of them (one brick will cover two burgers). Cook for 4 to 5 minutes. Remove the brick, flip the packets, place the brick on top, and cook for 3 to 4 minutes. Remove from the grill and let cool slightly. Tear open the foil and serve.

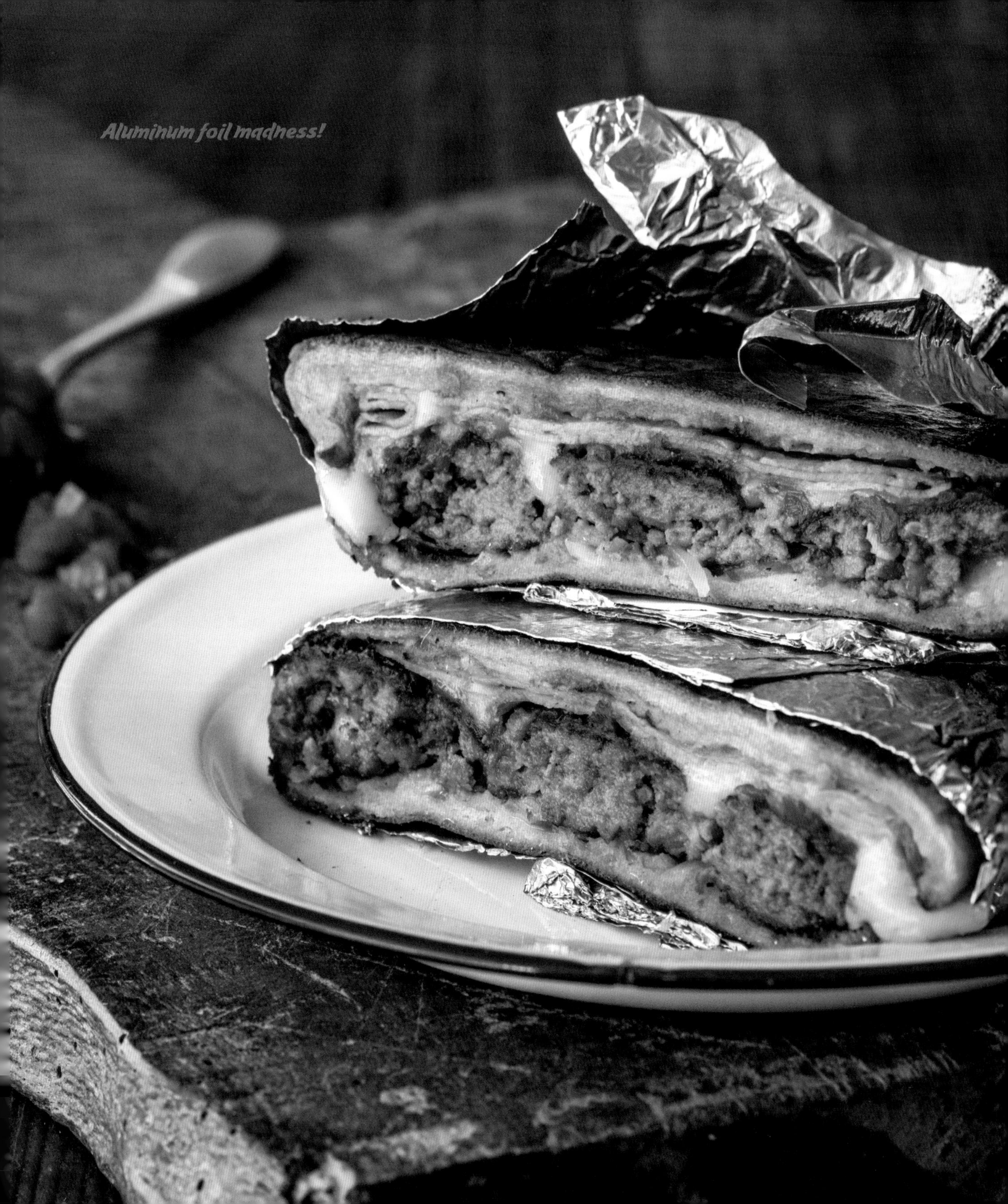
Aluminum foil madness!

We only took one picture. Right after we photographed this . . . I ate it!! All of it!!

Bacon Mac 'n' Cheese Burger

Is it a cheeseburger? . . . Is it mac 'n' cheese? . . . It's an award-winning, Burger Bash champion, cheese 'n' bacon mac 'n' cheese–topped burger! **Are you kiddin' me?!** Sign me up for some of *that* action.

BTW, you can make the bacon mac 'n' cheese a day or two ahead of time and the onion straws a few hours in advance. Just make sure they're in disguised containers. If anyone finds 'em before you need 'em, you won't have anything left for the burgers!

MAKES **4 servings** • ***TIME*** **1 hour 15 minutes**

Bacon mac 'n' cheese

16 slices applewood smoked bacon, cut crosswise into 1/4-inch-wide pieces

4 tablespoons (1/2 stick) unsalted butter

1/2 cup all-purpose flour

6 cups whole milk

3 ounces sharp white cheddar cheese, grated (about 3/4 cup)

2 ounces Fontina cheese, grated (about 1/2 cup)

2 ounces smoked Gouda cheese, grated (about 1/2 cup)

1 bay leaf

3 tablespoons yellow mustard

2 or 3 gratings of nutmeg

2 teaspoons kosher salt

5 or 6 turns freshly ground black pepper

1/2 pound small elbow pasta, cooked al dente

Crispy onion straws

Canola oil, for frying

1 large sweet onion, finely sliced

1 1/2 cups buttermilk

1 To prepare the mac 'n' cheese, in a large saucepan over medium-high heat, cook the bacon until it's crispy and the fat has rendered, 6 to 8 minutes. Using a slotted spoon, remove the bacon from the pan and set aside.

Reduce the heat to medium and add the butter to the pan. Whisking constantly, gradually add the flour to make a roux. Cook, whisking, until the mixture turns a light golden color and is the consistency of wet sand, 1 to 2 minutes. Whisking constantly, slowly add the milk, whisking to blend and prevent lumps. Bring the mixture to a simmer. Add the cheeses and the bay leaf and cook, whisking, until the cheese has melted. Whisk in the mustard, nutmeg, salt, and pepper. Add the cooked pasta and the bacon bits and stir to combine. Remove and discard the bay leaf. Set aside to cool. (This can be done a day or two ahead of time; store in a covered container in the refrigerator until you need it.)

2 To prepare the onion straws, in a deep cast-iron skillet, heat 2 to 3 inches of canola oil to 350°F. Have ready a plate topped with several layers of paper towels.

3 While the oil is heating, separate the layers of the sliced onion and soak them in the buttermilk in a medium bowl for 10 to 12 minutes. In a separate large shallow pan, combine the flour, cayenne, paprika, garlic powder,

RECIPE CONTINUES →

RECIPE CONTINUED FROM PREVIOUS PAGE

2 cups all-purpose flour

1 teaspoon cayenne pepper

1 teaspoon paprika

1 teaspoon garlic powder

1 tablespoon kosher salt

1 teaspoon freshly ground black pepper

Burgers

1¾ pounds ground beef (80% lean), divided into 4 even balls

1 tablespoon kosher salt

8 slices cheddar cheese

4 brioche hamburger buns

3 tablespoons Roasted Garlic Butter (page 298), melted

½ cup Donkey Sauce (page 296)

1 kosher dill pickle, thinly sliced

¼ cup thinly sliced sweet onion

8 slices applewood smoked bacon, cooked until crisp

1 large red heirloom tomato, thinly sliced

½ head iceberg lettuce, finely shredded

2 teaspoons of the salt, and the black pepper. Remove the onions from the buttermilk, shake off the excess, and dredge them in the flour mixture.

4 Working in small batches, fry the onions in the hot oil until golden brown, about 2 minutes. Use a spider or slotted spoon to remove them from the oil and transfer to the paper towels to drain. Season with the remaining 1 teaspoon salt. (These can be made a few hours ahead of time; cool and store in an airtight container at room temperature until ready to use.)

5 To cook the burgers, preheat a large cast-iron griddle or skillet over high heat. Season the burger balls all over with the salt. Place them on the hot griddle 3 to 4 inches apart. (If necessary, cook in batches so you don't overcrowd the burgers.) Cook for 90 seconds without moving to develop a crust. Then, using a heavy spatula, smash each burger, flattening it to ¼ inch thick. Cook until blood starts to come to the surface of the burger, 3 to 4 minutes. Flip to another part of the griddle (so it's hot) and cook on the second side for 2 to 3 more minutes. Top each burger with 2 heaping tablespoons of the mac 'n' cheese. Place 2 slices of cheddar on top of each to cover the mac 'n' cheese. Cover the burgers with a dome (or an upside-down metal mixing bowl), then lift one side of it quickly and add 2 tablespoons water to the pan under the dome to steam the burgers and help melt the cheese. Cook under the dome for 60 seconds. Remove the dome and transfer the burgers to a platter to rest.

6 Brush the cut sides of the brioche buns lightly with the roasted garlic butter. Toast the bun halves on the griddle until golden and crisp, about 45 seconds per side. Set aside.

7 To assemble the burgers, smear donkey sauce on the cut side of each bun half. Cover each of the bottom bun halves with 3 pickle slices and 1 or 2 onion slices. Top each with a burger, 2 slices of crisped bacon, 2 tomato slices, shredded lettuce, and some crispy onion straws. Place the top bun halves on top of the onion straws. Serve.

Turkey and Roasted Green Chile Burger
with Crushed Avocado

The turkey burger presents us with a different challenge than the beef burger: It's poultry, so you've *gotta* cook it all the way through, but it doesn't have as much of that good protective fat as 80% lean beef does, so it has a tendency to be dry as a bone. The key is first to make sure the griddle is blazin'-saddles-hot before the burgers meet up with it and then to press them nice and thin. The heat gives you the crust and the thin gives you the juicy. Now, that's a righteous burger!

MAKES 4 servings • **TIME** 1 hour

Burgers

1½ pounds ground turkey

2 poblano peppers, fire-roasted (see page 32) and coarsely diced

2 Hatch or Anaheim chiles, fire-roasted (see page 32) and coarsely diced

2 garlic cloves, minced

4 green onions (white and light green parts), finely sliced

Kosher salt and freshly ground black pepper

1 tablespoon extra-virgin olive oil

4 slices smoked Gouda cheese

4 slices pepper Jack cheese

4 whole-wheat burger buns

¼ cup Roasted Garlic Butter (page 298), melted

1 To prepare the turkey burgers, in a large bowl, combine the turkey, poblanos, Hatch chiles, garlic, and green onions. Mix until well combined and form into 4 equal balls. Cover and place in the fridge for 10 minutes to firm up.

2 Preheat a large cast-iron griddle or skillet over high heat.

3 To cook the burgers, season the burger balls all over with salt and black pepper. Add a little of the olive oil to the hot griddle. Place the burger balls on the griddle and cook for 90 seconds to develop a crust. (If necessary, cook in batches so you don't overcrowd the burgers.) Using a heavy spatula, smash each burger so it is slightly larger than the size of the bun (it will shrink back in size as it cooks). Cook until the underside of the burger is browned, 3 to 4 minutes. Flip to another part of the griddle (so it's hot), and cook on the second side for 2 to 3 more minutes. Top each burger with a slice of smoked Gouda and a slice of pepper Jack cheese. Cover the burgers with a dome (or an upside-down metal mixing bowl), then lift one side of it quickly and add 2 tablespoons water to the griddle under the

RECIPE CONTINUES →

RECIPE CONTINUED FROM PREVIOUS PAGE

Toppings

2 ripe Hass avocados, pitted and peeled

Juice of 1 lemon

Kosher salt and freshly ground black pepper

1 heirloom tomato

2 tablespoons Donkey Sauce (page 296)

1/4 red onion, thinly sliced

1/4 head iceberg lettuce, thinly sliced

dome to steam the burgers and melt the cheese. Remove the dome and transfer the burgers to a platter to rest.

4 Brush the cut sides of the buns lightly with melted garlic butter. Toast the bun halves on the griddle until golden and crisp, about 45 seconds per side. Set aside.

5 In a medium bowl, combine the avocado and lemon juice and season with salt and pepper. Using a fork, coarsely mash the avocado. Slice half the heirloom tomato into 4 thin slices and reserve for the burgers. Dice the rest of the tomato and fold it into the crushed avocado mixture.

6 To assemble the burgers, smear the cut sides of the buns with donkey sauce. Place some sliced red onion on the bottom bun halves and top each with a burger, a tomato slice, a big scoop of crushed avocado, and a large handful of sliced lettuce. Place the top bun halves on top and serve.

Fire-Roasting Peppers and Chiles

There is nothing, I mean nothing, that compares to the deep, smoky flavor that comes from fire-roasting. Yeah, I know you can *buy* roasted peppers, but do yourself a favor and find out how much better they are when ya do them yourself.

- Use a grill or, if you have a gas oven, the burners on your stovetop, or the broiler (set the rack about 4 inches from the flame). If using a grill or broiler, place the peppers or chiles directly on the rack. If using gas burners, you can place the peppers on the grate above the flame.
- Turn the grill, broiler, or a burner to high. Fire-roast the peppers over the open flame until the skins are charred and black all over, about 2 minutes per side; use tongs to turn the peppers.
- Remove the peppers from the heat and immediately place them in a large bowl. Cover tightly with plastic wrap and let stand for 3 to 4 minutes for small chiles and 8 to 10 for large bell peppers (the steam will help to loosen the skins), or until cool enough to handle. Remove the plastic and scrape away and discard the charred skin. Cut the peppers in half and remove and discard the seeds, stem, and membrane. Proceed as directed in the recipe.

The glasses in the back aren't blurry. You're just dazed and glazed by the beauty of these burgers.

PASTA & NOODLES
The Snockie.

La pasta non aspetta nessuno!

If you have an Italian grandmother, you might have heard her say once or a thousand times, "*La pasta non aspetta nessuno!*" (Pasta waits for no one!) Practically speaking, it means get every last darned thing ready *before* you cook your pasta. Get your sauce done, the salad dressed and tossed, the garlic bread warmed and sliced, call the family to the table, and make sure their butts are in those chairs. Then, *and only then,* drop the pasta. After a few minutes, start checking the pasta every 30 seconds so that you can drain it the minute it's al dente, toss it right in with the sauce, and serve it immediately.

One of the reasons pasta should be pulled exactly at this moment is that as long as it's warm and touching anything warm, it'll continue to cook, and overcooked, gummy pasta

→

oughta be a crime. And even if your Italian *nonna* wasn't thinking this when she said it, the rule applies across the international pasta and noodle spectrum. Whether we're talking about Italian pasta and red sauce, pad thai, lo mein, Polish *haluski*, or Ashkenazi *kasha varnishkes*, everything else can wait. The pasta or noodles cannot.

When you're cooking pasta, this is liquid gold.

Pasta 101

Remember *la pasta non aspetta nessuno*? If not, go back two pages and remind yourself. It means have **everything** ready before the pasta is ready, because that pasta will not wait around. The other big sin against pasta is boiling it in a too-small amount of undersalted water. **For every 1 pound of pasta, boil 1 gallon of water with 1 tablespoon of salt.** No exceptions. (And if I ever see anyone putting oil in the pot or rinsing cooked pasta, I cry salty Italian tears. *Don't do it.*)

One thing that you definitely should do, however, is use a glass measuring cup to pull out at least a cup of the pasta cooking water right before you drain it. You can use it to loosen up a thicker sauce and help it cling to the noodles. Plus, that hot pasta has a tendency to really chug the sauce; if the sauce is loosened up, the noodles won't get bogged down. Typically in Italy pasta is tossed with a modest amount of really flavorful sauce. An Italian chef once said to me: "Your pasta is not a castle; it shouldn't be sitting in a moat of sauce." He's 100 percent right. So do it like the Italians do.

What kind of pasta should you use? The answer is the best-quality dried noodles you can get. In a lot of situations, *fresh pasta can be overrated.* Sure, sheets of fresh pasta are great for making ravioli, and little pillows of fresh gnocchi can be amazing. But only use it when you really want that light and airy tenderness. In a lot of situations fresh pasta doesn't hold up against most big, heavy sauces. It's not a good choice for those *abbondanza* family pasta or noodle dishes like the ones in this chapter. So, purchase the best-quality dried pasta you can—it should be chalky and dry and rustic looking—and cook it right! *Buon appetito!*

That means "abundance," and it's said when someone is commenting on a fabulous spread of food.

Don't make a "mou-stake" and cook only one portion of this recipe. You will want two . . . trust me!

Chicken Mamou

The most famous version of this dish comes from the inimitable chef Paul Prudhomme of K-Paul's Louisiana Kitchen and Commander's Palace in New Orleans. I first learned about it from a chef buddy of mine named Gerard (from Sally Tomatoes) who made it so well he might as well have learned it from Chef Paul himself. It's such an amazing dish that when I make it, I purposely make too much just so I have some left over for the next day. The key is cutting the chicken small enough that the pieces become almost like crisp chicken cracklings.

***MAKES* 4 servings • *TIME* 1 hour**

Spice Mix

1 tablespoon dried basil
2 teaspoons dried thyme
2 teaspoons paprika
2 teaspoons ground cumin
1 teaspoon cayenne pepper
¼ teaspoon ground white pepper
1 teaspoon kosher salt
5 or 6 turns freshly ground black pepper

1½ pounds boneless, skinless chicken thighs, cut into ⅜-inch dice
8 slices applewood smoked bacon, diced
1 yellow onion, diced
2 red bell peppers, seeded and diced
6 garlic cloves, minced
1 cup dry white wine
2 tablespoons Worcestershire sauce
Two 28-ounce cans whole fire-roasted tomatoes, with their juice
2 cups finely sliced green onions (white and light green parts)
1 teaspoon plus 2 tablespoons chopped fresh oregano
1 tablespoon kosher salt
1 pound penne rigate
½ cup grated Parmesan cheese

1 To prepare the spice mix, combine all the ingredients in a small bowl. Sprinkle all over the chicken and set aside at room temperature.

2 In a large sauté pan over medium-high heat, cook the bacon until browned and crisp, 6 to 8 minutes. Remove from the pan with a slotted spoon and set aside. Add the chicken to the pan with the bacon fat. Cook until very well browned all over and almost crispy, 12 to 14 minutes. Remove from the pan and set aside.

3 Add the onion and bell peppers to the pan and sauté until the onion is translucent, 4 to 5 minutes. Add the garlic and sauté for 1 minute. Deglaze the pan by adding the wine and Worcestershire sauce and scraping up the browned bits from the bottom of the pan. Add the tomatoes. Simmer for 15 minutes, stirring and breaking up the tomatoes with a wooden spoon.

4 Add the chicken, half of the bacon, 1 cup of the green onions, and 1 teaspoon of the oregano to the pan. Simmer for 10 minutes. Remove the pan from the heat and set aside.

5 Meanwhile, in a large stockpot over medium-high heat, bring 1 gallon of water to a boil. Add the salt, then add the penne and stir. Cook the penne until al dente, 10 to 12 minutes. Drain thoroughly.

6 To serve, transfer the penne to a large serving bowl. Add the chicken Mamou mixture and toss to combine. Fold in the remaining bacon. Garnish with the remaining 1 cup green onions and 2 tablespoons oregano. Serve with the Parmesan cheese.

Fire-Roasted Fieri Lasagna

There's something about lasagna that makes it just like Chinese food and pizza. **When it's good, it's really good, and when it's bad, well, it's still good.** I've been loving lasagna as long as I can remember and making it myself almost as long. When I was in college I'd assemble a huge one in a big hotel pan, cook it off, let it cool, then cut it into squares to pack into resealable bags in the freezer. With just a couple of hours of work, I'd have a full week's worth of dinners that would **rock the socks** off my roommates. That's a trick that lasts; we still do it at home. It makes it so easy to pull together a quick but delicious dinner when Lori and the kids and I are running in every direction. And Hunter loves nothing more than to find half a lasagna in the freezer when he's hunting for a "snack" before dinner (teenagers . . .).

MAKES **8 servings** • ***TIME*** **2½ hours**

Meat ragu

Two 28-ounce cans whole fire-roasted tomatoes, with their juice

¼ cup extra-virgin olive oil

2 carrots, finely diced

1 medium onion, finely diced

4 garlic cloves, minced

10 ounces ground beef (80% lean)

10 ounces bulk sweet Italian pork sausage

6 ounces pepperoni, coarsely ground in a food processor

1½ teaspoons kosher salt

½ cup tomato paste

1½ tablespoons all-purpose flour

1 tablespoon julienned basil

1 tablespoon chopped marjoram

1 tablespoon chopped oregano

8 to 10 turns freshly ground black pepper

½ teaspoon red chili flakes

1 To prepare the ragu, place the tomatoes in a food processor and pulse until chunky. Set aside.

2 In a large Dutch oven over medium-high heat, heat the olive oil. Add the carrots and onion and cook until the onion is translucent, 4 to 5 minutes. Add the garlic and cook for 1 minute, until fragrant. Add the ground beef, sausage, and pepperoni and season with the salt. Cook for about 10 minutes, or until the meat is browned all over, using a wooden spoon to break up the meat as it cooks. Add the tomato paste and cook for 4 to 5 minutes, until fragrant.

3 Dust the flour over the mixture and stir well to combine. Stir in the reserved tomatoes, basil, marjoram, oregano, black pepper, and chili flakes. Bring to a boil, then cover and reduce the heat to a simmer. Cook for 45 minutes, stirring occasionally. Remove from the heat and set aside to cool. Using a large spoon, skim off any oil that accumulates on the surface. (The ragu can be prepared 2 to 3 days ahead of time; store it in a covered container in the refrigerator until ready to use.)

The flour in the sauce helps soak up the oil from the meat.

RECIPE CONTINUES 

Do not let your dad pick the crunchy cheese from all the sides!

RECIPE CONTINUED FROM PAGE 40

Lasagna

2 pounds good-quality lasagna noodles

2 tablespoons plus 1 teaspoon kosher salt

1 pound whole-milk ricotta cheese

½ pound Parmesan cheese, grated (about 2½ cups)

1 large egg, beaten

5 or 6 gratings of nutmeg

5 or 6 turns freshly ground black pepper

2 tablespoons extra-virgin olive oil

1 garlic clove, minced

1½ pounds baby spinach leaves

1 pound mozzarella cheese, grated (about 4 cups)

¼ cup julienned basil

1 tablespoon chopped marjoram

1 tablespoon chopped oregano

4 To prepare the lasagna, in a large stockpot over medium-high heat, bring 2 gallons of water to a boil. Add 2 tablespoons of the salt. Add the lasagna noodles and stir gently to separate. Cook the lasagna noodles until al dente, 8 to 9 minutes. Meanwhile, prepare a large bowl of ice water. When the noodles are done, drain them, then plunge them immediately into the ice water for 30 seconds to stop the cooking process. Drain and spread the noodles on a rack.

5 In a large bowl, combine the ricotta, half of the Parmesan, the egg, nutmeg, and pepper. Mix well to combine and set aside.

6 In a large sauté pan over medium-high heat, heat the olive oil. Add the garlic, spinach, and the remaining 1 teaspoon salt. Sauté the spinach until tender and wilted, 1 to 2 minutes. Remove the pan from the heat and pour off any liquid. Transfer the spinach to a clean kitchen towel and twist it into a ball to squeeze out any excess moisture. Set aside.

7 Preheat the oven to 350°F. Have ready a heavy 10 x 14 x 3-inch lasagna pan.

8 To assemble the lasagna, ladle 1 cup of the ragu into the bottom and around the sides of the pan. Arrange several lasagna noodles on top of the sauce, slightly overlapping them to create an even layer that completely covers the ragu. Spread 2 cups of the ragu over the lasagna noodles, followed by one-third of the ricotta mixture, one-quarter of the mozzarella, and one-third of the spinach.

You'll be forming four layers of noodles in all, so divvy up your noodles for each layer accordingly.

9 Arrange more noodles on top, overlapping to cover the spinach. Spread 2 cups ragu over the noodles, followed by half of the remaining ricotta, one-third of the mozzarella, and half of the spinach. Arrange more noodles on top. Spread 2 cups ragu over them, followed by the remaining ricotta, half of the remaining mozzarella, and the remaining spinach. Arrange more noodles on top. Spread the remaining ragu on top and sprinkle with the remaining mozzarella and Parmesan and the basil, marjoram, and oregano.

10 Cover the pan with heavy-grade plastic food wrap (or parchment paper), then wrap the whole pan tightly with aluminum foil. Place the pan on a baking sheet (to catch any drips) in the center of the oven. Bake for 1 hour. Remove the foil and plastic food wrap and bake for 20 minutes longer, until well browned around the edges and bubbling. Finish under the broiler if necessary. Cool for 20 minutes before serving.

The plastic wrap keeps the lasagna moist.

Morgan's Veggie Ragu

My incredible sister Morgan set a standard of kindness, generosity, and straight-up humanity that I try hard to honor and exemplify every day of my life.

She was also a lasagna thief.

When we'd all get together I never wanted her (as the only vegetarian in the group) to be forced to eat only the side dishes around a big meaty main course. So I'd make a giant veggie lasagna to add to the spread. I can't tell you how many times she'd have just one slice and then take the whole thing home! I'd be standing there like, "Yeah, sure, Morgan, take the entire lasagna home with you. That's just what I ***meant*** for you to do."

Aw, well, little sisters, right? This one's for you, Bips.

The biggest problem with most vegetarian lasagnas is their texture. All mush. The trick for kickass vegetarian lasagna is to roast all the liquid out of the vegetables before they get anywhere near the noodles. Use this ragu in place of the meat ragu in the recipe on page 40. And don't be surprised when your sister swipes the leftovers.

Veggie ragu

1 Japanese eggplant, cut lengthwise into ¼-inch-thick strips

1 small yellow squash, cut lengthwise into ¼-inch-thick strips

1 small zucchini, cut lengthwise into ¼-inch-thick strips

1 red bell pepper, seeded and cut into ¼-inch-thick slices

1 Preheat the oven to 425°F.

2 Place the eggplant, yellow squash, zucchini, bell pepper, fennel, celery, carrot, onion, kale, garlic, chili flakes, basil, marjoram, and oregano in a large bowl and mix well to combine. Spread the vegetables out on two large roasting pans and drizzle with the olive oil. Season with salt and pepper. Roast for 10 to 12 minutes, until well charred. Spoon the crushed tomatoes

RECIPE CONTINUES →

RECIPE CONTINUED FROM PREVIOUS PAGE

½ fennel bulb, cut into ¼-inch-thick slices

4 celery stalks, cut crosswise into ¼-inch-thick slices

1 carrot, cut into ¼-inch-thick coins

1 small onion, sliced into thin wedges

4 cups chopped kale leaves (ribs and stems removed)

2 garlic cloves, minced

½ teaspoon red chili flakes

1 tablespoon chopped basil

1 tablespoon chopped marjoram

1 tablespoon chopped oregano

¼ cup extra-virgin olive oil

1 tablespoon kosher salt

7 or 8 turns freshly ground black pepper

One 28-ounce can crushed fire-roasted tomatoes, with their juice

over the vegetables and bake until browned and bubbly, 10 to 12 minutes. Set aside to cool.

3 Working in batches, place the vegetables in a food processor and process until the vegetables are well broken down into a chunky-sauce consistency. Proceed with step 4 above, using this in place of the meat ragu.

We love you, Bips!

Chicken Rigatoni Saltimbocca Bake

The great thing about this dish (**besides everything, I mean**) is that you can make the sauce, pasta, and chicken a little ahead of time. Then when you're ready to serve, toss the pasta and sauce together, top with the chicken, and you're good to go. If you want to punch it up to the next level, after you crisp the sage leaves, sauté 2 or 3 cups of chopped cauliflower, broccoli, or green beans in the oil. Remove them before you add the prosciutto to the pan and continue with the recipe. Then fold it all into the rigatoni with the sauce and you've got your all-in-one starch, protein, and veggie-full meal!

MAKES **4 to 6 servings** • ***TIME*** **1 hour**

Pasta

1 tablespoon kosher salt

1 pound rigatoni pasta

Breaded chicken

1 cup all-purpose flour

2 teaspoons kosher salt

8 to 10 turns freshly ground black pepper

2 large eggs

1 cup seasoned Italian bread crumbs

1 cup panko bread crumbs

2 teaspoons granulated garlic

1 teaspoon onion powder

1 teaspoon dried sage

1 pound boneless, skinless chicken breast halves, sliced in half horizontally and cut against the grain into 1 x 2-inch strips

Olive oil, for frying

1/4 pound Parmesan cheese, grated (about 1 1/4 cups)

1 To prepare the pasta, in a large pot over high heat, bring 1 gallon of water to a boil. Add the salt. Add the rigatoni and stir. Cook the pasta until al dente, 8 to 10 minutes. Reserve 1 cup of the pasta water. Drain and cool the pasta. Set aside.

2 To prepare the chicken, place the flour in a shallow dish and season with 1 teaspoon of the salt and 4 or 5 turns pepper. In a second shallow dish, beat the eggs. In a food processor, pulse the Italian bread crumbs and panko a few times to break down and combine them. Transfer the bread crumbs to a third shallow dish and stir in the granulated garlic, onion powder, dried sage, remaining 1 teaspoon salt, and 4 or 5 turns pepper. Have a rimmed baking sheet ready.

3 Lightly coat a chicken strip in the flour, then dip it into the egg mixture, then into the seasoned bread crumbs. Gently press the bread crumbs onto the chicken so they stick well and coat evenly. Set aside on the baking sheet and repeat with the remaining chicken.

4 In a deep, heavy sauté pan, pour olive oil to a depth of 1 inch. Heat the oil to 350°F over medium-high heat. Line a baking sheet with paper towels.

RECIPE CONTINUES →

A boat-a Saltimbocca!

RECIPE CONTINUED FROM PAGE 45

¼ pound aged or regular Provolone cheese, grated (about 1 cup)

Sage and prosciutto beurre blanc

3 tablespoons extra-virgin olive oil

16 sage leaves

¼ pound Prosciutto di Parma, cut crosswise into thick julienne

1 large shallot, minced

2 tablespoons drained nonpareil capers

½ cup dry white wine

Juice and grated zest of 1 lemon

1 cup heavy cream

3 tablespoons chopped flat-leaf parsley

½ teaspoon kosher salt

5 or 6 turns freshly ground black pepper

¼ pound (1 stick) cold unsalted butter, cut into cubes

2 tablespoons grated Parmesan cheese

1 ounce aged or regular Provolone cheese, grated (about ¼ cup)

3 tablespoons finely sliced basil

Tip: When dried pasta is correctly dehydrated, it dries from the inside out, so it really becomes dry. When you reconstitute it, it ends up al dente, "to the tooth," meaning it's tender, but still has real bite to it. If you want truly toothsome pasta, you've gotta make sure that you start with really good dry pasta.

5 Working in batches, fry the breaded chicken strips until golden brown and crispy, turning once, 2 to 3 minutes per side. Use tongs or a slotted spoon to transfer to the paper towels. Set aside.

6 To make the beurre blanc, place the olive oil and sage leaves in a large sauté pan, and set the pan over medium-high heat. Fry until crispy, 3 to 4 minutes once the oil is hot. Remove the sage leaves with a slotted spoon and set aside on a paper towel. To the same pan with the oil, add the prosciutto and cook until it is crispy and the fat has rendered, 4 to 5 minutes. Remove the prosciutto with a slotted spoon and set aside on a paper towel. In the remaining olive oil and fat in the pan, cook the shallot and capers until the shallot is translucent, 2 to 3 minutes.

7 Remove the pan from the heat and let cool for a minute or two. Carefully add the wine, lemon juice and zest, reserved pasta water, and cream (watch out for hot bubbles from the pan). Return the pan to the heat and bring to a gentle simmer, stirring constantly. Cook until the mixture has reduced by two-thirds. Add the parsley, salt, and pepper. Over low heat, whisk in the cold butter one or two cubes at a time, letting each cube melt into the sauce before adding more. The sauce will emulsify. Add the Parmesan and Provolone and whisk until melted. Coarsely chop half of the sage leaves and the prosciutto and add them to the sauce along with half the basil. Stir well. Keep warm over very low heat, whisking occasionally to keep the sauce emulsified.

8 Preheat the oven to 350°F.

9 To assemble the chicken rigatoni saltimbocca, add the rigatoni to the beurre blanc and toss together. Transfer to an ovenproof baking dish and place the chicken on top of the pasta. Top with the grated Parmesan and Provolone and bake for 12 to 15 minutes to warm through and melt the cheeses. Garnish with the remaining crispy sage and prosciutto and serve.

Rhode Island Beef and Noodles

This was one of the first dishes my wife, Lori, ever cooked for me. Her original was more straightforward, pretty much just ground beef, onions, and jarred gravy tossed with egg noodles. As humble and not so exciting as those ingredients might sound, it's really good—just like the feeling I got when I realized the girl from Rhode Island was kinda making me a beef Stroganoff! Yeah, sure, I've taken it a little further here, but if there's one person who understands that I can't help "improving" any dish—even one that comes with perfect memories—it's Lori.

MAKES **4 to 6 servings** • ***TIME*** **1 hour**

1½ pounds top round beef, cut into 1½-inch cubes

2 tablespoons kosher salt, plus more for seasoning

6 to 8 turns freshly ground black pepper, plus more for seasoning

¼ cup extra-virgin olive oil

1 medium yellow onion, diced

3 cups sliced cremini mushrooms

4 garlic cloves, minced

2 tablespoons all-purpose flour

1 cup full-bodied red wine

1 quart Beef Stock (page 226 or low-sodium store-bought)

¼ cup Worcestershire sauce

1 pound egg noodles

¼ pound Parmesan cheese, grated (about 1¼ cups)

4 tablespoons (½ stick) cold unsalted butter, cut into cubes

1 cup sour cream, for garnish

1 Season the cubes of beef with 1 tablespoon of the salt and the pepper.

2 In a Dutch oven over medium-high heat, heat the olive oil. Working in batches so as not to crowd the pan, brown the beef well on all sides, 6 to 8 minutes. Use a slotted spoon to transfer the beef to a bowl and set aside. Add the onion and mushrooms to the pan and sauté until the mushrooms are well browned, about 5 minutes. Add the garlic and sauté for 1 minute, until fragrant. Add the flour and cook for 3 minutes, stirring, until nutty and fragrant. Add the wine, beef stock, and Worcestershire sauce and mix well, scraping up the browned bits from the bottom of the pan. Bring to a boil.

3 Return the beef (and any juices) to the Dutch oven, cover, and simmer over medium-low heat for 35 to 40 minutes, until the beef is tender when pierced with a fork. Uncover and simmer for 15 minutes, until the sauce has thickened to a gravy-like consistency. Season with salt and pepper.

4 In a large stockpot over medium-high heat, bring 1 gallon of water to a boil. Add the remaining 1 tablespoon salt, then add the egg noodles and stir. Cook the noodles until al dente, 8 to 10 minutes. Reserve 1 cup of the pasta water, then drain the noodles and transfer them to a large mixing bowl.

RECIPE CONTINUES 

The real deal Ryder Seal of Approval.

← RECIPE CONTINUED FROM PAGE 48

¼ cup chopped flat-leaf parsley, for garnish

¼ cup minced chives, for garnish

Add half of the Parmesan and the butter cubes. Toss to mix and coat the noodles evenly as the butter melts. Add the reserved pasta water as needed to create a light sauce that coats the noodles.

5 Transfer the noodles to a large serving platter and ladle the Rhode Island beef over the top. Garnish with the sour cream, remaining Parmesan, the parsley, and the chives. Serve immediately.

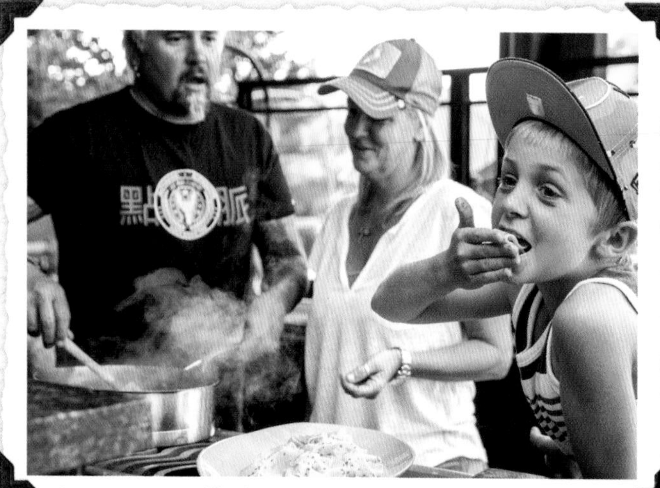

I can't believe he just did that.

Linguine with White Wine and Clams

For a few years we were a little worried about Ryder's picky eating. It's not easy to live with a reluctant eater when you cook like I do. Then one day when he was around five years old, the kid met a bowl of clams. Forty littlenecks later, I've got a whole new worry. . . .

Ryder has never looked back. That boy can stare down a bowl of linguine and clams from fifty paces. I always make double when he's around, just so the rest of us can have a bite.

There's another thing here I always make a lot of: garlic bread. Make more than you think you'll need. They'll eat it! But that cheese that's on it? Keep it on the bread. I don't have a lot of rules, but that's one I never stray from. **No cheese, ever, on linguine and clams!** You can't let anything get in the way of tasting those clams, man. Just ask Ryder.

MAKES **4 servings** • *TIME* **1 hour**

Linguine and clams

- 2 tablespoons extra-virgin olive oil
- 1 large shallot, minced
- 2 teaspoons thyme leaves
- ½ teaspoon red chili flakes
- 6 garlic cloves, minced
- 36 littleneck clams, cleaned (see page 52)
- 1 tablespoon plus 1 teaspoon kosher salt
- 1 cup dry white wine
- 1 cup bottled clam juice
- ½ cup Chicken Stock (page 228 or low-sodium store-bought)
- 4 or 5 turns freshly ground black pepper
- 2 lemons, quartered

1 To make the linguine and clams, heat the olive oil in a large sauté pan over medium-high heat. Add the shallot and sauté until translucent, 2 to 3 minutes. Add the thyme, chili flakes, garlic, clams, and 1 teaspoon of the salt. Toss a few times to mix, then cover with a lid and cook until the clams start to pop open, 5 to 7 minutes (do not stir the clams too vigorously or you risk pulling the meat out of the shells or cracking them). As soon as each clam opens, use tongs to transfer it to a large bowl. Set aside.

2 When all the clams have been removed, deglaze the pan by adding the wine, clam juice, and chicken stock and scraping up the browned bits from the bottom of the pan. Season with black pepper. Squeeze the lemon quarters over the pan (catch any seeds in your hand and discard them), then add the lemon quarters to the pan. Bring to a boil and cook for 6 to 8 minutes, until the liquid has reduced by half. Remove the pan from the heat and whisk in the butter a few cubes at a time.

3 Meanwhile, preheat the oven to 350°F. in a large pot over high heat, bring 1 gallon of water to a boil.

RECIPE CONTINUES →

RECIPE CONTINUED FROM PREVIOUS PAGE

4 tablespoons (½ stick) cold unsalted butter, cut into cubes

1 pound linguine

Garlic bread

¼ pound (1 stick) unsalted butter, at room temperature

¼ cup extra-virgin olive oil

6 garlic cloves, minced

¼ pound Parmesan cheese, grated (about 1¼ cups)

1 cup chopped flat-leaf parsley, plus more for garnish

2 tablespoons minced chives

2 tablespoons chopped oregano

1 sourdough baguette, cut lengthwise in half

¼ cup chopped flat-leaf parsley, for garnish

4 When the water is boiling, add the remaining 1 tablespoon salt, then add the linguine and stir. Cook the pasta until about 2 minutes before al dente, 8 to 10 minutes (the pasta should be soft and just pliable). Using tongs, transfer the linguine from the pasta water to the pan with the clam sauce. Add 1 cup of the pasta water to the pan. Return the pan to the heat and simmer the pasta for 2 minutes in the pan to finish cooking to al dente in the sauce.

5 To make the garlic bread, process the butter, olive oil, garlic, Parmesan, parsley, chives, and oregano in a food processor until well combined. Spread the mixture on the cut sides of the bread and place the bread on a baking sheet. Toast for 10 to 12 minutes, until warmed through.

6 To serve, use tongs to transfer the linguine to a large serving bowl. Return the clams to the pan with the sauce and toss to heat through. Arrange the clams on top of the pasta and ladle sauce on top. Garnish with the parsley and serve with the garlic bread.

Cleaning Clams 101

I **hate** sand in my shorts . . . I mean in my *clams.* Nothing throws off the whole clam experience for a diner more than sand between their teeth. And all it takes for a whole batch to get really sandy is for a single clam to be sandy. So do us all a favor and **clean your clams.** Putting some cornmeal in the water helps get the sand out: They suck up the cornmeal and then spit it out, along with the sand.

- Place the clams in a colander and run cold water over them while you scrub the shells with a stiff brush to remove any debris from the outside. Discard any that have cracked shells.
- For 36 littleneck clams, place ½ cup fine cornmeal and 1 gallon of cold water in a large bowl. Stir well, then add the clams. Let soak for 20 minutes to purge the salt and sand they have collected.
- When ready to use, drain the clams in a colander, rinse thoroughly with cold water, and drain again. Discard any clams that do not close even when tapped on the counter.

Pappardelle, Peas, and Sausage
with Roma Cream Sauce

Ribbons of fresh pappardelle are lapped by a light, creamy Roma tomato sauce, studded with sweet Italian sausage and peas, and covered generously with grated Parmesan cheese. . . .

Uh, is anyone else around here suddenly really hungry?

MAKES **4 servings •** ***TIME*** **45 minutes**

- 2 tablespoons extra-virgin olive oil
- 1 pound bulk sweet Italian sausage
- 1 large shallot, minced
- Kosher salt
- 4 garlic cloves, minced
- ½ cup sweet vermouth
- 2 cups diced cored Roma tomatoes (about 6 tomatoes)
- One 28-ounce can San Marzano tomatoes with their juice, pureed
- Freshly ground black pepper

1 To prepare the sauce, heat the olive oil in a large sauté pan over medium-high heat. Add the sausage and cook until well browned, breaking it up with a wooden spoon as it cooks, 6 to 8 minutes.

2 Add the shallot and 1 teaspoon salt. Sauté until the shallot is translucent, 3 to 4 minutes. Add the garlic and cook for 1 minute, until fragrant. Deglaze the pan by adding the vermouth and scraping up the browned bits from the bottom of the pan. Add the diced tomatoes, pureed tomatoes, black pepper, and chili flakes. Bring to a boil, then reduce the heat and simmer for 8 to 10 minutes, until the tomatoes start to break down and the sauce thickens.

RECIPE CONTINUES 

RECIPE CONTINUED FROM PREVIOUS PAGE

1/2 teaspoon red chili flakes

1 cup frozen peas

1 cup half-and-half

1/2 pound Parmesan cheese, grated (about 2 1/2 cups)

1 pound fresh egg pappardelle pasta

1/4 cup torn basil leaves, plus more for garnish

3 Stir in the peas, half-and-half, and two-thirds of the Parmesan and cook for 5 to 7 minutes to reduce the sauce. Remove the pan from the heat and set aside.

4 To prepare the pasta, in a large stockpot over medium-high heat, bring 1 gallon of water to a boil. Add 1 tablespoon salt, then add the pappardelle. Stir to loosen and separate the pasta and cook until about 2 minutes before al dente, 5 to 6 minutes (the pasta should be soft and just pliable). Using tongs, transfer the pasta from the pasta pot directly to the pan with the tomato sauce. Add 1/2 to 1 cup of the pasta water (depending on how thick your sauce is) to the tomato sauce. Add the basil and cook for 2 to 3 minutes to heat through and finish cooking the pasta in the sauce.

5 Transfer to a serving dish and garnish with the remaining Parmesan and basil. Serve.

Pasta Party

Sure, traditional spaghetti has its glorious place (under a giant pile of meatballs, ideally), but it's not the pasta shape that most rocks my world. What really get my attention are all the fun 'n' funky shapes that aren't as common as straight-up spaghetti. The different shapes aren't just for show, ya know—they actually have a purpose. Long, wide pastas like pappardelle and short, chunky pastas with lots of crevices are a good match for hearty sauces. Smoother, more delicate shapes such as capellini (angel-hair pasta) are meant for lighter sauces. Here are some of my faves, pictured beginning at the bottom right-hand corner of the page.

PAPPARDELLE: wide ribbons
RIGATONI: ridged tubes
MACARONI: curved "elbows"
MAFALDE: ribbons with curly edges
LONG FUSILLI: corkscrews
PENNE OR PENNETTE RIGATE: ridged quills
LASAGNA: wide sheets
LINGUINE: long and thin
ORECCHIETTE: little ears
COUSCOUS: tiny pasta beads

Seafood Salad
with Israeli Couscous

If you're wondering what couscous is doing in the pasta and noodles chapter, I'm here to tell ya that couscous *is* pasta. In fact, Israeli couscous is often sold as "pearl pasta." And it's one of the only kinds of pasta that I think should ever be served in a cool seafood salad. A lot of the others would be too heavy, but the couscous is perfect in this light, bright, fresh dish.

The other key to keeping it light and bright? **Don't shock the hell out of your fresh seafood.** More recipes than I can count tell you to throw the cold seafood into a hot court bouillon (fish broth) and then into a bowl of ice-cold water. Now you've shocked the bejeezus out of it twice. The seafood gets hard and chewy.

Instead, gently poach the seafood so lightly in the broth that it doesn't even notice it's cooking. Then let it cool down while still in the court bouillon. Now you have perfectly tender seafood with good bite. A perfect match for pearls of any kind.

MAKES **4 to 6 servings •** ***TIME*** **1 hour, plus chilling time**

½ pound cleaned calamari tubes and tentacles, tubes cut into 1-inch rings
2 cups buttermilk

Court bouillon

2 celery stalks, cut into ½-inch slices
½ fennel bulb, cut into ½-inch slices
1 onion, skin on, halved and quartered
4 flat-leaf parsley sprigs
4 dill sprigs
2 bay leaves
1 dried red chile
1 lemon, thinly sliced
½ teaspoon black peppercorns
1 cup dry white wine
4 cups ice

1 To tenderize the calamari, place the calamari and buttermilk in a large resealable plastic bag. Seal and massage the bag to ensure the calamari is well coated. Refrigerate for at least 30 minutes but no longer than 1 hour. Drain, rinse, and set aside.

2 Meanwhile, to make the court bouillon, place all the ingredients except the ice in a large stockpot. Add 2 cups cold water. Bring to a boil over high heat, then reduce the heat to medium-low and simmer for 10 to 12 minutes. Remove from the heat and add the ice to chill the liquid quickly. Stir when the ice has melted.

3 Place the shrimp, scallops, and calamari in a fine-mesh colander or strainer that fits in the stockpot. Lower the colander into the court bouillon, making sure the seafood is completely submerged. Place the pan over medium heat and slowly heat the bouillon until it is barely simmering and the shrimp has turned pink. Remove from the heat and let the seafood

RECIPE CONTINUES 

RECIPE CONTINUED FROM PREVIOUS PAGE

½ pound 21/25 shrimp, peeled and deveined, sliced lengthwise in half

½ pound sea scallops, quartered

Vinaigrette

1 cup extra-virgin olive oil

3 tablespoons white wine vinegar

2 sun-dried tomatoes (packed in oil)

2 large garlic cloves, minced

Juice and grated zest of 1 lemon

1 teaspoon Dijon mustard

½ teaspoon sugar

Kosher salt and freshly ground black pepper

Salad

1½ cups Israeli couscous

½ pound baby arugula

½ fennel bulb, finely sliced, fronds reserved for garnish

Kosher salt and freshly ground black pepper

1 Roma tomato, cored and diced, for garnish

2 green onions (white and light green parts), sliced on the bias, for garnish

1 lemon, cut into wedges, for garnish

steep in the broth for 5 minutes. Transfer the pot and colander setup to the refrigerator and chill completely, about 1 hour.

4 To prepare the vinaigrette, place all the ingredients in a blender. Puree until the sun-dried tomatoes and garlic are completely broken down and the vinaigrette is emulsified. Taste and adjust the seasoning. Let the vinaigrette sit in the fridge for at least 5 minutes before using. (The vinaigrette can be stored in an airtight container in the refrigerator for 2 to 3 days.)

5 When you're ready to make the salad, remove the colander with the seafood from the court bouillon and set aside to drain. Strain the bouillon and discard the solids. Return the bouillon to the stockpot and bring to a boil. Add the couscous and cook until tender, 12 to 14 minutes. Drain thoroughly and spread on a rimmed baking sheet to cool.

6 In a large mixing bowl, combine the arugula, fennel, enough vinaigrette to lightly coat, and salt and pepper to taste; toss gently to combine. Transfer to a large serving dish. To the mixing bowl add the reserved seafood and couscous and enough vinaigrette to coat the pasta evenly, about ¼ cup. Gently toss to combine. Arrange the seafood and couscous on top of the arugula. Garnish with the diced tomato, green onions, lemon wedges, and fennel fronds. Serve.

Island Shrimp and Lo Mein Noodles with Crispy Chiles

This is in the spirit of a dish we used to call Kung Pao Shrimp in the early days. So many people have asked me for the recipe over the years that I finally had to write it down here just so I have something to offer them. Now everyone can bring home a little of that Kung Pao magic!

MAKES 4 to 6 servings • TIME 45 minutes

Pineapple-teriyaki sauce

¼ cup sliced green onions (white and light green parts)

1 tablespoon grated ginger

1 tablespoon minced garlic

1 tablespoon toasted sesame oil

1 cup pineapple juice

Juice and grated zest of 1 orange

1 teaspoon red chili flakes

½ cup soy sauce

2 tablespoons hoisin sauce (Asian BBQ sauce)

5 or 6 turns freshly ground black pepper

2 tablespoons cornstarch

Canola oil, for frying

¼ cup buttermilk

1 jalapeño, seeded and thinly sliced

1 Fresno chile, seeded and thinly sliced

½ cup cornstarch

Kosher salt

1 To prepare the pineapple-teriyaki sauce, in a medium saucepan over medium-high heat, sauté the green onions, ginger, and garlic in the sesame oil until fragrant and just lightly golden in color, about 1 minute. Add half the pineapple juice, the orange juice and zest, the chili flakes, soy sauce, hoisin sauce, and black pepper. Bring to a boil, then reduce the heat to a simmer and cook for 5 to 7 minutes, until slightly reduced.

2 Meanwhile, in a small bowl, combine the remaining pineapple juice and the cornstarch and stir into a well-blended slurry. Whisk the slurry into the sauce and stir well to avoid lumps. Cook for 2 to 3 minutes, until thickened. Remove the pan from the heat and set aside. (This can be done a day in advance; store in a covered container in the refrigerator until ready to use.)

3 In a wok, pour canola oil to a depth of ½ inch. Heat the oil to 350°F. Line a plate with paper towels.

4 While the oil is heating, in a small bowl, mix the buttermilk, jalapeño, and Fresno to coat. Drain the chiles and lightly dredge them in the cornstarch, shaking off any excess.

RECIPE CONTINUES →

RECIPE CONTINUED FROM PREVIOUS PAGE

1 tablespoon grated ginger

1 tablespoon minced garlic

1½ pounds 21/25 shrimp, peeled, deveined, and butterflied

1 medium red onion, thinly sliced

2 medium carrots, julienned

4 celery stalks, julienned

1 small zucchini, julienned

½ cup bias-cut asparagus

1 pound dried lo mein noodles

½ cup chopped cilantro

½ cup finely sliced green onions (white and light green parts)

5 Working in small batches, fry the chiles in the hot oil until golden brown and crisp, 2 to 3 minutes. Use a slotted spoon to transfer the chiles to the paper-towel-lined plate. Season with salt and set aside.

6 Pour off all but 2 to 3 tablespoons of oil from the wok and return the wok to high heat. Add the ginger and garlic and stir-fry until the garlic is fragrant, about 2 minutes. Add the shrimp and stir-fry until the shrimp turns pink and is curled, 3 to 4 minutes. Set the shrimp aside on a plate. Add to the wok the onion, carrots, celery, zucchini, asparagus, and 1 teaspoon salt. Stir-fry the vegetables until lightly charred around the edges, 5 to 6 minutes. Return the shrimp to the wok and add the pineapple-teriyaki sauce. Toss well to combine.

7 Meanwhile, in a large stockpot over medium-high heat, bring 1 gallon of water to a boil. Add 1 tablespoon salt, then add the noodles and stir. Cook the noodles until al dente, 5 to 6 minutes. Drain the noodles and add them to the wok. Toss everything together.

8 Serve the noodles garnished with the crispy chiles, cilantro, and green onions.

Don't know how the forks made it in
the pic . . . Where are my chopsticks?

Marsala Madness!

Chicken Marsala Radiatori

We eat this at home once a week . . . every week. No other dish can bring that coast of Marsala, Sicily,* feeling into your kitchen like this one can.

MAKES **4 to 6 servings •** ***TIME*** **1 hour**

1½ pounds boneless, skinless chicken breast halves, cut into roughly 1 x 2-inch, ⅜-inch-thick strips

¼ cup all-purpose flour

Kosher salt and freshly ground black pepper

4 tablespoons extra-virgin olive oil

2 cups tightly packed baby spinach leaves

3 cups sliced cremini mushrooms

1 large red bell pepper, seeded and julienned

¼ cup minced shallot

1 tablespoon tomato paste

2 garlic cloves, minced

1 teaspoon thyme leaves

1 cup sweet Marsala wine

1 cup Chicken Stock (page 228 or low-sodium store-bought)

2 tablespoons cold unsalted butter, cut into cubes

3 tablespoons chopped flat-leaf parsley, plus more for garnish

1 pound radiatori pasta

**Yep, it's a place, not just a wine.*

1 Using the flat side of a meat mallet, lightly pound the chicken pieces.

2 In a large dish, combine the flour, 1 teaspoon salt, and ½ teaspoon black pepper. Lightly dredge the chicken pieces in the flour and set aside.

3 In a large nonstick sauté pan over medium-high heat, heat 1 tablespoon of the olive oil. Sauté the spinach until wilted, 1 to 2 minutes. Season with salt and black pepper and set aside. Add 2 tablespoons of the olive oil to the pan and, working in batches, brown the chicken pieces all over, 3 to 5 minutes. Remove the chicken from the pan and set aside.

4 Add the remaining 1 tablespoon olive oil to the pan, then add the mushrooms, bell pepper, shallot, and salt to taste. Sauté until the mushrooms are lightly browned, 6 to 8 minutes. Stir in the tomato paste, garlic, and thyme and cook for 1 minute, until fragrant. Deglaze by adding the Marsala and scraping up the browned bits from the bottom of the pan.

5 Return the chicken to the pan, then add the chicken stock. Bring to a boil and simmer until reduced by half, 6 to 8 minutes. Season with salt and pepper and return the cooked spinach to the pan. Stir in the butter cubes a few at a time until melted. Stir in the parsley.

6 Meanwhile, to cook the radiatori, in a large stockpot over medium-high heat, bring 1 gallon of water to a boil. Add 1 tablespoon salt, then add the pasta. Cook according to the package directions (timing will vary depending on the size of the radiatori) until al dente. Drain.

7 Toss the radiatori with the chicken and sauce, and garnish with more chopped parsley. Serve.

ONE FOR THE WEEK

Because Nobody Digs Ordinary Leftovers

I don't have to tell you that I love just about everything about cooking. When I'm home on a Sunday and I can put the game on, crank up the tunes, and cook up a storm all afternoon, that is 100 percent my happy place. But there's one thing I'm not a big fan of about cooking—or should I say "reheating." Leftovers. As soon as I look at a plate of last night's dinner, I'm disenchanted.

This doesn't mean that I don't *eat* last night's dinner. It just never *looks* like last night's dinner. When it comes to leftovers, **I am the king of repurposing.** It's a good talent to have for someone like me who never wants to see the same dish two nights in a row. But for busy parents, working people, and anyone trying to feed a family on a budget (so, like, pretty much everyone), it's fundamental, the most economical and time-saving way to cook because it makes the most of your food money and time in the kitchen. And in my house, it helps keep the peace when I'm on the road. I try to be home with Lori and the boys on weekends, but during the week I'm often traveling. I don't like to leave them high and dry to cook from scratch every night I'm gone. So on the weekend, I'll cook up a meal with dishes that can be easily turned into other stuff later in the week. I might roast a few chickens, fire-roast a bunch of corn on the cob, and make a big pot of quinoa pilaf. On the first night I'll serve some of the corn Mexican-style, spreading the ears with mayonnaise and sprinkling them with ground chile and fresh lime juice. The rest of it I cut off the cob. The next night some of the chicken, corn, and quinoa can be turned into a big salad with a bunch of basil or other herbs. And then a night or two later, the rest of the corn and quinoa become a soup topped with shredded chicken. In this chapter I lay out four big meals, each one followed by three spin-offs that use up all the leftovers and **are just as finger-lickin' good as the first night's meal.**

This kind of cooking is easy to do once you get the hang of it, but it does require a little foresight. The recipes here do all the planning for you, but when you're winging it on your own, follow my three **Rules for Repurposing** on page 70.

That's my middle name (and Ryder's too)!

Guy Ramsay's Rules for Repurposing

Planning and cooking with repurposing in mind isn't difficult. All it takes is a little foresight. So just follow my rules, and you're halfway there.

This goes for the grill, too. Gas and charcoal cost money, man, and once it's hot, you can throw on double the number of chicken breasts or a couple bunches of asparagus. Now tomorrow night's dinner is halfway done.

If you're cooking one thing, multiply it with tomorrow's dinner in mind. In the cases I mentioned a couple of pages ago, make at least twice as much corn and potatoes as you'll eat the first night. Coat just half the corn and use half of the potatoes in the salad. Save the other half for the rest of the week.

When the oven is on, you're cooking for the week. That means that even if you're not going to eat roasted squash tonight, cook it while the oven is hot. It saves time and it saves money.

Don't overseason, overdress, or overcommit. When you make a dish that will be repurposed in a night or two, don't season it in a way that gets you stuck in one flavor profile and makes it harder to use in a different cuisine. So, if you're making Mexican-style corn on the cob on the first night, don't slather every last cob with mayonnaise. And don't make a huge batch of vinegary or creamy potato salad with those potatoes, because you can't turn that into hash or pancakes later in the week.

Twins!

Oven-Roasted Chicken

Main Recipe

with Roasted Red Bliss Potatoes and Cauliflower Florets

It's an all-you-can-roast dinner tonight, perfect for cooler weather. And you can become a roasting ninja while you make it: First, get the chickens in the oven. While they're roasting, prep the potatoes and toss them in the oven, too. Then cut up the cauliflower. By the time you've set the table, it's all ready to go *and* you've laid the groundwork for three more meals this week.

MAKES **4 to 6 servings •** ***TIME*** **2½ hours**

Roasted chickens

¼ pound (1 stick) unsalted butter, at room temperature

2 to 3 thyme sprigs, plus 1 tablespoon thyme leaves

1 tablespoon minced flat-leaf parsley

Juice and zest of 2 lemons

Two 4½- to 5-pound free-range, organic chickens, rinsed and dried

2 tablespoons kosher salt

2 teaspoons freshly ground black pepper

1 large onion, coarsely chopped

4 medium carrots, coarsely chopped

4 celery stalks, coarsely chopped

1 cup dry white wine

Roasted Red Bliss potatoes

1 tablespoon kosher salt

2 teaspoons freshly ground black pepper

1 tablespoon granulated garlic

1 tablespoon granulated onion

1 Preheat the oven to 375°F.

2 To prepare the chickens, in a small bowl, combine the butter, thyme leaves, parsley, and lemon juice and zest and mix well. Rub the herb butter under the skin of the breast and over the meat of the chickens. Season all over with the salt and pepper.

3 Tuck the wing tips under the backs of the chickens and use kitchen twine to tie the legs together. Put the onion, carrots, celery, thyme sprigs, and wine in a large roasting pan. Cover with a roasting rack and place the chickens on the rack breast side up. Roast in the center of the oven until the chickens are golden brown, their skin is crispy, and a thermometer inserted into the thickest part of the thigh joint registers 165°F to 170°F, about 1 hour 15 minutes. Discard the onion, carrots, celery, and thyme.

Truss the chicken so it cooks evenly!

4 While the chickens are roasting, make the potatoes. In a small bowl, combine the salt, pepper, garlic, onion, oregano, and paprika and mix well. Spread the potatoes evenly on two large rimmed baking sheets and drizzle them with the olive oil. Sprinkle the spice mixture over the potatoes and shake the pans to coat evenly. Roast, turning the potatoes halfway through

RECIPE CONTINUES 

Roasted to the mosted . . . ed!?
Or toasted? Ha ha.

RECIPE CONTINUED FROM PAGE 71

1 tablespoon dried oregano

2 teaspoons paprika

5 pounds small Red Bliss potatoes, scrubbed and rinsed

¼ cup extra-virgin olive oil

Roasted cauliflower florets

2 large cauliflower heads

½ cup extra-virgin olive oil

1 tablespoon kosher salt

1 teaspoon freshly ground black pepper

1 tablespoon granulated garlic

1 tablespoon granulated onion

2 tablespoons chopped flat-leaf parsley

½ teaspoon red chili flakes

cooking, until tender when pierced with a knife and browned in spots, about 45 minutes.

5 To prepare the cauliflower, remove the outer green leaves from both heads, leaving the cores intact. Place one cauliflower head on its base on a cutting board. Using a sharp knife, cut it into 1-inch, bite-size florets. Transfer the florets to a large bowl. Repeat with the other cauliflower. Add the olive oil, salt, black pepper, garlic, onion, parsley, and chili flakes and toss until well coated. Spread the cauliflower evenly on two large rimmed baking sheets. Roast until tender and golden brown around the edges, 20 to 25 minutes.

6 Transfer one roasted chicken to a platter, tent loosely with aluminum foil, and let stand for 15 minutes. To serve, carve the chicken into 10 pieces and serve with half of the roasted potatoes and cauliflower.

Tip: If you can't fit everything in your oven at the same time, just hold back about half of the potatoes and cauliflower and roast them while you eat dinner.

Prep for the Week

- Set the second chicken aside to cool completely.
- Cut some of the breast into 2½-inch-long and ¼-inch-wide strips (you should have 2 cups) for the Roasted Chicken Spring Rolls with Spicy Peanut Dipping Sauce (page 77).
- Pull the remaining chicken meat (you should have 4 cups) for the Chicken Chile Verde Enchiladas (page 74), discarding the bones and skin.
- Set aside 3 cups each of the potatoes and cauliflower for the Curried Cauliflower and Potato Salad (page 80).
- Store everything in airtight containers in the refrigerator until needed.

Chicken Chile Verde Enchiladas

There's something about enchiladas that makes them just fly out of restaurant kitchens. So here's a real-deal enchilada recipe you can use to blow everybody away at home. Creamy, tangy cilantro crema is so on point here and on any Tex-Mex or Mexican-inspired dish, such as Mexican Pork Pozole (page 85) and Roasted Turkey Chilaquiles with Chipotle Queso (page 106).

***MAKES* 4 to 6 servings • *TIME* 1 hour**

Chile verde

1 pound tomatillos, husked, washed, and halved

4 poblano peppers, fire-roasted (see page 32)

1 Anaheim chile, fire-roasted (see page 32)

2 serrano chiles, fire-roasted (see page 32)

1 jalapeño, fire-roasted (see page 32)

1 bunch cilantro, washed

1/4 cup canola oil

1 medium sweet onion, minced

2 teaspoons kosher salt

4 garlic cloves, minced

4 cups Chicken Stock (page 228 or low-sodium store-bought)

2 tablespoons ground cumin

Cilantro crema

1 1/2 cups sour cream

1/4 cup buttermilk

1 To make the chile verde, in a food processor, puree the tomatillos, poblanos, Anaheim, serranos, jalapeño, and cilantro until smooth. In a large saucepan over medium-high heat, heat the canola oil until hot. Add the onion and salt and cook until the onion is translucent, 5 to 6 minutes. Add the garlic and cook for 1 minute, until fragrant. Add the pureed tomatillo-pepper mixture, chicken stock, and cumin and bring to a boil, then reduce the heat to a simmer and cook until the chile verde has reduced and thickened, 25 to 30 minutes. Set aside off the heat.

2 Meanwhile, to make the cilantro crema, place all the ingredients in a blender and pulse several times. Scrape down the sides and pulse again until completely pureed, about 1 minute. Transfer to a covered container and refrigerate until needed.

3 To make the enchiladas, heat the olive oil in a large sauté pan over medium-high heat until hot. Add the chicken, salt, and pepper and sauté until the chicken is browned and crispy around the edges, 4 to 5 minutes. Add 2 cups of the chile verde sauce and toss well to coat evenly. Heat through. Set aside off the heat.

4 Preheat the oven to 425°F. Have ready a large rimmed baking sheet.

½ bunch cilantro, washed

Juice of 1 lime

1 teaspoon kosher salt

Enchiladas

2 tablespoons extra-virgin olive oil

4 cups pulled reserved Oven-Roasted Chicken meat (page 71)

1 teaspoon kosher salt

5 or 6 turns freshly ground black pepper

¼ pound Oaxaca cheese, grated (about 1 cup)

¼ pound Jack cheese, grated (about 1 cup)

Twelve 6-inch corn tortillas

½ pound sharp white cheddar cheese, grated (about 2 cups)

2 ounces Cotija cheese, crumbled (about ½ cup), for garnish

½ cup finely sliced green onions (white and light green parts), for garnish

¼ cup pepitas, toasted (see page 22), for garnish

2 radishes, thinly sliced, for garnish

2 limes, cut into wedges

5 Combine the Oaxaca and Jack cheeses in a medium bowl. Lightly toast one corn tortilla in a dry pan for about 10 seconds on each side. Lay the tortilla flat on a clean surface. Place about ⅓ cup of the roasted chicken mixture across the middle, spreading it end to end. Top with a generous sprinkle of the cheese mixture. Tightly roll up the tortilla around the filling and transfer to the baking sheet. Repeat with the remaining tortillas and fillings, spacing the enchiladas 1 inch apart and arranging them in two rows.

Make sure they stay pliable so they don't crack when you roll them.

6 Lightly spoon the remaining chile verde sauce over the enchiladas, then sprinkle with the cheddar. Bake until the cheese is melted and lightly browned, 8 to 10 minutes. Let rest for 5 minutes.

7 Transfer the enchiladas to a platter using a large spatula. Drizzle with the cilantro crema and garnish with the crumbled Cotija, green onions, pepitas, and radishes. Serve with lime wedges on the side.

Roasted Chicken Spring Rolls

with Spicy Peanut Dipping Sauce

You wanna know the best way to hide leftovers? Tuck 'em in a place no one will ever find them. . . . Extra points for making their hiding place so flavorful that everyone begs for seconds.

MAKES **4 to 6 servings •** ***TIME*** **45 minutes**

Dipping sauce

1 tablespoon toasted sesame oil

2 garlic cloves, minced

1 tablespoon grated ginger

2 tablespoons hot water, plus more as needed

½ cup creamy peanut butter

Juice and zest of 1 lime

2 tablespoons low-sodium soy sauce

1 tablespoon seasoned rice vinegar

1 teaspoon sriracha sauce

1 tablespoon hoisin sauce

2 tablespoons coarsely chopped roasted peanuts, for garnish

Spring rolls

¼ pound maifun noodles (thin dried rice noodles)

½ cup hoisin sauce

1 tablespoon sriracha sauce

Twelve 8-inch round rice paper sheets, or as needed

12 small butter lettuce leaves, rinsed and dried, plus 2 cups julienned butter lettuce leaves

1 To make the dipping sauce, pour the sesame oil in a small sauté pan and set over medium heat. Add the garlic and ginger and sauté lightly until just fragrant, about 1 minute. Transfer to a blender and add the hot water, peanut butter, lime juice and zest, soy sauce, vinegar, sriracha, and hoisin. Puree until smooth, adding a little extra hot water if necessary to keep the mixture moving. Transfer to a bowl and garnish with the chopped peanuts. Set aside.

2 To make the spring rolls, place the noodles in a small bowl. Add hot water to cover them and set them aside to soften, 10 to 12 minutes. Drain.

3 In a small bowl, combine the hoisin and sriracha.

4 Have ready all the spring roll ingredients and a serving platter for the finished rolls, and take a look at "Spring Rolls 101" on page 79 for pointers before you begin. Fill a shallow pie dish with lukewarm tap water and submerge one rice paper wrapper for about 10 seconds to soften. Place the wrapper on a clean work surface. In the center of the wrapper, place a lettuce leaf to create a layer of protection. Place some shredded lettuce, a few cilantro sprigs, and 4 chicken strips on top. Lightly brush with the hoisin-sriracha mixture. Top with some maifun noodles, then 3 pieces each cucumber, carrot, and bell pepper, a sprinkling of green onion, and finally a pinch of torn basil (see page 78, fig. a).

RECIPE CONTINUES →

RECIPE CONTINUED FROM PREVIOUS PAGE

½ cup cilantro sprigs

2 cups 2½-inch-long, ¼-inch-wide strips reserved Oven-Roasted Chicken (page 71)

½ seedless hothouse cucumber, cut into 2½-inch-long, ¼-inch-wide strips

1 large carrot, julienned

1 red bell pepper, seeded and julienned

2 green onions (white and light green parts), thinly sliced diagonally

½ cup torn Thai basil leaves

For serving

2 limes, cut into wedges

¼ cup cilantro sprigs

5 Fold in both sides of the rice paper. Fold the top tightly over the filling to seal it in (fig. b), then roll the filling over onto the wrapper to seal tightly (fig. c), finishing the roll when the seam side is down. Roll as tight as you can without tearing, but don't worry if the wrapper does tear. Save the filling and get another wrapper. After two or three times you will get it. Transfer the completed rolls to the serving platter. Repeat with the remaining wrappers and filling.

6 Serve the rolls with the spicy peanut dipping sauce, lime wedges, and cilantro.

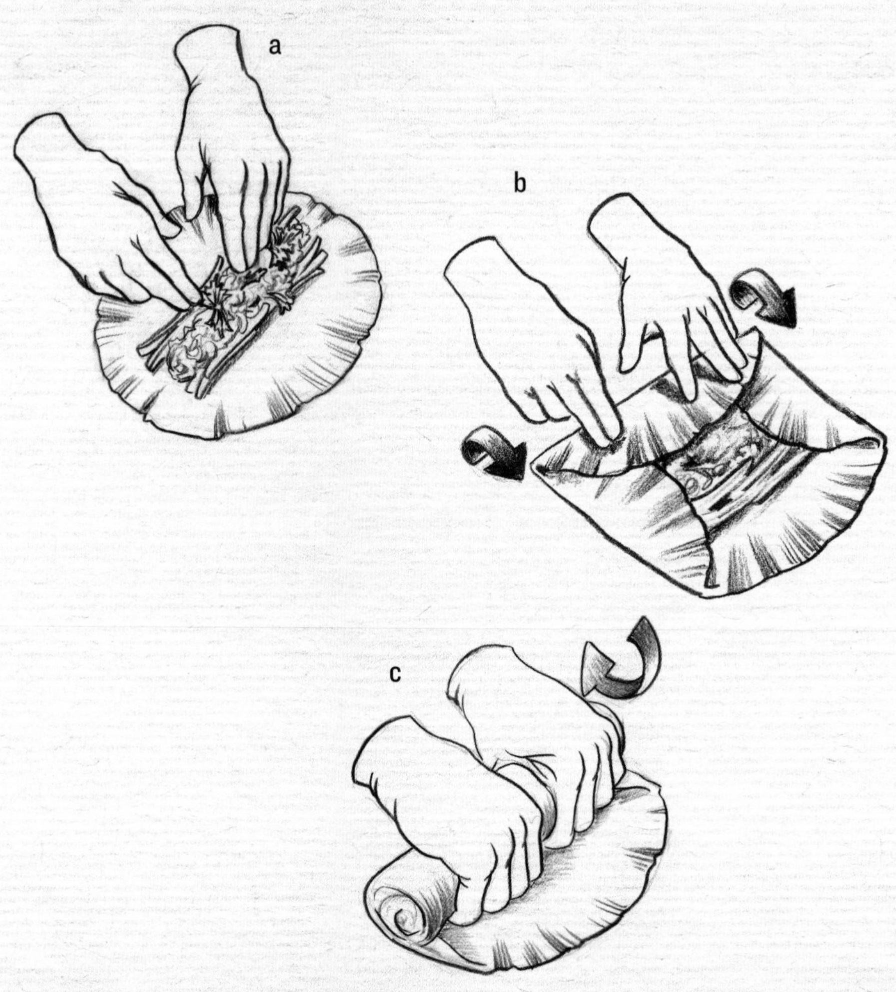

Spring Rolls 101

I think a lot of people believe there's some secret to forming spring rolls that makes it impossible for regular mortals to do it. I'm here to tell ya that's not the case at all. You've just gotta handle the rice paper sheets right, and **the rest is easy.**

Actually the "rest" comes first—in that you've gotta **have everything you need ready to go before you begin.** So get your workstation in order. Line up all the fillings, ideally in the order they'll go into the rolls. Get your rice paper sheets ready—but keep them in their package or covered with a kitchen towel, because if you get water on them, they'll stick together. Have the platter for the finished rolls dry and ready. Ditto for the work surface you're about to stuff and roll all these babies on.

The very last thing to do before you begin is prepare a shallow dish of water for softening the rice paper sheets. The key to properly softening rice paper for spring rolls is not to **over**soften it. So use *lukewarm* water—not hot! If you use hot water, one, you'll burn yourself, and two, your rice paper will go from nice flat sheet to floppy slop in about 5 seconds.

Put the sheet in the *lukewarm* water, and as soon as you can take it out of the water and it'll fold over itself, it's good to go. If you leave it in the water until it's as soft as you eventually want it, it'll tear on you when you try to roll it up with the filling. It will keep hydrating out of the water, so take it out before it's all the way there. Don't worry if some of your rice paper sheets tear; it happens to everyone. Just move the filling to another paper and try again. It takes a little practice, but after you've made this recipe just once, you'll be a regular pro.

Curried Cauliflower and Potato Salad

Serve this smoky curried salad with sliced chicken or sandwiches.

MAKES **4 to 6 servings** • ***TIME*** **20 minutes**

3 cups reserved Roasted Cauliflower Florets (page 73)

3 cups reserved Roasted Red Bliss Potatoes (page 73)

1 teaspoon coriander seeds

1 teaspoon cumin seeds

1 teaspoon fennel seeds

1 tablespoon curry powder

¼ teaspoon cayenne pepper

¾ cup diced fire-roasted red bell peppers (see page 32)

¼ cup chopped cilantro

½ cup mayonnaise

¼ cup plain yogurt

½ small red onion, julienned

½ cup thinly sliced celery

Juice and zest of 1 lemon

Kosher salt and freshly ground black pepper

¼ cup finely sliced green onions (white and light green parts), for garnish

1 Coarsely chop the cauliflower and potatoes into ½-inch chunks and set aside.

2 In a dry skillet over medium heat, toast the coriander seeds, cumin seeds, and fennel seeds until fragrant, shaking the pan frequently, 2 to 3 minutes. Transfer them to a spice grinder and pulse until ground to a fine powder, then pour them into a small dish and mix in the curry powder and cayenne.

3 Set aside about 1 tablespoon each of the bell peppers and cilantro for garnish and place the rest in a large bowl. Add the mayonnaise, yogurt, red onion, celery, lemon juice and zest, reserved spices, and salt and black pepper to taste. Stir until smooth. Add the cauliflower and potatoes and mix well to coat evenly. (The salad can be stored in an airtight container in the refrigerator for up to 1 day.)

4 Transfer the salad to a large serving bowl. Garnish with the green onions and the reserved cilantro and bell peppers. Serve.

Tip: A blade coffee grinder can also be used as a spice grinder. If you also use the grinder for coffee, when you're done grinding the spices, put a handful of dry rice in the empty grinder. Grind it up, discard the rice, and then wipe out the grinder with a dry paper towel. This'll keep the spicy kick where it belongs—in this salad—and away from where it doesn't belong—in tomorrow morning's cuppa joe.

The bottom of the plate has blurry curry!
Ha ha!

Prized pork
platter perfection!

Slow-Roasted Pork Shoulder

with Green Vegetable Succotash and Basmati Rice Pilaf

Main Recipe

This menu and its spin-offs put crazy-versatile pork through its paces all week long. You've gotta make a lot of pork the first night, because it's gonna get devoured.

MAKES **4 to 6 servings** • *TIME* **5½ hours**

Pork shoulder

2 large onions, sliced

4 medium carrots, coarsely chopped

6 celery stalks, coarsely chopped

1 quart Chicken Stock (page 228 or low-sodium store-bought)

3 tablespoons granulated garlic

2 tablespoons onion powder

2 tablespoons paprika

2 tablespoons Italian seasoning

2 tablespoons kosher salt

1 tablespoon freshly ground black pepper

One 6-pound boneless pork shoulder, trimmed of excess fat, cut into 4 equal pieces

¼ cup extra-virgin olive oil

1 Preheat the oven to 425°F.

2 Place the onions, carrots, and celery in the bottom of a large roasting pan and pour in the chicken stock.

3 In a small bowl, combine the garlic, onion powder, paprika, Italian seasoning, salt, and pepper to make a dry rub. Rub the pork all over with the olive oil, then season all over with the dry rub. Place the pork on top of the vegetables in the pan and roast for 30 minutes.

4 Reduce the heat to 325°F and roast, adding water to the bottom of the pan if it becomes dry, until the pork is very tender when pierced with a fork, 4 to 5 hours. Let stand until cool enough to handle, about 30 minutes.

5 Toward the end of roasting, prepare the rice pilaf. In a large saucepan, bring the stock and 2½ cups water to a simmer over medium heat.

6 Meanwhile, place the rice in a mesh strainer and rinse under cold running water until the water runs clear. Drain well.

This removes any excess starch, which makes the rice gummy.

7 Place the olive oil, onion, and salt in a medium saucepan and cook over medium heat until the onion is just translucent, 4 to 5 minutes. Add the rice and bay leaves and mix well to combine and coat evenly. Add the warm

RECIPE CONTINUES

← RECIPE CONTINUED FROM PREVIOUS PAGE

Basmati rice pilaf

2½ cups Chicken Stock (page 228 or low-sodium store-bought)

3 cups basmati rice

1 tablespoon extra-virgin olive oil

¼ cup finely diced onion

1 teaspoon kosher salt

2 bay leaves

¼ cup chopped cilantro

Succotash

1 tablespoon plus 1 teaspoon kosher salt

1 cup shelled and hulled fresh or frozen fava beans

2 cups shelled fresh or frozen edamame beans

2 cups fresh or frozen peas

1 cup diced green beans

1 cup diced asparagus

2 tablespoons extra-virgin olive oil

½ red bell pepper, seeded and diced

1 large shallot, minced

4 garlic cloves, minced

4 to 5 turns freshly ground black pepper

2 tablespoons unsalted butter

stock and water and bring to a boil. Boil, uncovered, until most of the liquid has evaporated, about 10 minutes. Reduce the heat to a simmer, cover, and cook for 15 minutes, or until the liquid has been completely absorbed. Let the pan sit off the heat, still covered, for 7 to 8 minutes. When ready to serve, discard the bay leaves, fluff the rice with a fork, and fold in the cilantro.

8 While the pork is resting, prepare the succotash. In a medium saucepan, bring 4 to 5 inches of water and 1 tablespoon of the salt to a boil over medium-high heat. Have ready a large bowl of ice water. Add the fava beans, edamame, peas, green beans, and asparagus to the boiling water and boil for 2 minutes. Drain and immediately plunge into the ice water (this "blanching" locks in the bright green color). Drain and let stand to dry.

9 Set a large sauté pan over medium-high heat and add the olive oil. When it is hot, add the bell pepper and shallot. Sauté until the shallot is translucent, 3 to 4 minutes. Add the blanched vegetables, garlic, remaining 1 teaspoon salt, and the black pepper and sauté until heated through, 5 to 6 minutes. Add the butter and toss until the butter has melted. Remove the pan from the heat.

10 To serve, pull two pieces of the pork into bite-size pieces and transfer to a serving platter. Spoon the juices from the pan over the top. Serve with the pilaf and succotash.

Prep for the Week

- Cut some of the pork into 4 cups ¾-inch cubes for the Mexican Pork Pozole (opposite).
- Pull 2 cups of the pork and set aside with 1 cup basmati rice pilaf for the Sweet Italian Pepper Poppers (page 88).
- Set aside 4 cups green vegetable succotash for the Green Pea Patties with Sriracha Ranch (page 87).
- Store everything in separate airtight containers in the refrigerator until needed.

Mexican Pork Pozole

Nothing chases away the cold night shivers like a rich, meaty stew, especially when it's *this* stew, every bite of which is studded with chewy hominy and cubes of flavorful roasted pork.

MAKES **4 to 6 servings** • ***TIME*** **1 hour**

2 tablespoons extra-virgin olive oil

1 large sweet onion, coarsely chopped

2 large celery stalks, coarsely chopped

2 medium carrots, coarsely chopped

3 teaspoons kosher salt

4 garlic cloves, minced

4 cups ¾-inch-cubed reserved Slow-Roasted Pork Shoulder (page 83)

1 tablespoon ground cumin

1 tablespoon ancho chile powder

1 tablespoon dried Mexican oregano

1 teaspoon freshly ground black pepper

One 28-ounce can whole fire-roasted tomatoes, halved, with their juice

2 quarts Chicken Stock (page 228 or low-sodium store-bought)

One 25-ounce can hominy, rinsed and drained

Canola oil, for frying

8 corn tortillas, cut into strips

2 Hass avocados, pitted, peeled, and diced

½ small head green cabbage, thinly sliced

4 radishes, thinly sliced

1 jalapeño, seeded and thinly sliced

½ cup finely sliced green onions (white and light green parts)

½ cup chopped cilantro

1 cup Cilantro Crema (page 74)

1 In a large Dutch oven over medium-high heat, heat the olive oil until hot. Add the onion, celery, carrots, and 2 teaspoons of the salt and sauté until the onion is translucent, 4 to 5 minutes. Add the garlic, pork, cumin, ancho, oregano, and pepper and sauté until the pork is browned on all sides, 6 to 8 minutes. Add the tomatoes, chicken stock, and hominy, mix well, and bring to a boil. Reduce the heat and simmer until the stock has thickened, 35 to 40 minutes. Set the pan aside off the heat.

2 Pour canola oil into a deep cast-iron skillet to a depth of 2 inches and heat it over high heat to 350°F. Line a plate with paper towels and set it next to the stove.

3 Working in batches, fry the tortilla strips in the hot oil until crispy and golden brown, stirring often, 1 to 2 minutes. Using a slotted spoon or spider, transfer the strips to the paper towels. Season with the remaining 1 teaspoon salt and set aside.

4 Serve the stew, garnishing each serving with the avocado, cabbage, radishes, jalapeño, green onions, cilantro, cilantro crema, and crispy tortilla strips.

That's a fatty green pea patty!

Green Pea Patties
with Sriracha Ranch

Sufferin' succotash, where'd all the succotash *go*?! Oh, of course, it's right here in these gorgeous green patties. Better not blink, though, 'cause they're topped with this spicy-tangy sriracha ranch, and **they're gonna be gone in a flash.**

MAKES **4 to 6 servings** • ***TIME*** **45 minutes, plus chilling time**

Sriracha ranch

1½ cups Ranch Dressing (page 292)

¼ cup sriracha sauce

Green pea patties

4 cups reserved Green Vegetable Succotash (page 83)

¼ cup all-purpose flour

½ cup panko bread crumbs

1 ounce Parmesan cheese, grated (about ⅓ cup)

2 large eggs, beaten

1 teaspoon baking powder

½ teaspoon kosher salt

4 or 5 turns freshly ground black pepper

Extra-virgin olive oil

¼ cup chopped dill, for serving

1 To prepare the sriracha ranch, in a medium bowl, whisk together the ingredients until well combined. Cover and refrigerate until ready to serve.

2 Line a baking sheet with parchment paper.

3 To make the patties, put the succotash in a food processor and pulse 7 or 8 times to chop coarsely. Do not overprocess, as you want some of the texture of the vegetables in the patties. Transfer to a large bowl and add the flour, panko, Parmesan, eggs, baking powder, salt, and pepper and mix well until evenly incorporated.

4 Form the mixture into about 12 patties that are 3 inches across and about ¾ inch thick and set them on the prepared baking sheet. Refrigerate for 20 to 30 minutes to firm up and chill.

5 Line a platter or baking sheet with paper towels. Set a large nonstick skillet over medium heat. Coat with a light layer of olive oil. Working in batches (4 or 5 patties at a time), cook on one side until lightly golden and crisp around the edges, 3 to 4 minutes. Turn and cook for 2 to 3 minutes on the other side. Drain on the paper towels.

6 Serve with the sriracha ranch and a sprinkle of dill.

Sweet Italian Pepper Poppers

With stuffed peppers on the menu, you become a magician—totally transforming dinner from a night or two ago into something that is so different, **no one will ever know they're eating leftovers.** Don't worry, your secret is safe with me.

MAKES **4 to 6 servings •** ***TIME*** **45 minutes**

1 pound mini tricolor sweet Italian peppers*

2 tablespoons extra-virgin olive oil

½ cup minced sweet onion

1 teaspoon thyme leaves

2 teaspoons kosher salt

4 garlic cloves, minced

2 cups reserved pulled Slow-Roasted Pork Shoulder (page 83)

1 cup reserved Basmati Rice Pilaf (page 83)

1 cup whipped cream cheese

1 cup Provolone cheese, grated

1 large egg, beaten

2 tablespoons chopped flat-leaf parsley

¼ teaspoon red chili flakes

5 to 6 turns freshly ground black pepper

½ cup panko bread crumbs

1 lime, cut into wedges

***It's easier than ever to find bags of mini sweet peppers in grocery stores these days, but if they've gone missing in your neighborhood, you can use four bell peppers in their place. Cut off the top quarter of each one instead of cutting a strip out and increase the baking time to 20 to 25 minutes.**

1 Preheat the oven to 375°F.

2 To prepare the peppers for stuffing, use a paring knife to cut out a lengthwise strip (about one-quarter of the pepper) to create a long opening. Repeat with the remaining peppers, reserving the pepper strips. Carefully remove the membranes and seeds from inside of each pepper, then arrange the peppers cut side up on a rimmed baking sheet. Dice the pepper strips and set aside.

3 To prepare the filling, in a large sauté pan over medium-high heat, heat the olive oil until hot. Add the diced peppers, onion, thyme, and 1 teaspoon of the salt and sauté until the onion is translucent, 2 to 3 minutes. Add the garlic and cook until fragrant, about 1 minute. Set aside to cool.

4 In a large bowl, combine the pork, rice, cream cheese, cooled onion mixture, Provolone, egg, parsley, chili flakes, remaining salt, and the black pepper. Mix well.

5 Using a teaspoon, stuff each pepper with a generous amount of the filling so it domes on top of the pepper. Sprinkle with the panko.

6 Bake until the panko and peppers are browned around the edges, 8 to 10 minutes. (Or, to make ahead, wrap the baking sheet with the unbaked stuffed peppers in plastic wrap and refrigerate for up to 1 day; bake for 15 to 17 minutes straight from the refrigerator.) Serve with lime wedges.

Pick a pepper!

This beef will have you in disbelief.

Roasted Beef Top Round with Toasted Farro and Fennel Salad and Spicy Utica Greens

Main Recipe

With top round you get really nice, sliceable beef after it's roasted. Sure, it's perfect for sandwiches, but we're looking for something more from our leftovers this week, so check out the three awesome dishes that follow this menu for some real-deal ideas of what to do with leftover roast beef.

About the Utica greens—they're Italian-style braised greens that originated in Utica, New York, and we're all better off for it. If you don't believe me, go to Utica yourself and check them out. And while you're up there, stop in at the Turning Stone Resort and Casino in Verona, where they make the most *un-be-liev-able* version of Utica greens.

MAKES **4 to 6 servings** • ***TIME*** **2 hours, plus 1 to 2 hours of cure time**

Roasted beef

3 tablespoons kosher salt

2 tablespoons freshly ground black pepper

3 tablespoons onion powder

3 tablespoons garlic powder

2 tablespoons dried oregano

1 tablespoon paprika

One 8-pound beef top round roast, trimmed, cut into 2 equal pieces

2 tablespoons extra-virgin olive oil

2 tablespoons rosemary needles

2 tablespoons thyme leaves

1 large sweet onion, sliced

4 large carrots, sliced ½ inch thick

6 celery stalks, sliced ½ inch thick

4 parsnips, peeled and sliced ½ inch thick

1 To cure the top round, mix together the salt, pepper, onion powder, garlic powder, oregano, and paprika in a small bowl. Rub the beef with the olive oil, then rub on the spice mix and the rosemary and thyme, coating the meat well. Place the meat on a wire rack set on a baking sheet and refrigerate, uncovered, for 1 to 2 hours.

2 Preheat the oven to 450°F.

3 Place the onion, carrots, celery, parsnips, and turnips in a large roasting pan and pour in the beef stock. Place the meat on top of the vegetables and roast for 20 minutes. Reduce the heat to 275°F and roast for 55 to 60 minutes, or until the internal temperature reaches 135°F. Transfer one piece of meat to a platter and loosely tent it with aluminum foil (set the other aside to cool and store for later in the week). Rest for 15 to 20 minutes before carving.

4 Meanwhile, to make the farro, in a large, heavy pot over medium-high heat, heat the olive oil until hot. Add the farro and lightly toast until nutty

RECIPE CONTINUES 

 RECIPE CONTINUED FROM PREVIOUS PAGE

2 medium turnips, peeled and quartered

1 quart Beef Stock (page 226 or low-sodium store-bought)

Farro and fennel salad

¼ cup extra-virgin olive oil

2 cups farro

½ fennel bulb, trimmed and diced

1 small red onion, diced

2 medium carrots, diced

1 celery stalk, diced

¼ teaspoon dried oregano

2 garlic cloves, minced

1 tablespoon kosher salt

½ teaspoon freshly ground black pepper

Utica greens

1 tablespoon extra-virgin olive oil

1½ cups julienned assorted spicy, salty salumi, such as country ham, spicy capicola, and/or Genoa salami

1 medium onion, thinly sliced

1 green bell pepper, seeded and julienned

¼ small fennel bulb, trimmed and thinly sliced lengthwise

3 tablespoons minced garlic

3 pounds rainbow chard or any broad, leafy greens, thin stems and leaves coarsely chopped

½ cup Chicken Stock (page 228 or low-sodium store-bought)

¼ cup red wine vinegar

1 tablespoon fresh lemon juice

2 tablespoons unsalted butter

and fragrant, stirring often, 1 to 2 minutes. Add the fennel, onion, carrots, celery, and oregano and sauté until the vegetables are translucent, 3 to 4 minutes. Add the garlic and cook for 1 minute, until fragrant. Add 5 cups water and the salt and pepper. Stirring often, bring to a boil over high heat, then reduce the heat, cover, and simmer until the farro is tender, 35 to 40 minutes. Drain and transfer to a bowl. Set aside to cool.

5 To make the greens, in a large sauté pan over medium-high heat, heat the olive oil and salumi. Cook until the fat begins to render, 4 to 5 minutes. Add the onion, bell pepper, and fennel and sauté until the onion begins to brown, 7 to 8 minutes. Add the garlic and sauté until fragrant, 1 to 2 minutes. Add the chard and toss together well. Deglaze the pan by adding the chicken stock and scraping up the browned bits from the bottom of the pan. Cover the pan and cook until the vegetables are wilted, 5 to 6 minutes. Add the vinegar, lemon juice, butter, salt, black pepper, garlic, chili flakes, and sugar, stir to combine, and cook until heated through, 3 to 4 minutes.

6 To serve, cut the top round into thick slices and arrange them on a serving platter. Ladle some of the juices from the roasting pan over the meat. Serve with the farro and fennel salad and the spicy Utica greens, with grated Parmesan sprinkled over the greens.

1 teaspoon kosher salt

1 teaspoon freshly ground black pepper

½ teaspoon granulated garlic

½ teaspoon red chili flakes

½ teaspoon sugar

1¾ ounces Parmesan cheese, grated (about ½ cup), for serving

Prep for the Week

- Coarsely chop 3 cups of the reserved top round and set aside 3 cups of the greens for the Chopped Beef and Greens Mac 'n' Cheese (page 97).
- Slice the top round into 3 cups bite-size strips for the Spicy Thai Red Beef Curry (page 94).
- Cut the top round into 4 cups 4-inch dice and reserve 2 cups of the farro salad for the Beef and Crispy Farro Bake (page 99).
- Store everything in tightly covered containers in the refrigerator until needed.

100 percent undeniably a crazy family.

Spicy Thai Red Beef Curry

Keeping a jar of Thai curry paste and a couple cans of coconut milk in your pantry is like taking out insurance against ever having bland food, and it's just what you need to turn some of the roast beef from the other night into this lip-smackin' curry.

MAKES **6 servings** • *TIME* **45 minutes**

3 tablespoons canola oil

1 small onion, thinly sliced

2 cups trimmed and halved green beans

1 large red bell pepper, julienned

1 tablespoon minced ginger

4 garlic cloves, minced

1 serrano chile, seeded and finely sliced

1 lemongrass stalk, trimmed and smashed

One 4-ounce jar Thai red curry paste

2 pounds reserved Roasted Beef Top Round (page 91), cut into bite-size strips (about 3 cups)

Two 13.5-ounce cans coconut milk

3 cups Chicken Stock (page 228 or low-sodium store-bought)

2 tablespoons fish sauce

Juice and zest of 1 lime

1/4 teaspoon sugar

1/2 teaspoon kosher salt

Basmati Rice Pilaf (page 83), warmed, for serving

1 Heat the canola oil in a large, heavy pot over high heat. Add the onion, green beans, and bell pepper and sauté until well charred, 2 to 3 minutes. Transfer to a bowl and reduce the heat to medium. Add the ginger, garlic, chile, lemongrass, and red curry paste. Fry until fragrant, 2 to 3 minutes.

2 Add the beef and mix well to coat evenly. Add the coconut milk, chicken stock, and fish sauce and mix well. Raise the heat to high and bring to a boil. Boil for 15 to 20 minutes, until the coconut milk has reduced and thickened.

3 Reduce the heat to a simmer and return the vegetables to the pot along with the lime juice and zest, sugar, and salt. Simmer until the vegetables are warmed through. Serve at once with the rice pilaf.

That's beef curry in a hurry.

Looks crazy . . . tastes even crazier!

Chopped Beef and Greens Mac 'n' Cheese

I love a meal with lots of components, but there's definitely a place (*home*) and a time (*now*) for the good ol' one-pot supper. I'm not the kinda guy to tell you what to do, but if I were, I'd say you should definitely serve this with a big green salad tossed with good vinaigrette, like the one on page 60.

MAKES **4 to 6 servings •** ***TIME*** **1 hour**

Mac 'n' cheese

2¼ teaspoons kosher salt

1½ cups penne rigate

Olive oil

3 tablespoons unsalted butter

3 tablespoons all-purpose flour

1 quart whole milk

1 pound sharp white cheddar cheese, grated (about 4 cups)

7 to 9 turns freshly ground black pepper

2 or 3 gratings of nutmeg

Pinch of cayenne pepper

3 cups coarsely chopped reserved Roasted Beef Top Round (page 91)

3 cups reserved Spicy Utica Greens (page 91), coarsely chopped

1 tablespoon Worcestershire sauce

1 teaspoon Dijon mustard

1 Preheat the oven to 350°F.

2 In a large saucepan over medium-high heat, bring 2 quarts of water to a boil. Add 1½ teaspoons of the salt, then add the penne and stir. Cook the penne until al dente, 10 to 12 minutes. Drain thoroughly. Toss with a small amount of olive oil and spread in a single layer on a rimmed baking sheet. Set aside.

3 Meanwhile, in a large saucepan over medium heat, melt the butter, then whisk in the flour to make a roux. Cook, whisking constantly, until it turns pale yellow in color, about 5 minutes. Slowly add the milk and cook, whisking constantly, until you have a smooth, medium-thick sauce, about 10 minutes. Add the cheddar and whisk until melted. Whisk in ½ teaspoon of the salt, 3 or 4 turns of the black pepper, the nutmeg, and the cayenne. Set aside to cool to room temperature.

4 In a large bowl, combine the pasta, beef, greens, and cheese sauce. Stir in the Worcestershire sauce, mustard, remaining ¼ teaspoon salt, and remaining 4 or 5 turns black pepper. Pour the mixture into a wide, large casserole dish (or individual crocks) and spread it out evenly.

5 To make the Parmesan panko crust, in a large nonstick sauté pan, heat the olive oil, butter, and garlic until the butter has melted. Remove from

RECIPE CONTINUES →

RECIPE CONTINUED FROM PREVIOUS PAGE

Parmesan panko crust

1/4 cup extra-virgin olive oil

2 tablespoons unsalted butter

1 garlic clove, minced

2 cups panko bread crumbs

1/4 cup chopped flat-leaf parsley

3/4 ounce Parmesan cheese, grated (about 1/4 cup)

1/4 teaspoon kosher salt

4 or 5 turns freshly ground black pepper

the heat and add the panko, parsley, Parmesan, salt, and pepper. Toss until well mixed together. Spread the panko evenly over the pasta.

6 Cover the dish (or crocks) with foil and bake in the center of the oven until heated through, about 25 minutes. Remove the foil and cook for 8 to 10 minutes more, until the sauce is bubbling and the top is golden and crispy. Serve hot.

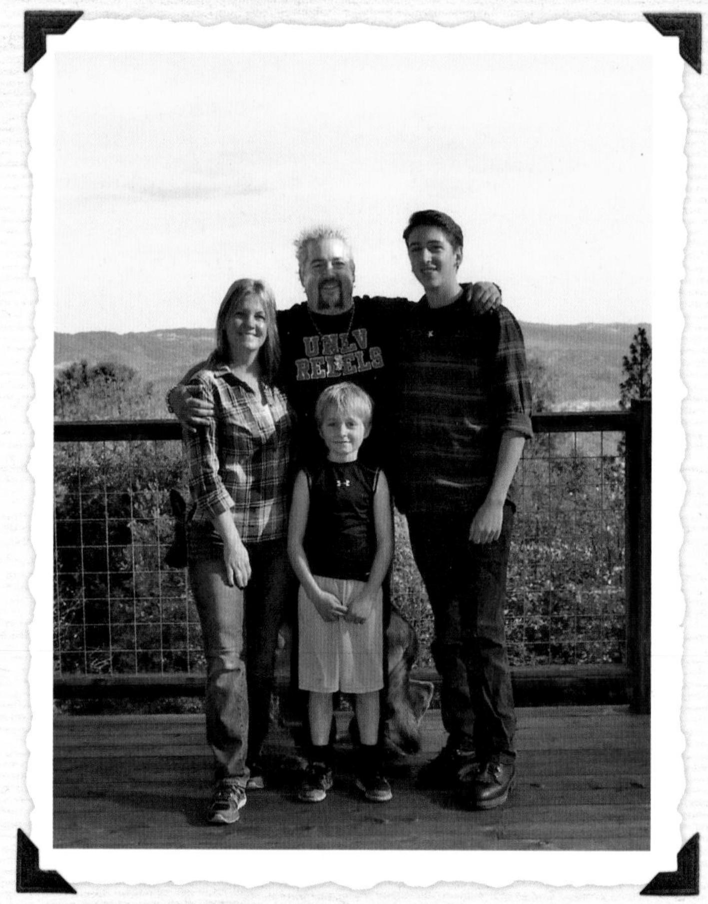

At the ranch . . . our favorite place in the world.

Beef and Crispy Farro Bake

Not too many people consider using cooked grains in this way, as a crunchy topping for stews. Farro in particular has a warm, nutty flavor and a great chewy texture. When baked on top of this rich and fragrant Guinness-enhanced beef stew, it crisps up beautifully.

MAKES 4 to 6 servings • TIME 45 minutes

1/2 cup extra-virgin olive oil
1/2 sweet onion, cut into 1/4-inch dice
2 celery stalks, cut into 1/4-inch dice
1 medium carrot, cut into 1/4-inch dice
1 russet potato, peeled and cut into 1/4-inch dice
2 1/2 teaspoons kosher salt
10 to 12 turns freshly ground black pepper
2 pounds reserved Roasted Beef Top Round (page 91), cut into 1/4-inch dice (about 4 cups)
3 garlic cloves, minced
2 teaspoons thyme leaves
1 teaspoon chopped rosemary
2 tablespoons all-purpose flour
One 12-ounce bottle Guinness or other stout beer
3 cups Beef Stock (page 226 or low-sodium store-bought)
3 tablespoons Worcestershire sauce
2 tablespoons demi-glace
1 tablespoon Dijon mustard
2 cups reserved Farro and Fennel Salad (page 92)
3 tablespoons chopped flat-leaf parsley
1 3/4 ounces Parmesan cheese, grated (about 1/2 cup)

1 Preheat the oven to 375°F.

2 Heat 1/4 cup of the olive oil in a large Dutch oven or other heavy pot over medium-high heat until hot. Add the onion, celery, carrot, potato, 2 teaspoons of the salt, and 6 to 8 turns pepper and sauté until the onion is translucent, 5 to 6 minutes.

3 Add the beef and sauté until well browned on all sides, 7 to 8 minutes. Add the garlic, thyme, and rosemary and cook for 1 minute, until fragrant. Add the flour and stir well to coat all the ingredients evenly; this will help prevent lumps. Deglaze the pan by adding the Guinness and beef stock and scraping up the browned bits from the bottom of the pan. Add the Worcestershire sauce, demi-glace, and mustard and stir well to combine. Bring to a boil, then reduce the heat and simmer until the potatoes have started to break down and the sauce is thick and rich, 18 to 20 minutes. Set aside off the heat.

4 Meanwhile, in a large bowl, combine the farro salad, parsley, Parmesan, and the remaining 1/4 cup olive oil. Season with the remaining 1/2 teaspoon salt and the remaining 4 to 6 turns pepper and stir to combine.

5 Pour the beef mixture into a 9 x 13-inch casserole or baking dish and spread it out evenly. Sprinkle the farro salad on top. Bake until the farro is golden brown and crispy, 10 to 12 minutes. Serve hot.

Bacon-wrapped anything is great!

Bacon-Roasted Turkey

Main Recipe

with Scalloped Potatoes and Caramelized Balsamic Brussels Sprouts

Who says you have to wait until Thanksgiving to have roasted turkey with trimmings, not to mention the awesome leftovers? Not me. I often like to pair Brussels sprouts with bacon, but in this menu the turkey is wrapped in bacon (ooooh, yeah), so a balsamic and honey dressing caramelizes with the Brussels sprouts as they roast and adds that deep, savory kick. I'll say it again: *ooooh, yeah.*

MAKES **4 to 6 servings** • ***TIME*** **2½ hours, plus overnight brining**

Bacon-roasted turkey

Two 2½- to 3-pound bone-in, skin-on turkey breasts, washed and patted dry

1 gallon All-Purpose Brine (page 300)

¼ cup extra-virgin olive oil

2 garlic cloves, minced

1 teaspoon thyme leaves, minced

1 tablespoon kosher salt

1 teaspoon freshly ground black pepper

1 pound thick-cut applewood smoked bacon

Scalloped potatoes

6 cups heavy cream

3 teaspoons kosher salt

½ teaspoon freshly ground black pepper

5 or 6 gratings of nutmeg

5 pounds Idaho potatoes, peeled, rinsed, and cut into ¼-inch-thick slices

¼ cup minced chives, plus 1 tablespoon for garnish

1 Place the turkey breasts in the chilled brine and refrigerate overnight.

2 Preheat the oven to 350°F. Place a large roasting rack in a large roasting pan.

3 Remove the turkey breasts from the brine and pat dry (discard the brine). In a small bowl, whisk together the olive oil, garlic, thyme, salt, and pepper. Rub all over the turkey.

4 Shingle the bacon over the skin of the turkey breasts, tucking the ends underneath to secure them. Place the turkey breasts on the roasting rack set in the roasting pan. Roast in the center of the oven until the bacon is crispy and the interior temperature of the breasts reaches 165°F on an instant-read thermometer, about 1 hour 10 minutes. Remove the breasts from the oven and rest for 20 minutes before carving.

5 Meanwhile, to make the scalloped potatoes, combine the cream, 1½ teaspoons of the salt, the pepper, and nutmeg in a large pot. Bring to a simmer over medium-high heat. Add the potatoes and chives, reduce the heat to medium-low, and cook until barely fork-tender, 10 to 12 minutes. Set aside.

6 Butter a 10 x 14 x 3-inch heavy baking pan, ensuring that the bottom and sides of the dish are well coated. In a medium bowl, combine the Gruyère and

RECIPE CONTINUES 

RECIPE CONTINUED FROM PREVIOUS PAGE

2 tablespoons unsalted butter, for the pan

½ pound Gruyère cheese, grated (about 2 cups)

½ pound white cheddar cheese, grated (about 2 cups)

Brussels sprouts

4 garlic cloves, minced

2 tablespoons chopped flat-leaf parsley

½ cup extra-virgin olive oil

¼ cup good-quality balsamic vinegar

2 tablespoons honey

2 teaspoons kosher salt

½ teaspoon freshly ground black pepper

½ teaspoon red chili flakes (optional)

3 pounds Brussels sprouts, outermost leaves discarded, trimmed and halved lengthwise

1 medium red onion, thinly sliced

cheddar. Transfer one-third of the potatoes and cream mixture to the buttered baking dish, spreading it in an even layer. Top with a third of the cheese. Repeat the layering process with the potatoes and cheese twice more, ending with cheese on top. Cover the dish with foil and place it on a baking sheet to catch any bubbling overflow. Bake until the potatoes are tender, about 45 minutes. Remove the foil and bake until the top is golden brown and bubbling, another 15 to 20 minutes. Let stand while you roast the Brussels sprouts. Garnish with the remaining 1 tablespoon chives before serving.

7 Increase the oven temperature to 375°F.

8 To make the Brussels sprouts, in a medium bowl, combine the garlic, parsley, olive oil, vinegar, honey, salt, black pepper, and chili flakes (if using). Add the Brussels sprouts and onion and toss well to coat. Spread the mixture evenly on a rimmed baking sheet and roast until the Brussels sprouts are well browned, 30 to 35 minutes. Transfer to a large bowl and toss again before serving.

9 To serve, slice 1 turkey breast (reserving the other for later meals) and arrange the slices on a platter. Serve with the potatoes and Brussels sprouts.

Prep for the Week

- Dice 2 cups of the reserved turkey and reserve 1 cup of the Brussels sprouts for the Stuffed Acorn Squash with Roasted Turkey, Brussels Sprouts, and Farro (page 104).
- Pull 3 cups of the turkey and reserve 3 cups of the scalloped potatoes for the Spicy Turkey, Corn, and Poblano Stew (page 109).
- Pull 2 cups of the turkey into 1-inch strips for the Roasted Turkey Chilaquiles with Chipotle Queso (page 106).
- Store everything in tightly covered containers in the refrigerator until needed.

Ready to roast!

Stuffed Acorn Squash
with Roasted Turkey, Brussels Sprouts, and Farro

Stuffed squash is one of those great "kitchen sink" dishes that allows you to repurpose all kinds of leftovers without anyone being the wiser. In fact, whenever I have a little extra room in the hot oven, I'll bake off a few squash and then store them in the refrigerator. Later in the week, when I've got a few nights' worth of leftovers, those squash'll be ready and waiting to be stuffed and baked. An aioli like the one here adds an awesome creamy-spicy kick.

MAKES **4 servings** • ***TIME*** **1 hour 15 minutes**

Red pepper aioli

2 red bell peppers, fire-roasted (see page 32)

4 garlic cloves, minced

Juice and zest of 1 lemon

1 cup mayonnaise

1/4 cup pine nuts, toasted (see page 22)

3/4 ounce Pecorino Romano, grated (about 1/4 cup)

1 teaspoon kosher salt

1/2 teaspoon freshly ground black pepper

1 teaspoon red chili flakes

Stuffed squash

4 acorn squash, washed

4 tablespoons extra-virgin olive oil

2 tablespoons kosher salt

1 teaspoon freshly ground black pepper

1/2 medium sweet onion, minced

1 To prepare the aioli, place all the ingredients in a food processor and process until smooth. Transfer to a bowl, cover, and refrigerate until needed.

2 Preheat the oven to 350°F.

3 Cut off and discard the top third of each squash. Cut a thin slice from the bottom, pointed end to create a flat surface. Scoop out and discard the seeds and pulp. Stand the squash cavity side up on a rimmed baking sheet. Drizzle with 2 tablespoons of the olive oil and season with 1 tablespoon of the salt and 1/2 teaspoon of the black pepper. Bake until tender, 25 to 30 minutes. Set aside on the baking sheet.

4 Meanwhile, in a large sauté pan over medium-high heat, heat the remaining 2 tablespoons olive oil. Add the onion, bell pepper, remaining 1 tablespoon salt, and remaining 1/2 teaspoon black pepper and sauté until the onion is translucent, 4 to 5 minutes. Add the garlic and sauté for 1 minute, until fragrant. Transfer to a large bowl and add the farro, turkey, Brussels sprouts, cranberries, chili flakes, and Parmesan. Mix well to combine.

1 medium red bell pepper, seeded and diced

2 garlic cloves, minced

1 cup cooked farro or Toasted Farro and Fennel Salad (page 91)

2 cups diced reserved Bacon-Roasted Turkey (page 101)

1 cup reserved Caramelized Balsamic Brussels Sprouts (page 101), julienned

¼ cup chopped dried cranberries

¼ teaspoon red chili flakes

1¾ ounces Parmesan cheese, grated (about ½ cup)

¼ cup chopped flat-leaf parsley, for garnish

5 Using a large spoon, divide the stuffing evenly among the squash. Loosely tent the entire baking sheet with foil. Bake for 15 minutes, then remove the foil and bake until the top of the stuffing is golden brown, about 10 minutes.

6 Garnish with the parsley and serve with the red pepper aioli.

A stuffed jack-o'-lantern in Flavortown.

Roasted Turkey Chilaquiles
with Chipotle Queso

It's hard to know what I love best—crunchy fried tortillas; spicy, smoky salsa rojo; fresh pico de gallo; or creamy chipotle-queso sauce? A big dish of chilaquiles means I never have to choose.

MAKES **4 servings** • ***TIME*** **45 minutes**

Chipotle queso

1 tablespoon unsalted butter

1/4 cup minced chipotle peppers in adobo

2 garlic cloves, minced

1 teaspoon kosher salt

1 1/2 cups half-and-half

1 cup crumbled queso fresco

1 1/2 cups grated Jack cheese

1 tablespoon minced cilantro

Chilaquiles

Canola oil, for frying

Eighteen 6-inch corn tortillas, cut into 1-inch-thick strips

Kosher salt

2 cups 1-inch strips reserved Bacon-Roasted Turkey (page 101)

2 cups Salsa Rojo (page 291)

1 cup Pico de Gallo (page 290)

1/2 cup finely sliced green onions (white and light green parts)

1/2 cup drained Pickled Red Onions (page 294)

1/4 cup chopped cilantro

1/4 cup crumbled queso fresco

1/2 cup Cilantro Crema (page 74)

1 To make the chipotle queso, in a medium saucepan over medium heat, melt the butter. Add the chipotle, garlic, and salt and cook until fragrant, 1 to 2 minutes. Add the half-and-half, bring the mixture to a simmer, and cook until reduced by one-third, 7 to 8 minutes. Add the queso fresco, Jack cheese, and cilantro and cook, stirring, over medium-low heat, until the cheeses have melted and the sauce is smooth. Set aside and keep warm.

2 To make the chilaquiles, pour canola oil into a Dutch oven to a depth of 3 inches and heat it over high heat to 350°F. Line a plate with paper towels.

3 Working in batches, fry the tortilla strips until crispy and golden brown, stirring often, 1 to 2 minutes. Using a slotted spoon or spider, transfer the strips to the paper towels and season immediately with salt.

4 Preheat the oven to 350°F.

5 Heat 1 tablespoon canola oil in a nonstick sauté pan over high heat. Add the turkey and cook, stirring occasionally, until a little crispy, about 2 minutes. Set aside.

To get a nice crust on the already-cooked meat, the pan should be nonstick.

6 In a large, heavy baking pan, arrange a third of the tortilla strips and scatter a third of the turkey on top. Spoon 2/3 cup of the salsa rojo over the turkey. Spread a third of the chipotle queso over the salsa and top with 1/3 cup of the pico de gallo. Repeat these layers twice more, ending with pico de gallo.

7 Bake until heated through, about 15 minutes.

8 Top with the green onions, pickled red onions, cilantro, crumbled queso fresco, and cilantro crema. Serve hot.

Spicy Turkey, Corn, and Poblano Stew

This is turkey stew with attitude. Grab yourself a bowl and a spoon, quick, because this won't last long. At least, it never does in my house.

MAKES **4 to 6 servings** • ***TIME*** **1 hour**

- 4 tablespoons (1/2 stick) unsalted butter
- 1 medium sweet onion, diced
- 1 teaspoon kosher salt
- 4 garlic cloves, minced
- 2 tablespoons fine cornmeal
- 1 1/2 quarts Chicken Stock (page 228 or low-sodium store-bought)
- 6 poblano peppers, fire-roasted (see page 32), seeded and diced
- 1 serrano chile, fire-roasted (see page 32), seeded and diced
- 1 1/2 cups sweet corn kernels
- 1 tablespoon ground cumin
- 3 cups reserved Scalloped Potatoes (page 101)
- 3 cups pulled reserved Bacon-Roasted Turkey (page 101)
- 5 or 6 turns freshly ground black pepper
- 1 tablespoon Tabasco sauce
- 1/4 cup crumbled queso fresco, for garnish
- 1/4 cup chopped cilantro, for garnish
- 1 lime, cut into wedges, for serving
- 10 to 12 corn tortillas, grilled, for serving

1 In a large Dutch oven over medium-high heat, melt the butter. Add the onion and salt and cook until the onion is translucent, 4 to 5 minutes.

2 Add the garlic and cook for 1 minute, until fragrant. Stir in the cornmeal, then whisk in the chicken stock until smooth. Bring to a boil.

3 Add the poblanos, serrano, corn, cumin, and scalloped potatoes. Return the mixture to a boil, then reduce the heat and simmer for 20 to 25 minutes, stirring often and breaking up the potatoes slightly with a wooden spoon as the vegetables cook down and soften.

4 Add the turkey and simmer until heated through, about 5 minutes.

5 Season with the black pepper and Tabasco. Serve hot, garnished with the queso fresco and cilantro and with the lime wedges and tortillas alongside.

GRAINS &
GREENS
Namaste

Healthy Is Not a Bad Word

Here's the deal. We Americans all need to eat way more greens and vegetables of all kinds. And we also need to eat way more of those kick-butt superfoods known as grains. And I'm not talking here just about green beans and rice. **You've gotta branch out beyond the bland and usual.**

→

There's kale, asparagus, Brussels sprouts, fresh summer squash "pasta," artichokes! And the world of grains is huge.

My sister became a vegetarian when she was still just a kid—so I grew up eating all sorts of grains and greens. (You can see some of my favorites on the opposite page and on page 125.) I didn't appreciate it when I was a kid (sorry, Mom and Dad), but I know now how lucky I was to have a super-health-conscious family.

Guido's Ode to Salad

(Yeah, you read that right!)

When I was a kid, my parents made sure we had salad Every Single Night. The thing is, I thought everybody did—until my buddies began coming over for dinner and wigging out when they saw the giant mountain of greens in the middle of the table. At the time I thought, *Like I needed proof we're the craziest damn family in town.*

But what's truly crazy is that the constant salads didn't make me hate them. In fact, I love salad. It seems like whenever I say this to someone, they look at me cross-eyed, like I just grew an extra head or something. So I'm going to speak it loud and proud now, people. **I Love Salad.** And not those macaroni, pasta, or potato salads drowning in mayo. Don't get me wrong; they have their place. But my hands-down favorite salad is tossed greens with all sorts of veggies. I'm talking real variety here. I love a bowl full of hearts of romaine or baby arugula or mesclun; marinated or pickled something, such as artichokes or sun-dried tomatoes or olives; cooked white or red beans; green veggies like asparagus, green beans, peas, and edamame; and sweet veggies like carrots, corn, and roasted beets. I skip a few things people seem to think "should" be in salads, like cucumbers and mushrooms and croutons. **I don't let myself be hemmed in by what's considered normal—and neither should you.** Then I toss it all with a spicy, sharp dressing made with red wine vinegar and olive oil, a bunch of chopped herbs, and a lot of freshly cracked pepper. I'm talking a *lot* of black pepper. I mean, until it hurts.

The gnarlier, the better.

Pan-Fried Artichokes
with Meyer Lemon Aioli

Artichokes have got to be just about the gnarliest vegetable there is to look at. But to eat? **There's nothin' better.** Take it from me, though—the best way to get the fam on board with eating these crazy-lookin' things is to first get rid of those prickly tops (the kiddos don't love food that pinches) and the rough "choke" at the center of each one. Then serve 'em up with a creamy sauce like this sweet-n-tangy Meyer lemon aioli. These are great with Roasted Spatchcock Chickens Three Ways (page 233).

MAKES **4 to 6 servings** • ***TIME*** **45 minutes**

Meyer lemon aioli

1/2 cup extra-virgin olive oil

1/2 cup canola oil

2 large eggs yolks

Juice and grated zest of 3 Meyer lemons

1 tablespoon Dijon mustard

Pinch of cayenne pepper

1/4 teaspoon Worcestershire sauce

1 teaspoon kosher salt

3 or 4 turns freshly ground black pepper

1 teaspoon chopped flat-leaf parsley

Artichokes

2 regular lemons, quartered

4 medium globe artichokes

1 teaspoon kosher salt

5 or 6 turns freshly ground black pepper

3 tablespoons extra-virgin olive oil

1 small onion, diced small

4 garlic cloves, minced

2 anchovies, minced

1 To make the aioli, combine the olive oil and canola oil in a measuring cup. In a blender, place the egg yolks, lemon juice and zest, mustard, cayenne, and Worcestershire sauce and blend until combined. With the blender running on medium speed, slowly add the oils in a steady stream. Blend for 2 to 3 minutes, until the mixture is smooth and creamy. Transfer to a small bowl. Season with salt and black pepper and fold in the parsley. Cover and refrigerate. The aioli can be stored in an airtight container for 2 to 3 days.

2 To prepare the artichokes, fill a large bowl with cold water. Squeeze the juice from the lemon quarters into the water, and then add the quarters to the water.

3 Working with one artichoke at a time, remove the two bottom layers of hard, outer leaves. Use a serrated knife to trim off the top third of the artichoke and discard. Use a vegetable peeler to peel off the tough outer fibers from the stem. Trim a little off the stem end and then cut the artichoke in half lengthwise through the stem. With a small spoon, dig out the inner fibers from the center of the artichoke heart. Submerge the artichoke in the bowl of lemon water to prevent browning. Repeat with

RECIPE CONTINUES →

RECIPE CONTINUED FROM PREVIOUS PAGE

Pinch of red chili flakes

1 cup lager beer

1 tablespoon unsalted butter

1 teaspoon chopped flat-leaf parsley, for garnish

1 teaspoon chopped chives, for garnish

Ryder's all-time FAVE!!

the remaining artichokes. Keep them in the water until you're ready to cook them.

4 Drain the artichokes on paper towels until they are well dried. Season with the salt and pepper.

5 In a large sauté pan over medium-high heat, heat the olive oil until smoking. Add the artichokes to the pan, cut side down, and cook for 4 to 5 minutes, until golden brown. While cooking, use a large spoon to baste the tops of the artichokes with oil from the pan. Flip the artichokes, reduce the heat to medium, and add the onion, garlic, anchovies, and chili flakes. Cook until the onion and garlic are fragrant and lightly colored, 2 to 3 minutes, continuing to baste the tops of the artichoke halves with the oil from the pan.

6 Pour out any oil from the bottom of the pan, then deglaze the pan by carefully pouring in the beer. Scrape up the browned bits from the bottom of the pan. Cover the pan with a lid or loosely with foil and steam until the artichokes are cooked through and the liquid in the pan has almost completely evaporated, 5 to 6 minutes.

7 Uncover the pan, reduce the heat to medium, and cook until all the liquid has evaporated. Add the butter and swirl the pan to baste the artichokes. Cook until slightly crisp, 1 to 2 minutes, flipping the artichokes a few times and basting with melted butter from the pan.

8 Transfer the artichokes to a serving platter. Spoon the sauce from the pan over them, garnish with the chopped parsley and chives, and serve with the aioli on the side.

Broccoli Slaw
with Roasted Cashews and Cranberries

Giving broccoli the slaw treatment is so tasty that you might even find yourself adding it to the Thanksgiving menu.

MAKES **4 to 6 servings** • ***TIME*** **45 minutes**

Yogurt honey Dijon dressing

3/4 cup plain Greek yogurt
2 tablespoons Dijon mustard
2 tablespoons honey
Juice and grated zest of 1 lemon
1 tablespoon finely sliced chives
1 teaspoon kosher salt
4 or 5 turns freshly ground black pepper

Broccoli slaw

2 broccoli heads
2 medium carrots, julienned
1/4 red cabbage head, finely sliced
1/2 medium onion, thinly sliced
1 teaspoon kosher salt
5 or 6 turns freshly ground black pepper
1/2 cup coarsely chopped roasted cashews
1/2 cup dried cranberries

1 To make the dressing, combine all the ingredients in a medium bowl and whisk well to blend. Cover and set aside.

2 To make the slaw, remove the broccoli stems from the heads. Coarsely chop the heads into bite-size pieces. Peel the stems and cut them into thin matchsticks. Transfer the broccoli to a large bowl.

3 Add the carrots, cabbage, onion, salt, pepper, and enough dressing to coat the vegetables (you'll likely use it all). Toss to combine well. Cover the bowl and refrigerate for 15 to 20 minutes to let the vegetables soften.

4 Top with the cashews and dried cranberries and serve.

Looks like the real deal . . . 'cuz it is.

Roasted Spaghetti Squash

with Kale and Parm

This crazy-simple recipe is the best way I know to show off one crazy vegetable; it starts out looking like a perfectly ordinary squash, but after cooking can easily be shredded into long ribbons of "spaghetti." If that transformation alone doesn't blow their minds, generously topping the nest of earthy-sweet spaghetti squash with crispy kale chips and freshly grated Parm surely will.

MAKES **4 servings** • ***TIME*** **1 hour**

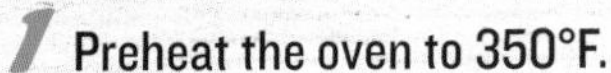

1 large spaghetti squash

2 tablespoons plus 1 teaspoon extra-virgin olive oil

2 teaspoons oregano leaves

2 garlic cloves, minced

½ teaspoon red chili flakes

2 teaspoons kosher salt

6 to 8 turns freshly ground black pepper

1 large bunch kale

1¾ ounces Parmesan cheese, finely grated (about ½ cup)

1 Preheat the oven to 350°F.

2 Split the spaghetti squash in half lengthwise. Use a large spoon to scrape out the seeds and discard.

3 Place the spaghetti squash cut side up on a rimmed baking sheet and drizzle with 2 tablespoons of the olive oil. Sprinkle with the oregano, garlic, chili flakes, 1 teaspoon of the salt, and 3 or 4 turns of the black pepper. Turn over so they are cut side down (this will enable them to cook faster). Bake in the center of the oven until the squash flesh is fork-tender, about 45 minutes. Set aside to cool slightly, about 5 minutes. Use a large spoon and fork to scrape out the fibers from the squash halves and place them in a large bowl. Toss gently to separate the strands so they resemble spaghetti.

4 Meanwhile, wash the kale and remove and discard the stems. Tear the leaves into large bite-size pieces (about 1 inch). Dry completely in a salad spinner. Transfer the kale to a large bowl. Dress very lightly with the remaining 1 teaspoon olive oil, so the leaves are barely coated. Season with the remaining 1 teaspoon salt and 3 or 4 turns black pepper. Spread the leaves evenly on two rimmed baking sheets and roast until crispy and bright green, 12 to 14 minutes. Set aside.

5 To assemble, place the spaghetti squash on a large platter and top with the crispy kale chips. Sprinkle with the Parmesan and serve.

Kale and Hominy Succotash

If you've ever heard me talk about kale, this won't come as a surprise, but I get killer kravings for kale all the time. Whip up a batch of this (it's krazy easy) so you can eat it for both of us. And if you're one of those holdouts who's sure you'll never learn to love kale, no matter what . . . **prepare to be converted, baby.**

MAKES **4 servings** • *TIME* **45 minutes**

- 3 tablespoons extra-virgin olive oil
- One 15-ounce can hominy, drained
- 2 cups pulled rotisserie chicken meat (optional)
- 1/2 medium onion, finely diced
- 1/4 cup finely diced red bell pepper
- 1 teaspoon thyme leaves
- 1/4 teaspoon red chili flakes
- 1 teaspoon kosher salt
- 3 or 4 turns freshly ground black pepper
- 2 garlic cloves, minced
- 6 cups coarsely chopped kale leaves (stems discarded)
- 1/4 cup Chicken Stock (page 228 or low-sodium store-bought)
- 2 teaspoons cornstarch
- 1 teaspoon fresh lemon juice
- 1 tablespoon minced chives, for garnish
- 2 tablespoons chopped flat-leaf parsley, for garnish

1 Set a large cast-iron skillet over medium-high heat. Add the olive oil and heat until smoking. Add the hominy and the chicken (if using) and cook until they are golden brown around the edges, 4 to 5 minutes. Add the onion, bell pepper, thyme, chili flakes, salt, and black pepper and cook until the onion is translucent, 4 to 5 minutes. Add the garlic and kale and mix well. Cook until the kale is bright green, 5 to 6 minutes.

2 Deglaze the pan by adding the chicken stock and scraping up the browned bits from the bottom of the pan. Cook until the liquid has reduced by half, 3 to 4 minutes.

3 In a small dish, mix the cornstarch with 2 teaspoons water. Stir this slurry into the pan sauce and simmer, stirring, until the sauce has thickened, about 2 minutes.

4 Transfer to a serving dish. Finish with the lemon juice and garnish with the chives and parsley. Serve.

Serious succotash,
Sylvester.

Quick Cracked Bulgur Wheat Salad

You've gotta groove on a salad (or any dish) that comes together this quickly and tastes this good. White balsamic vinegar is lighter and a little less sweet than regular balsamic. And unlike the deep brown of regular balsamic, white balsamic is a pale golden color, so it keeps the salad nice and bright.

MAKES **4 servings** • ***TIME*** **30 minutes**

White balsamic vinaigrette

¼ cup white balsamic vinegar

Juice of 1 lemon

2 garlic cloves, minced

1 small shallot, minced

1 teaspoon sugar

½ teaspoon Dijon mustard

½ teaspoon kosher salt

4 or 5 turns freshly ground black pepper

½ cup extra-virgin olive oil

Bulgur salad

1 teaspoon kosher salt

1 cup cracked bulgur wheat

2 cups baby arugula

1 cup halved cherry tomatoes

¼ cup thinly sliced red onion

½ cup chopped dried apricots

2 tablespoons coarsely chopped smoked almonds

2 tablespoons sliced green onions (white and light green parts)

1 To make the vinaigrette, in a medium bowl, whisk together the vinegar, lemon juice, garlic, shallot, sugar, mustard, salt, and pepper. Whisking constantly, add the olive oil in a slow, steady stream to lightly emulsify. Cover and set aside. The vinaigrette can be stored in an airtight container in the refrigerator for up to 2 days.

2 To make the salad, in a medium saucepan over medium-high heat, bring 2½ cups water to a boil, then add the salt. Add the bulgur and stir. Cover the pan and reduce the heat to medium. Simmer the bulgur until tender, about 15 minutes. Let stand, covered, for 5 minutes. Fluff the bulgur with a fork and spread it out on a rimmed baking sheet to cool.

3 Transfer the cooled bulgur to a large bowl. Add the arugula, tomatoes, onion, and apricots. Pour over enough vinaigrette to coat and gently toss to mix.

4 Top with the almonds and green onions and serve.

Farro Salad with Kale and Pickled Vegetables

Farro is one of those ancient grains that everyone's talking about these days. I don't usually go in much for hype, but this stuff actually deserves all the noise. I'm telling you, farro has got *attitude*—the good kind, I mean, not the kind the teenagers can sometimes bring. Farro is like a grain on steroids; its nutty chewiness is just the thing to anchor this salad of shredded kale and those zippy quick pickles you just made.

MAKES **4 to 6 servings** • ***TIME*** **1 hour 15 minutes**

- 2 cups farro
- 2 tablespoons extra-virgin olive oil
- 2 garlic cloves, minced
- 1 shallot, finely diced
- 1 teaspoon kosher salt
- 2 cups low-sodium vegetable stock
- 1 cup dry white wine
- 2 cups Quick Pickled Vegetables (page 293), coarsely chopped, plus some pickling brine from the jar
- 3 cups thinly sliced kale leaves
- 2 tablespoons chopped flat-leaf parsley, for garnish

1 In a large dry saucepan over medium-high heat, toast the farro, stirring occasionally, until fragrant and slightly golden, about 2 minutes. Add the olive oil, garlic, shallot, and salt and cook for 2 to 3 minutes, until the shallot is softened.

2 Deglaze the pan by adding the vegetable stock, wine, and 3 cups water and scraping up the browned bits from the bottom of the pan. Bring to a boil, then reduce the heat, cover, and simmer until the farro is al dente and the liquid has evaporated, 30 to 35 minutes. Remove the pan from the heat, fluff the farro with a fork, and transfer it to a large bowl. Refrigerate until cool.

3 Add the pickled vegetables, a few spoonfuls of the pickling brine, and the kale leaves to the bowl with the farro. Toss to combine the ingredients and coat thoroughly with the brine. Garnish with the parsley and serve.

Great Grains

I never realized how much incredible flavor and chewy texture grains like bulgur and barley and brown rice have until I tasted that quick-cooking rice in the big red box for the first time and I was like, "What *is* this fluffy-mushy stuff you're calling rice?!" If that's your nightly grain, you're missing out. Big time. There's nothing better than cooking up a big old pot of farro one night or over the weekend and storing it in the fridge. Talk about versatile! You can warm it up and put a fried egg on top of it for breakfast. (I said *you* can. As you may know, I don't dig fried eggs.) Let it come to room temp and mix it into a green salad. Let it stand in for the rice in fried rice. Stir it into chili to take the place of some or all of the ground meat. I've just gotta say, **there are *far-ro* too many ideas to even mention them all here.** So I'll stop the talking and let you get cooking.

Zucchini Pappardelle
with Shaved Asparagus and Ricotta Salata

A mandoline is the absolute best way to cut vegetables into thin, uniform slices. There's no need for a fancy, expensive mandoline. Pick up a lightweight version like the one I'm using below and you'll be slicing like a pro in no time. Just make sure you get the kind with a blade, not that musical one with the strings. A stringed mandolin might be great for playing the blues, but it'll make a mess outta your zucchini.

MAKES **4 servings** • ***TIME*** **1 hour**

2 medium zucchini

1½ teaspoons kosher salt

1 bunch medium-thick asparagus, woody stems trimmed

1 large carrot

Juice and grated zest of 1 orange

Juice and grated zest of 1 lemon

3 tablespoons extra-virgin olive oil

4 or 5 turns freshly ground black pepper

¼ teaspoon red chili flakes

1 tablespoon chopped flat-leaf parsley

1 teaspoon honey

¾ ounce ricotta salata cheese, shaved (about ¼ cup)

¼ cup pine nuts, toasted (see page 22) and coarsely chopped

1 Line two rimmed baking sheets with clean kitchen towels. Use a mandoline or sharp knife to slice the zucchini lengthwise into very thin strips (about ⅛ inch). Arrange the zucchini slices on the prepared baking sheets. Sprinkle the slices evenly with ½ teaspoon of the salt. Let stand for 15 minutes, or until you see moisture beads on the surface of the zucchini slices and the slices become pliable.

2 Prepare a large bowl of ice water. Use a vegetable peeler to shave the asparagus and carrot lengthwise into long, thin strips, placing the strips in the ice water as you cut them. Set aside.

3 In a large bowl, whisk together the orange and lemon juices and zests, olive oil, the remaining 1 teaspoon salt, the black pepper, chili flakes, parsley, and honey.

4 Drain the asparagus and carrot well and add them to the bowl with the dressing. Add the zucchini. Gently toss to coat with the vinaigrette.

5 Top with the ricotta salata and pine nuts. Serve at once.

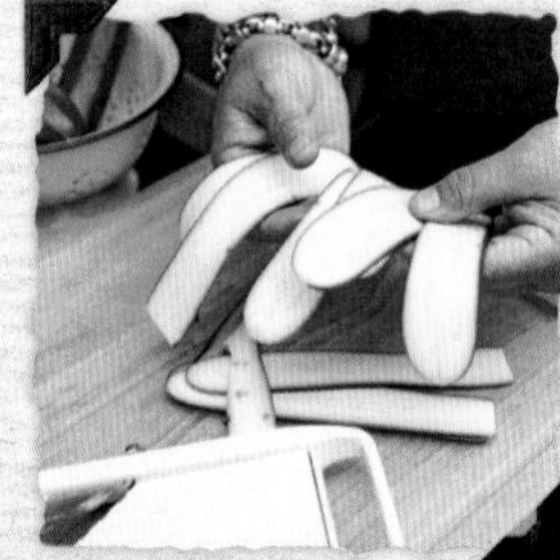

Grilled Asparagus
with Bacon, Brie, and Crunchy Quinoa

You're gonna love how the creamy Brie and crispy bacon goodness gets all melted and clings to the asparagus spears. The key is to be sure to toss the asparagus with the toppings as soon as possible after it comes off the grill.

MAKES **2 to 4 servings** • ***TIME*** **35 minutes**

Brie béchamel

5 slices applewood smoked bacon, cut crosswise into 1/2-inch-wide pieces

1 1/2 teaspoons all-purpose flour

1/2 cup milk

6 ounces Brie cheese, cubed (about 1 1/2 cups)

Asparagus

1/4 cup steamed red quinoa

1 tablespoon extra-virgin olive oil, plus more for grilling

1 bunch jumbo asparagus

1 teaspoon kosher salt

4 or 5 turns freshly ground black pepper

1 tablespoon minced chives, for garnish

Tip: For real asparagus flavor and texture, you want something about the width of a thick pencil. And when they're going to be grilled, as in this recipe, make sure they're even thicker, so they can stand up against the heat of the fire.

1 Set a medium sauté pan over medium-high heat. Place the bacon in the hot pan and cook, turning as needed, until the fat has rendered and the bacon is crispy, 8 to 10 minutes. Using a slotted spoon, transfer the bacon to a plate lined with paper towels.

2 Add the flour to the bacon fat in the pan and mix together to make a roux. Add the milk and whisk until smooth. Fold in the cubed Brie and remove the pan from the heat so the cheese softens slightly but doesn't melt completely. Set aside.

Don't add the Brie until the sauce is completely smooth; if you add it too early, the Brie will get too hot and "break," which'll leave you with gloppy sauce.

3 Meanwhile, place the cooked quinoa and the olive oil in a medium nonstick skillet. Cook over medium-high heat until golden and crispy, 8 to 10 minutes. Set aside in the pan.

4 Preheat a grill to high. While the grill is heating, remove and discard the woody ends of the asparagus stems. Brush the asparagus with olive oil and season with the salt and pepper. Grill until well charred all over, 3 to 4 minutes per side.

5 Transfer to a large bowl. While still hot, add half of the bacon and all the Brie béchamel sauce. Toss well to coat the asparagus evenly.

6 Transfer the asparagus to a serving platter and sprinkle with the toasted red quinoa and the remaining bacon. Garnish with the chives and serve.

Green Papaya Salad
with Lime and Pepitas

Your mother may have always told you that eating unripe fruit would give you a stomachache, but I'm here to tell ya she was wrong—but *only* about that, and only when it comes to this salad. Green, unripe papaya is the star ingredient in this iconic Southeast Asian dish. You can find unripe papaya at Asian grocery stores. To make quick work of julienning it, make sure you get yourself a mandoline like the one I talked about on page 126.

MAKES **4 to 6 servings** • ***TIME*** **45 minutes**

Lime vinaigrette

¼ cup olive oil

Juice and grated zest of 2 limes

2 tablespoons seasoned rice vinegar

2 tablespoons mirin (Japanese rice wine)

2 tablespoons fish sauce

1 tablespoon low-sodium soy sauce

2 teaspoons sugar

½ teaspoon toasted sesame oil

Kosher salt and freshly ground black pepper

Papaya salad

3 tablespoons uncooked jasmine rice

2 teaspoons toasted sesame oil

2 cups trimmed and halved green beans

½ teaspoon kosher salt

5 or 6 turns freshly ground black pepper

2 green unripe papayas

1 small red bell pepper, seeded and cut into thin matchsticks

1 To make the vinaigrette, combine all the ingredients in a medium bowl and whisk to blend. Set aside or store in a covered container in the refrigerator for up to 2 days.

2 To make the salad, in a dry cast-iron skillet set over medium heat, toast the rice until nutty and fragrant, 10 to 12 minutes, stirring frequently so it doesn't burn. Transfer to a bowl to cool.

Toasted rice adds roasty fragrance and crunchy texture that ya don't wanna miss.

3 Transfer the cooled rice to a spice grinder and pulse until ground into fine pieces (the size of kosher salt). Set aside.

4 In a medium sauté pan over high heat, heat the sesame oil and green beans and cook until the beans are well charred on the outside but still almost raw in the middle so they remain crunchy, about 2 minutes. Season with the salt and black pepper. Transfer to a large bowl.

5 Use a sharp knife to cut off the top and bottom ends of one papaya so it can sit upright on your cutting board. With a vegetable peeler, peel off and discard the dark green outer skin. Repeat with the other papaya.

6 Set a mandoline to the julienne cut and slide a papaya lengthwise down the mandoline, rotating it when you reach the center and start to see the

½ unpeeled hothouse seedless cucumber, cut into thin matchsticks

1 cup mung bean sprouts

1 cup halved cherry tomatoes

¼ cup thinly sliced red onion

4 green onions (white and light green parts), thinly sliced diagonally

1 red Thai bird's-eye chile, finely sliced

¼ cup chopped Thai basil

¼ cup chopped mint

¼ cup pepitas, toasted (see page 22), for garnish

seeds. Continue all the way around the papaya; discard the seeds. Repeat with the other papaya. (If you don't have a mandoline, use a sharp knife to cut the trimmed and peeled papaya lengthwise into thin planks, rotating when you reach the seeds. Stack several planks on top of each other and cut lengthwise again into thin matchsticks. Repeat with all of the planks and the other papaya.)

7 To the bowl with the green beans, add the papaya, bell pepper, cucumber, bean sprouts, tomatoes, red onion, green onions, chile, basil, and mint. Drizzle with the lime vinaigrette and mix well.

8 Transfer the salad to a large serving platter. Garnish with the toasted pepitas and sprinkle with the ground toasted rice. Serve at once.

Mimi, Jamps, and Jules.

Dad's Green Beans

I know what you're thinking. Putting butter and soy sauce together sounds too weird for words. But these are, in fact, the green beans I grew up on, and the combination of flavor and texture is like taking the best savory umami taste you've ever had and wrapping it in the food equivalent of velvet. It's that good. Don't believe me? Go ask Jamps (that's what everyone calls my dad). Or just make this—it only takes a few minutes.

MAKES **6 servings** • ***TIME*** **25 minutes**

- 1 tablespoon plus ½ teaspoon kosher salt
- 2 pounds green beans, ends trimmed
- 2 tablespoons canola oil
- ¼ cup finely sliced yellow onion
- ¼ cup red bell pepper, cut into thin matchsticks
- 4 garlic cloves, minced
- 2 tablespoons unsalted butter
- 3 tablespoons low-sodium soy sauce
- 1 green onion (white and light green parts), finely sliced on the bias, for garnish
- 2 teaspoons sesame seeds, toasted (see page 22), for garnish

1 In a large stockpot over medium-high heat, bring 1 gallon water to a boil and season with 1 tablespoon of the salt. Prepare a large bowl of ice water. Add the green beans to the boiling water and cook until al dente, about 1 minute. Drain and immediately plunge the beans into the ice water. When cool, drain the beans in a colander and lay them out to dry on paper towels.

This stops the cooking process and locks in the texture and color.

2 In a large sauté pan over high heat, heat the canola oil until smoking. Add the green beans, onion, and bell pepper and sauté until the vegetables are charred all over, 1 to 2 minutes. Add the garlic and cook for 30 to 40 seconds, until fragrant. Add the butter, soy sauce, and the remaining ½ teaspoon salt and toss to mix and coat the beans evenly. Reduce the heat and cook until the sauce is thick enough to coat and stick to the vegetables, about 1 minute.

3 Transfer to a serving bowl. Garnish with the green onions and sesame seeds and serve.

This is actually my parents' copper pan.

SOUPS &
STEWS

The Righteous Bowl

There's something about soups and stews that takes you right back to your childhood. Maybe it was chicken noodle soup when you weren't feeling well, or a hearty bowl of beef stew on a cold night, or that chunky minestrone that your mom made. For my part, the word "stew" always makes me think of the fall, and especially late October. After a brisk night of trick-or-treating in

→

Ferndale, California, we'd head back to a cozy house where there would be something warm and delicious on the stove.

It almost doesn't matter what kind of soup or stew you're talking about—they give instant gratification. From the first bite, a good soup is warm, rich, and totally satisfying. Ready to dive into a bowlful right now? No worries if you don't have a family heirloom recipe for minestrone. I've got you 100 percent covered with the recipes here—and my minestrone might turn out to be *your* family's favorite.

Guy's Soup Rules

It seems as if more and more these days we are confronted with soups and stews—whether they're from cans or boxes or even when we go out to eat—that just aren't that memorable. They're processed, over- or underseasoned, have lousy textures, and are served at the wrong temperature. They've got too much of the ingredients that should be supporting players and too little of the ingredients that should be the rock stars of the bowl. Last but definitely not least, they're utterly lacking in creativity.

Here's the thing. There's nothing much new under the sun . . . or in the soup bowl. All the recipes have probably been written. I mean, sure, there's always room for a "new" spin, but usually it's just one that's new *again* (because our great-grandmothers knew it but then everybody forgot about it until last week) or new to us (because they've been doing it this way in a tiny village in Italy since the Middle Ages). Someone today might even be using his grandma's famous minestrone recipe, but when he makes it, it never tastes the same as it did when he was a kid. This is not because everything in the past was in black-and-white and looked and tasted better. **It's about discipline in how you make the soup.** *That* is what gets you the right result.

So many shortcuts are marketed to us these days that it's easy for people to begin to think that quicker really is better. It's not. The way to great soup and stew is taking the time to properly sear the meat; pulling the thickening roux off the stove when it's just right; cooking the pasta so it's not mushy; seasoning well so that everything tastes better; garnishing simply but appropriately. And, especially, using a great stock. If you don't have time to make your own stock, buy high-quality stock. Don't skimp! It's the base that everything else depends on. If it's lousy, the soup will be lousy. **You wouldn't buy cheap cement for the foundation of your house, so don't buy cheap stock for the foundation of your soup.**

Buffalo Chicken Soup

You know that tangy-creamy-spicy, lip-smacking goodness that comes on a platter of red-hot Buffalo wings with blue cheese dressing and crunchy cooling celery sticks? This soup puts it all in a bowl. Grab a spoon, man, 'cuz it's gonna go fast.

MAKES **4 servings** • ***TIME*** **50 minutes**

Soup

- 4 tablespoons (1/2 stick) unsalted butter
- 1 medium onion, diced
- 2 carrots, diced
- 2 celery stalks, diced
- 6 garlic cloves, minced
- 1 teaspoon kosher salt
- 4 or 5 turns freshly ground black pepper
- 1/4 cup all-purpose flour
- 2 quarts Chicken Stock (page 228 or low-sodium store-bought)
- 1 cup heavy cream
- 1/2 cup Frank's Red Hot sauce, or your favorite hot sauce
- 1/4 teaspoon celery seed
- Pinch of cayenne pepper

Croutons

- 2 tablespoons unsalted butter
- 2 tablespoons extra-virgin olive oil
- 1/4 sourdough baguette, cut into 2 cups of 1/2-inch cubes
- 1/2 teaspoon kosher salt
- 3 to 4 turns freshly ground black pepper

1 To make the soup, set a large, heavy pot over medium heat. Add the butter, onion, carrots, celery, garlic, salt, and black pepper and stir well. Cook, stirring occasionally, until the onion is translucent and the vegetables are tender but not browned, 6 to 7 minutes.

2 Add the flour and stir to coat the vegetables. Cook until the flour is fragrant but still light in color, 4 to 5 minutes.

3 Whisk in the chicken stock, cream, and hot sauce. Bring to a boil, then reduce the heat to a simmer. Add the celery seed and cayenne and simmer until the soup has reduced and slightly thickened, about 30 minutes.

4 Meanwhile, to prepare the croutons, in a large sauté pan over medium-high heat, melt the butter in the olive oil. Add the bread cubes to the pan and toss to coat evenly. Cook until golden all over, 7 to 8 minutes. Transfer the croutons to a bowl and season with the salt and pepper. Set aside.

5 Remove the soup from the heat and let cool slightly. Working in batches, puree about three-quarters of the soup in a blender until smooth and creamy. Return to the pot with the unblended soup and keep warm over low heat.

6 To serve, divide the pulled chicken among four bowls. Ladle the hot soup over the chicken. Garnish with the croutons, blue cheese crumbles, sour cream, green onions, celery leaves, and a sprinkle of celery seeds. Serve.

For serving

2 cups pulled chicken meat from Oven Roasted Chicken (page 71) or a rotisserie chicken

2 ounces blue cheese, crumbled (about ½ cup)

1 cup sour cream

¼ cup finely sliced green onions (white and light green parts)

Leaves from 2 celery hearts

1 teaspoon celery seed

Real-Deal Clam Chowder

I can safely say that I've had clam chowder all over the country, and I'll tell you right here and now that **the secret to great chowder isn't so much *where* it's made, but *how* it's made**—specifically, don't overdo it on the smoky bacon and, at all costs, avoid the dreaded and far-too-common Chewy Clam Calamity. There's nothin' worse than a mouthful of rubber when all you want is briny clam goodness. This real-deal recipe does it right: Make a tasty clam broth using soft-shelled steamers, then pull 'em and chop 'em really small so you get all the flavor and none of the chew. In the last few minutes, steam a bunch of littlenecks right in there so you get reinforced flavor, tender clams, and a gorgeous presentation. That's what I call the best of all worlds.

MAKES **4 to 6 servings •** ***TIME*** **1 hour**

5 pounds steamer clams

36 littleneck clams

¼ cup plus 1 teaspoon kosher salt

1 cup cornmeal

1 cup dry white wine

Juice and grated zest of 1 lemon

6 ounces thick-cut applewood smoked bacon, cut into ¼-inch dice

4 tablespoons (½ stick) unsalted butter

1 large sweet onion, cut into ¼-inch dice

4 celery stalks, cut into ¼-inch dice

5 or 6 turns freshly ground black pepper

2 cups heavy cream

1 quart clam juice

1½ pounds unpeeled Yukon Gold potatoes, cut into ½-inch cubes

Leaves from 3 thyme sprigs

2 bay leaves

¼ cup finely sliced mixed herbs, such as chives, parsley, and/or chervil, for garnish

1 Clean the steamer and littleneck clams in two separate bowls as directed on page 52. For the steamer clams, add ¼ cup kosher salt along with ½ cup cornmeal; for the littlenecks, use just ½ cup cornmeal as directed.

2 In a large stockpot, combine 2 cups water, the wine, and the lemon juice and zest and bring to a boil over medium-high heat. Place the drained steamer clams in the pot. Cover the pot and steam the clams for 4 to 5 minutes. Remove the lid and stir the clams with a wooden spoon. Cover and steam for another 4 to 5 minutes, until all the clams have opened. Transfer the clams to a large bowl, discarding any that have not opened. Strain the broth into another bowl through a mesh sieve lined with cheesecloth to catch any sand or debris. Reserve the broth.

3 When the clams have cooled, remove the meat from the shells. Cut off and discard the siphon from each clam. Coarsely chop the meat. Set aside.

4 Place the bacon in a large pot and set it over medium-high heat. Cook, stirring the bacon occasionally to separate it and ensure it doesn't burn, until golden brown and crispy, 6 to 7 minutes. Add the butter, onion, and celery and season lightly with the remaining 1 teaspoon salt and the pepper. Sauté until the onion is translucent, 5 to 6 minutes.

RECIPE CONTINUES →

RECIPE CONTINUED FROM PREVIOUS PAGE

5 Deglaze the pan by adding the reserved clam broth and scraping up the browned bits from the bottom of the pan. Add the cream and clam juice. Stir well and bring to a boil. Add the potatoes, thyme, and bay leaves. Cover and cook until the potatoes are tender, 10 to 12 minutes.

6 Add the chopped steamer clam meat and the drained littleneck clams. Cover and simmer until the littleneck clams pop open, about 12 minutes. Discard any clams that have not opened and remove and discard the bay leaves.

7 Ladle the chowder into large soup dishes and garnish with the herbs. Serve.

When it comes to wine, Sonoma County truly has "the Bounty of the County." Great soil, awesome weather, and some real-deal artisans come together to make some of America's greatest wines. If you dig wine, you're gonna love our Hunt & Ryde wines . . . named after Hunter and Ryder, of course. www.huntrydewinery.com

The wine guru, Mr. Guy Davis, of www.davisfamilyvineyards.com.

Green Curry Coconut Soup
with Artichoke Hearts and Crispy Chickpeas

Creamy coconut, tangy Thai curry, toasty sesame oil, fragrant crispy chickpeas . . . *need I say more?*

Yeah, actually, I do have one more thing to say. Make sure you do what it says down below here and warm up the onion and oil together, instead of heating the oil first and then adding the onion. This prevents the onion from browning, and that **keeps your creamy, tangy, toasty, fragrant soup clean and green, not down and brown.** And *that,* my friend, is worth saying just one more thing.

MAKES **4 to 6 servings** • ***TIME*** **1 hour**

One 15-ounce can chickpeas, rinsed and drained

3 tablespoons extra-virgin olive oil

1 teaspoon ground cumin

2 teaspoons garlic powder

1 teaspoon plus a pinch of kosher salt

1 tablespoon toasted sesame oil

1 medium onion, finely diced

4 garlic cloves, minced

One 15-ounce can artichoke hearts, drained

One 15-ounce can coconut milk

2 tablespoons green Thai curry paste

2 quarts vegetable stock

Juice of 1 lime

4 cups lightly packed baby spinach

1/4 cup finely sliced Thai basil leaves, for garnish

1 serrano chile, thinly sliced crosswise, for garnish

1 Preheat the oven to 400°F.

2 Spread half the chickpeas on paper towels and pat dry. Transfer to a rimmed baking sheet. Drizzle with 2 tablespoons of the olive oil and mix well to coat. Roast until the chickpeas are golden brown and crunchy, 20 to 25 minutes. Remove from the oven and season with the cumin, garlic powder, and a pinch of the salt. Toss well to coat and set aside to cool.

3 In a large pot over medium-high heat, combine the remaining 1 tablespoon olive oil, the sesame oil, and the onion. Cook, stirring, until the onion is translucent, 6 to 7 minutes. Add the garlic, artichoke hearts, remaining chickpeas, coconut milk, curry paste, and vegetable stock and bring to a boil. Reduce the heat and simmer until the soup has reduced and slightly thickened, about 30 minutes.

4 Add the lime juice and spinach and cook until the spinach is just wilted. Let the soup cool slightly off the heat, then puree it in batches in a blender until smooth and creamy. Season with the remaining 1 teaspoon salt. Return to the pan to reheat if necessary.

5 Ladle the soup into bowls. Garnish with the crispy chickpeas, Thai basil, and serrano slices. Serve.

Italian Wedding Soup
with Turkey Meatballs

During all the years I've been lucky to travel around Flavortown to meet and eat with so many different people, I've found out a lot about what they like. One thing I've learned is that people—whether they're young or old—*love* delicious little surprises in their soup, **especially things like these turkey meatballs.**

MAKES **4 to 6 servings •** ***TIME*** **1½ hours**

Turkey meatballs

Extra-virgin olive oil, for the pan

1 pound lean ground turkey

½ teaspoon Italian seasoning

½ teaspoon paprika

1 large egg

½ cup panko bread crumbs

¼ cup whole milk

2 garlic cloves, minced

2 tablespoons chopped flat-leaf parsley

¾ ounce Parmesan cheese, grated (about ¼ cup)

½ teaspoon red chili flakes

1½ teaspoons kosher salt

4 or 5 turns freshly ground black pepper

1 Preheat the oven to 350°F. Grease a rimmed baking sheet with olive oil.

2 To make the turkey meatballs, place all the ingredients in a large bowl and use your hands to mix together until combined. The milk and panko mixture, called "panade," makes the meatballs nice and light. Keep 'em that way by working gently—don't overmix!

3 Scoop out approximately 2 tablespoons (1 ounce) of the turkey mixture and form into a meatball. Place on the greased baking sheet. Repeat to form about 18 meatballs. Bake until well browned, 15 to 18 minutes. Set aside.

4 To prepare the soup, heat the olive oil in a large pot over medium-high heat. Add the onion, carrots, celery, zucchini, bell pepper, salt, and black pepper and sauté until the onion is translucent, 8 to 9 minutes. Add the garlic, chicken stock, and bay leaves. Use kitchen twine to tie the thyme and rosemary together and add them to the pot. Bring to a boil.

5 Add the meatballs and the escarole. Reduce the heat to a gentle simmer and cook for 25 minutes.

Soup

2 tablespoons extra-virgin olive oil

1 large sweet onion, cut into 1/4-inch dice

2 large carrots, cut into 1/4-inch dice

8 celery stalks, trimmed and sliced 1/4 inch thick

1 medium zucchini, cut into 1/4-inch-thick half-moons

1 large red bell pepper, seeded and cut into 1/4-inch dice

1 teaspoon kosher salt

6 or 7 turns freshly ground black pepper

4 garlic cloves, minced

3 quarts Chicken Stock (page 228 or low-sodium store-bought)

2 bay leaves

4 thyme sprigs

2 rosemary sprigs

2 heads escarole, trimmed and chopped into 1-inch pieces

1/2 pound whole-wheat orecchiette, cooked al dente

1 3/4 ounces Parmesan cheese, grated (about 1/2 cup)

1/4 cup chopped flat-leaf parsley

6 Stir in the orecchiette and cook for 3 to 4 minutes, to heat through. Remove and discard the bay leaves and herb bundle.

7 Ladle the soup into bowls. Top generously with the Parmesan and parsley and serve.

Charred Tomato and Red Bell Pepper Soup

Remember that tomato soup from a can that you got with a grilled cheese sandwich when you were a kid? Yeah, well, this is at the next level.

***MAKES* 4 to 6 servings • *TIME* 45 minutes**

2 pounds Roma tomatoes* (about 12 tomatoes), halved lengthwise

1 large sweet onion, cut crosswise into thick slices

3 large red bell peppers,* quartered and seeded

2 Fresno chiles,* halved and seeded

2 dried guajillo chiles, seeded

6 garlic cloves

1/4 cup extra-virgin olive oil

2 quarts vegetable stock

2 tablespoons aged or regular sherry vinegar

2 tablespoons unsalted butter, cubed

1 teaspoon kosher salt

5 or 6 turns freshly ground black pepper, plus more for serving

1/4 cup Basil Oil (page 297), for serving

*If you're pressed for time, skip the grill and instead of the tomatoes, bell peppers, and chiles, use a 28-ounce can of fire-roasted tomatoes, a 16-ounce can of roasted peppers (drained), and good-quality chili powder to taste.

1 Preheat a grill to high.

2 Squeeze the seeds out of the halved tomatoes. Grill the tomatoes for 4 to 5 minutes, until well charred around the edges. Remove from the grill and set aside.

I mean a heavy char here. Don't be afraid if it's got a little burn on it. That's exactly the good stuff we're lookin' for.

3 Grill the onion, bell peppers, chiles, and garlic until the skin of the peppers blisters and the onion is lightly browned, turning once or twice, 7 to 8 minutes. Remove from the grill and set aside.

4 In a large pot over medium-high heat, combine the olive oil, charred tomatoes, grilled vegetables, vegetable stock, and 1 quart water. Bring to a boil, reduce the heat, and simmer for 20 to 25 minutes.

5 Remove from the heat and let cool slightly. Stir in the vinegar and puree in batches in a blender until smooth and creamy.

6 Return the soup to the pot. Whisk in the butter and season with the salt and black pepper.

7 Ladle into soup bowls. Drizzle with some basil oil and top with a few grinds of black pepper. Serve.

This is ten-year-old-Ryder-approved soup!

Smoked Turkey and Hatch Chile Stew

Smoked turkey and fire-roasted Hatch chiles are the star players in this variation on green chile stew, a dish that's practically an institution in New Mexico—but that doesn't mean we can't have a little fun with it, right? Especially when the result is so much smoky, savory, blow-your-mind goodness. Lots of grocery stores and big box stores carry smoked turkey legs, or you can buy 'em online. Chiles labeled "Hatch" are ubiquitous on the West Coast but can be harder to find in other parts of the country. You can use fresh New Mexico or Anaheim chiles.

MAKES **4 to 6 servings** • ***TIME*** **1 hour**

1/4 cup extra-virgin olive oil

1 large sweet onion, cut into 1/2-inch dice

2 large carrots, sliced into 1/2-inch-thick rounds

6 celery stalks, trimmed, cut into 1/2-inch-thick slices

4 garlic cloves, minced

1 teaspoon kosher salt

7 or 8 turns freshly ground black pepper

1/4 cup all-purpose flour

2 tablespoons ground cumin

1 tablespoon smoked paprika

2 quarts Turkey or Chicken Stock (page 228 or low-sodium store-bought)

2 smoked turkey legs

1 pound russet potatoes, scrubbed and cut into 1/2-inch cubes

8 Hatch chiles, fire-roasted (see page 32) and cut into strips

1 cup fresh or frozen corn kernels

1/4 cup minced chives, for garnish

1 Heat the olive oil in a large, heavy pot over medium-high heat. Add the onion, carrots, and celery and cook until the onion is translucent, 7 to 8 minutes. Add the garlic, salt, black pepper, flour, cumin, and smoked paprika and stir to coat all the ingredients. Cook until the flour is nutty and fragrant, 5 to 6 minutes.

2 Deglaze the pan by adding the turkey stock and scraping up the browned bits from the bottom of the pan. Stir well until smooth and lump-free. Add the smoked turkey legs and enough water to just cover them. Bring to a boil, then reduce the heat to a simmer. Add the potatoes and Hatch chiles and simmer until the potatoes are tender and the stew has thickened, 35 to 40 minutes.

3 Remove the turkey legs and set aside until cool enough to handle. Pull the meat from the bones and return the meat to the stew; discard the bones. Add the corn to the stew and stir well. Simmer for 5 to 7 minutes, until heated through.

4 Ladle the stew into bowls. Garnish with the chives and serve hot.

Lentil Dal Chowder
with Grilled Garlic Naan

One of the best ways I know to get kids to eat a soup or stew that is new or unusual is to serve it with some can't-be-resisted bread, and tell them they can have it *only* if they dip it in the soup at least once. When the bread in question is this grilled garlic naan, and when the soup is this creamy dal, they'll buckle in a minute. Ya see, kiddos? Resistance is futile. . . .

MAKES **4 servings** • ***TIME*** **1 hour**

Lentil dal chowder

1 pound red lentils

2 tablespoons canola oil

2 shallots, minced

1 tablespoon minced ginger

3 cups ¼-inch-diced russet potatoes

2 cups coarsely chopped cauliflower

4 garlic cloves, minced

3 Roma tomatoes, cored and finely diced

1½ tablespoons curry powder

2 teaspoons ground turmeric

1 cup fresh or frozen corn kernels

1 cup fresh or frozen peas

Grilled garlic naan

4 tablespoons (½ stick) unsalted butter

4 garlic cloves, minced

One 9-ounce package naan bread or other flat bread

3 tablespoons minced cilantro

1 To prepare the dal, place the lentils in a strainer and rinse them under cold running water. Place the lentils in a medium bowl, cover with water, and let soak for 30 minutes. Drain and set aside.

2 When the lentils have 10 to 15 minutes left to soak, in a large pot over medium-high heat, heat the canola oil until hot. Add the shallots and ginger and sauté until the shallots are translucent, 3 to 4 minutes. Add the potatoes and cauliflower and sauté until the vegetables are lightly browned, 7 to 8 minutes. Add the garlic and cook lightly until fragrant, about 1 minute.

3 Add the drained lentils, tomatoes, curry powder, turmeric, corn, peas, and 2 quarts cold water. Bring to a boil, then reduce the heat. Simmer, skimming off any foam that appears as it cooks, until the lentils are tender, 35 to 40 minutes.

4 Remove from the heat. Using an immersion blender, pulse the mixture 4 or 5 times, until it is partially pureed and thickened, like a chowder. Set aside, keeping it warm.

5 Preheat a grill to medium.

6 To make the garlic naan, in a small saucepan over medium-high heat, heat the butter and garlic until the garlic is fragrant, 4 to 5 minutes.

Toasted chile and spice garnish

1 tablespoon canola oil

1 serrano chile, seeded, if desired, and minced

1 teaspoon coriander seeds

2 teaspoons cumin seeds

½ cup cilantro leaves, for serving

7 Cut the naan into quarters and brush on both sides with the garlic butter. Grill on both sides until the naan wedges are golden and have crosshatch grill marks, 3 to 4 minutes. Sprinkle with the cilantro. Set the naan aside, keeping it warm by covering it with a clean kitchen towel.

8 To make the garnish, heat the canola oil in a medium sauté pan over medium heat until shimmering. Carefully add the serrano, coriander seeds, and cumin seeds. Toast until the seeds are browned and fragrant, about 2 minutes. Remove from the heat.

Be careful: the seeds might pop.

9 To serve, stir the toasted serrano and spice garnish into the dal. Ladle into bowls and garnish with the cilantro. Serve with the garlic naan on the side.

Short Rib Shepherd's Stew

So when you make a stew of cubed short ribs simmered with a platoon of vegetables until it's falling-apart tender, and then you top that stew with the creamiest mashed potatoes, parsnips, and turnips, and then you brown it quick so it's got a nice crust on top . . . do you know what you've done? You've created the greatest comfort food ever eaten by man, woman, or child.

MAKES **4 to 6 servings •** ***TIME*** **1½ hours**

2½ pounds boneless short rib beef, cut into ½-inch cubes*
2 teaspoons kosher salt
8 to 10 turns freshly ground black pepper
2 tablespoons extra-virgin olive oil
1 medium onion, cut into ¼-inch dice
6 celery stalks, cut into ¼-inch dice
2 medium carrots, cut into ¼-inch dice
4 garlic cloves, minced
2 tablespoons tomato paste
¼ cup all-purpose flour
3 cups Beef Stock (page 226 or low-sodium store-bought)
1 tablespoon Worcestershire sauce
1 teaspoon thyme leaves
2 bay leaves
1 cup fresh or thawed frozen corn kernels
1 cup fresh or thawed frozen peas
2 cups Mashed Root Vegetables (recipe follows)
¼ cup chopped flat-leaf parsley, for garnish
¼ cup chopped chives, for garnish

*Or pick up 4 pounds of bone-in short ribs. Cut the meat off the bones to use here and use the bones to make stock (page 226).

1 Season the beef with the salt and pepper. Toss to mix well.

2 Heat the olive oil in a large Dutch oven over medium-high heat until smoking. Add the beef and brown on all sides, 8 to 9 minutes. Add the onion, celery, and carrots and sauté until lightly browned, 6 to 7 minutes. Add the garlic and tomato paste and cook until fragrant, about 2 minutes. Add the flour and mix well to coat the meat and vegetables. Cook until the flour is browned and fragrant, about 5 minutes.

3 Deglaze the pan by adding the beef stock and scraping up the browned bits from the bottom of the pan. Bring to a boil, then reduce the heat to a simmer. Add the Worcestershire sauce, thyme, and bay leaves. Cover and simmer, stirring often, until the meat is tender, about 1 hour.

4 Remove the stew from the heat and add the corn and peas. Cover and let stand for 10 minutes. Remove and discard the bay leaves.

5 Place an oven rack 6 inches from the heat source and preheat the broiler. Ladle the stew into oven-safe bowls. Top each serving with a scoop of the mashed root vegetables. Place the bowls on a rimmed baking sheet and place under the broiler. Broil for 1 to 2 minutes, or until the mashed vegetables are lightly browned, taking care not to burn them.

6 Garnish with the parsley and chives and serve.

Mashed Root Vegetables

MAKES **4 to 6 servings**

1 quart whole milk

2 cups heavy cream

4 thyme sprigs

2 bay leaves

1 pound parsnips, peeled and cut into 1-inch chunks

1 pound turnips, peeled and cut into 1-inch chunks

1 tablespoon kosher salt, plus more to taste

1½ pounds Yukon Gold potatoes, peeled and cut into 1-inch chunks

2 tablespoons unsalted butter, cubed

4 or 5 gratings of nutmeg

6 or 7 turns freshly ground black pepper

1 Place the milk, cream, thyme, bay leaves, parsnips, turnips, and salt in a large pot. Bring to a boil over medium-high heat, then reduce the heat and simmer for 20 minutes.

2 Add the potatoes and simmer until all the vegetables are fork-tender, about 20 minutes.

3 Discard the bay leaves and thyme sprigs.

4 Drain the vegetables, reserving 2 cups of the cooking liquid. Pass the vegetables through a ricer into a bowl or place in a bowl and use a masher to mash until smooth. Add the butter and a little of the reserved cooking liquid and stir well until smooth and creamy, adding more of the reserved liquid as necessary to achieve the desired consistency.

5 Season with the nutmeg, pepper, and salt to taste. Serve at once or let cool, cover with plastic wrap, and store in the refrigerator for up to 2 days. Reheat in the microwave or in a large saucepan; add a little milk if necessary to loosen the texture.

Spinach and Spring Vegetable Quinoa Minestrone

This may not be your grandma's minestrone, but then again, I'm not your grandma. Still, I'm pretty sure she'd approve of this spring vegetable style, which is not as heavy as what many people consider "classic" minestrone. Quinoa and fresh tomatoes add great texture and keep it light. And the crazy-simple step of simmering the rind of the Parmesan cheese with the soup adds crazy-good deep flavor.

MAKES **4 to 6 servings •** ***TIME*** **1 hour**

1 cup uncooked white quinoa

One 6-ounce piece Parmesan cheese (with rind)

6 Roma tomatoes

1/4 cup extra-virgin olive oil

1 medium sweet onion, diced

2 large carrots, cut into 1/4-inch dice

6 celery stalks, trimmed and cut into 1/4-inch dice

1 cup sliced cremini mushrooms

1 small zucchini, cut into 1/4-inch-thick half-moons

2 cups 1/2-inch pieces trimmed green beans

6 garlic cloves, minced

2 teaspoons kosher salt

6 or 7 turns freshly ground black pepper

2 quarts Chicken Stock (page 228 or low-sodium store-bought)

1/4 teaspoon red chili flakes

1 cup fresh or frozen corn kernels

1 Preheat the oven to 375°F.

2 Place the quinoa on a rimmed baking sheet and toast in the oven until fragrant and nutty, 8 to 10 minutes. Set aside to cool.

3 Cut off the rind from the Parmesan wedge. Finely grate the Parmesan. Set the rind and grated cheese aside.

4 Over the open flame of a grill or gas stove, or under a gas broiler, char the tomatoes until the skins are blackened and blistered. Let stand until cool enough to handle, then cut each one in half and squeeze out and discard the seeds. Coarsely chop the tomatoes and set aside.

5 In a large pot, heat the olive oil over medium-high heat. Add the onion, carrots, celery, mushrooms, zucchini, and green beans and cook until the onion is translucent, 6 to 7 minutes. Add the garlic, season with salt and pepper, and stir well. Add the reserved toasted quinoa, Parmesan rind, tomatoes, chicken stock, chili flakes, and 1 quart water. Bring to a boil, then reduce the heat and simmer for 30 to 35 minutes, until the vegetables are tender and the quinoa has popped open.

RECIPE CONTINUES →

← RECIPE CONTINUED FROM PAGE 155

4 cups lightly packed baby spinach

¼ cup chopped flat-leaf parsley, for garnish

¼ cup chopped basil leaves, for garnish

Tip: When you buy a chunk of true Parmesan cheese, it always comes with a piece of the rind attached; that's how you know you're gettin' the real thing. Don't throw away that rind! When you're done with the cheese, store the rind in the freezer—I have a resealable plastic bag dedicated to Parm rinds in my freezer. Then whenever you've got a soup or stew (or stock, page 228) simmering on the stove, toss a rind in there. It adds a rich, savory flavor that isn't at all obviously "cheesy" but is definitely there. Just make sure you throw out the rind before you serve the soup!

6 Add the corn and spinach and simmer for 2 to 3 minutes, until the spinach is just wilted. Remove and discard the Parmesan rind. Taste and adjust the seasoning as desired.

7 Ladle the soup into soup bowls and garnish with the grated Parmesan, parsley, and basil. Serve.

ALL HANDS ON DECK

This is the name of the actual sub my dad served on!

How to Make Sure EVERYONE Gets Their Hands Dirty

This chapter holds a bunch of recipes that are really more like plans for events, and they're inspired by a couple of different things. First, when I was a kid, my old man, a former Navy guy, used to holler "All hands on deck!" to call us out and make us do all sorts of work in the kitchen and around the house. Now I'm the guy in charge, and

→

No one in the family approved of this sketch. Ha ha.

I love nothing more than having my kids and nephew and their buddies in the kitchen working with me to prep dinner.

The other big inspiration is the many times when we have an even larger crowd of family and friends in the house. On a regular night, the crew may try to scatter as soon as you start moving toward dinner prep, but **when it's a family gathering, whether it's a reunion, vacation, or the holidays, suddenly everybody—young, old, and in between—wants to be in the kitchen.**

When I was a little kid, the adults in the house used to congregate around the person cooking while we ran wild outside. But today kids are watching food television, asking for cookbooks, and even going to cooking classes. And it's great, because for at least a couple of generations people were learning less and less about how to cook at home. Now we've got this whole young generation that's totally motivated to learn this stuff, but they don't know how to begin, and we don't always know how or when to involve and teach them.

So how do you make that happen? You give them experience that they'll remember for the rest of their lives by providing the opportunities for them to gain some know-how, make some mistakes, share in the successes, and build self-confidence. And, best of all, you do all of this while you feed the masses. This calls for big, glorious spreads that can be easily done when there's a battalion of helpers. I don't know who first said **many hands make light work,** but this chapter is dedicated to that person.

Tamale Night

My boys and I love to set up shop and make dozens of these babies at a time. (More than even my gang can eat in a single sitting. Good thing steamed tamales freeze so well. With just a couple of hours of work, you can make enough tamales for a month of Sundays.)

So I know from experience that the best way to make a whole lotta tamales at once is to form an assembly line where each person does the same thing for *all* the tamales. Have someone spread the masa, someone else add the filling, a third someone fold them up, and even assign someone just to tie them off. When each person is doing only one job, you get consistency, which means they'll cook evenly, rather than when everyone just fills their own. Then you end up with a half dozen different styles filled with varying amounts of each item that won't cook at the same rate.

The filling instructions and masa (tamale dough) recipe on pages 164–165 will make 20 tamales, using whichever one of the three fillings you like. But you can very easily double or triple it if you want to throw a full tamale-filling party and use two or all three fillings—just don't forget to double or triple both the masa and number of cornhusks.

When choosing cornhusks, make sure you get nice, big ones that can hold generous amounts of masa and filling; in a pinch you can overlap two smaller husks and treat them like a single bigger one. In any case, you'll want a few extras on hand, both because they can tear and because one or two can be pulled into skinny strips that you can use to tie them off.

The Tamale Setup

MAKES **about 20 tamales, to serve 6 to 8**

TIME **1 hour, plus 45 minutes for the masa and 15 minutes to 1 hour for the fillings**

About 20 dried cornhusks (about 6 inches wide and 7 to 8 inches long), plus one or two extra for making strips for tying (or use kitchen twine)

Masa (page 165)

One recipe tamale filling (pages 166–168)

Tamale steamer (or stockpot with a metal colander to fit it)

Boiling water

RECIPE CONTINUES →

RECIPE CONTINUED FROM PREVIOUS PAGE

1 Place the corn husks in a pan and cover with hot water. Set a plate or weight on top to keep them submerged. Soak for 1 hour or until soft and pliable.

2 To form the tamales, use paper towels to pat the cornhusks dry. Tear one or two of the extra husks lengthwise into thin strips for tying the finished tamales; set aside.

3 Holding a cornhusk with the tapered end toward you, place a heaping ¼ cup of the masa dough in the center of the cornhusk. Spread the mixture to within 1 inch of the sides of the husks, creating a 4 x 5-inch rectangle.

4 Place 2 tablespoons of filling down the middle of the dough. Fold 1 long edge of the husk to the center, covering the filling by about 2 inches, then fold the other side over to completely cover and encase the filling. Fold the bottom of the husk up and over to completely seal the bottom (leave the top open). Secure the tamale by lightly tying a strip of husk around it. Transfer to a large platter and repeat with the remaining corn husks, masa, and filling. (You can wrap the whole platter of filled, uncooked tamales in plastic wrap and refrigerate for up to 1 day.)

5 To steam the tamales, use a tamale steamer or place a metal colander in a large stockpot filled with just enough water that it does not touch the bottom of the colander. Cover and bring to a boil. Place the tamales upright in the colander, leaving a little room for them to expand and working in batches as needed. Cover and steam the tamales until the dough is firm and pulls away easily from the husk, 35 to 40 minutes. Set additional water to boil to use as needed. Monitor the water level in the pot as they cook and add more boiling water if necessary to keep them steaming. Transfer the tamales to a bowl. Cover with a clean kitchen towel to keep warm, if necessary, while you steam the remaining tamales.

6 Serve warm. To store leftovers, or to make ahead, freeze the steamed tamales in their husks in freezer bags for up to 1 month. Defrost in the refrigerator and reheat in the microwave or by steaming as directed above for a couple of minutes.

Masa (Tamale Dough)

MAKES enough for about 20 tamales

- 1 cup lard
- 2 jalapeños, seeded and minced
- ½ medium sweet onion, minced
- 1 tablespoon kosher salt
- 2 garlic cloves, minced
- 4 cups masa harina (fine corn flour)
- 1½ teaspoons baking powder
- 2 cups Chicken Stock (page 228 or low-sodium store-bought), or as needed

1 In a medium sauté pan, heat 1 tablespoon of the lard over medium-high heat until hot. Add the jalapeños, onion, and a pinch of the salt and sauté until the onion is translucent, 4 to 5 minutes. Add the garlic and cook until fragrant, about 1 minute. Remove from the heat and set aside to cool.

2 In a large bowl, use your hands to combine the masa and 3 cups water to form a thick paste that holds together as a single mass and is slightly tacky to the touch but not so wet that it's messy and hard to hold; add up to 1 cup more water as needed to achieve the right texture. Set aside.

3 In the bowl of a stand mixer fitted with the paddle attachment, beat the remaining lard on high speed until it is light in texture and fluffy, 2 to 3 minutes.

4 Stop the mixer. Add half the masa mixture and beat on medium speed until it is fully incorporated into the lard. Stop the mixer and add the remaining masa mixture, along with the baking powder, remaining salt, and cooked jalapeño-onion mixture. Beat on low speed for 3 to 4 minutes, until it comes together as an evenly blended mass.

5 Beating on low speed, gradually add the chicken stock until the dough is smooth and pulls away from the bowl (you may not need the full 2 cups). Turn the masa out into a bowl, cover, and let rest at room temperature for at least 10 minutes and up to a couple of hours before using.

Beef Picadillo Tamale Filling

MAKES **about 3½ cups, enough for 20 tamales**

2 tablespoons extra-virgin olive oil
1½ pounds ground chuck
1 tablespoon kosher salt
4 or 5 turns freshly ground black pepper
½ sweet onion, minced
1 large Idaho potato, peeled and cut into ¼-inch cubes
1 serrano chile, seeded and minced
1 poblano pepper, seeded and minced
2 garlic cloves, minced
2 Roma tomatoes, cored and cut into ¼-inch dice
1 cup tomato puree
¼ cup raisins
½ cup sliced green olives
2 teaspoons dried Mexican oregano
½ teaspoon ground cinnamon
½ teaspoon ground cumin
1 teaspoon sugar
Pinch of ground cloves

1 Heat the olive oil in a large sauté pan over medium-high heat until shimmering. Add the ground chuck and brown all over, 6 to 7 minutes, breaking it up with a wooden spoon as it cooks. Season with salt and black pepper.

2 Add the onion, potato, serrano, poblano, and garlic and sauté until the beef is well browned and the onion is translucent, 8 to 10 minutes.

3 Add the tomatoes, tomato puree, raisins, olives, oregano, cinnamon, cumin, sugar, and cloves and mix well. Bring to a boil, then reduce the heat and simmer until the potato is tender and almost completely broken down, about 20 minutes. Remove from the heat and set the picadillo aside to cool. (You can transfer the filling to an airtight container and refrigerate it for up to 3 days or freeze for up to 2 weeks.)

Achiote Chicken Tamale Filling

MAKES **about 3½ cups, enough for 20 tamales**

Achiote rub

1 tablespoon paprika

1½ teaspoons ancho chili powder

1 teaspoon ground cumin

1 teaspoon granulated garlic

½ teaspoon ground cloves

½ teaspoon dried marjoram

½ teaspoon dried thyme

1 tablespoon achiote paste

2 teaspoons kosher salt

4 or 5 turns freshly ground black pepper

2 tablespoons extra-virgin olive oil

Filling mixture

1½ pounds boneless, skinless chicken thighs

1 tablespoon extra-virgin olive oil

½ sweet onion, minced

½ cup peeled and ¼-inch-diced Idaho potato

2 guajillo chiles, seeded and minced

1 teaspoon kosher salt

4 or 5 turns freshly ground black pepper

4 garlic cloves, minced

1 cup Chicken Stock (page 228 or low-sodium store-bought)

2 tablespoons fresh lime juice

1 To prepare the achiote rub, combine all the ingredients in a small bowl and mix well to form a paste. Set aside.

2 To make the filling mixture, dice the chicken into ½-inch pieces and combine with the achiote rub. Mix well to coat evenly all over. Place in the refrigerator for at least 15 minutes and up to 1 hour.

3 Heat the olive oil in a large sauté pan over medium-high heat until shimmering. Add the chicken, onion, potato, and guajillo chiles and season with salt and black pepper. Sauté until the chicken is browned and the onion is translucent, 7 to 8 minutes. Add the garlic and cook for 1 minute more, until fragrant.

4 Add the chicken stock. Bring to a boil and add the lime juice. Reduce the heat and simmer until the chicken is tender, the potato has begun to break up, and the liquid has reduced almost completely, about 20 minutes. Remove from heat and set aside to cool. (You can transfer the filling to an airtight container and refrigerate it for 3 to 4 days.)

Oaxaca Cheese and Cilantro Pesto Tamale Filling

MAKES about 3 cups, enough for 20 tamales

4 cups lightly packed cilantro leaves and stems
1/4 cup lightly packed basil leaves
1/4 teaspoon dried Mexican oregano
1/4 cup pepitas, toasted (see page 22)
1 teaspoon kosher salt
Pinch of red chili flakes
1 teaspoon ground cumin
3 or 4 turns freshly ground black pepper
2 garlic cloves, minced
Juice and grated zest of 1 lime
1/4 cup extra-virgin olive oil
6 ounces Cotija cheese, crumbled (about 1 1/2 cups)
1/4 pound Jack cheese, grated (about 1 cup)

1 To prepare the cilantro pesto, combine all the ingredients except the cheeses in a food processor. Pulse 8 to 10 times, until the mixture is finely chopped but still has good texture; don't overprocess and puree it.

2 Transfer to a bowl and fold in the cheeses. Cover and set aside. Store in an airtight container and refrigerate for 1 to 2 days.

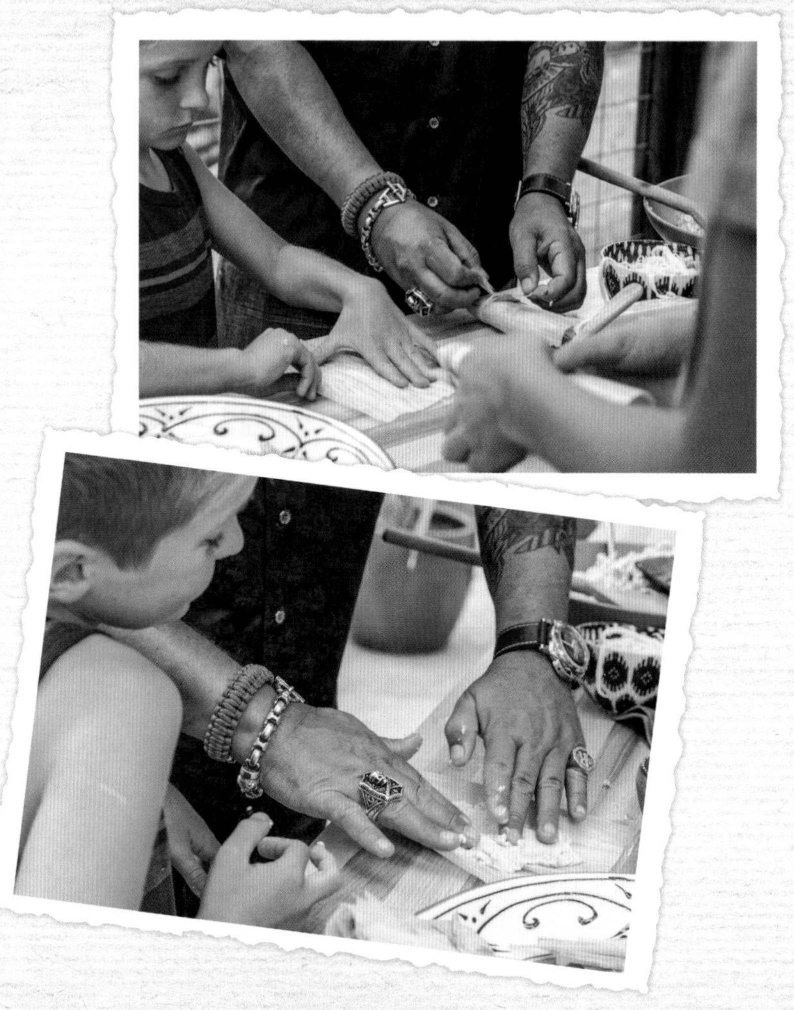

Kebab Night

I think just about everyone loves to eat with their hands, but it's not always obvious when it's appropriate to do so, and we don't get nearly enough opportunities to roll up our sleeves and really go for it. Enter kebabs, the best way I know to give people a formal introduction to the informal (and fun!) process of eating with your hands. And it's not just the eating that's fun here; the making of kebabs is a fine example of how entertaining all-hands-on-deck cooking can be. Just ask any kid you know how cool they think it would be to skewer all sorts of tasty ingredients with long, pointy sticks—and right away you'll see in their eyes what I'm talkin' about.

Plus, having that knowledge of how to set up good kebabs is an important and overlooked kitchen skill for an economizing family. The beauty of kebabs is that you don't have to have huge pieces of meat and bountiful amounts of each item; "kebabing" is a great way to utilize multiple small quantities of items. Say you open your freezer and fridge and you've got a couple of chicken breasts, one pork chop, a handful of mushrooms, a couple of potatoes, one zucchini, and some onions. You can turn this random collection of ingredients into a fantastic meal!

Now, if you want precise guidelines, use any or all of the recipes that follow; they'll give you fantastic results. You can even set up stations for each type of kebab so that they're made just as written here. But if you prefer (or the contents of your refrigerator require) more of a free-form approach, then cut up a bunch of ingredients, set out skewers, and let the crew have at it (just the way we did one afternoon at the ranch, as you can see in the photos here). If you go the free association route, be sure to check out my 101 on page 171 for a few guidelines that'll ensure your kebabs come out great.

Kebabs 101

Whether you're following a prescribed recipe with specific ingredients called for or you're just winging it, using up what's in your refrigerator and pantry, here are the details you need to know to keep your kebabs in line:

Choose the right skewer for the job. You'll see in the photo opposite some of my favorite skewers. There are no hard-and-fast rules for which one of these will always work in one situation or another, but there are a few good general guidelines, starting with the fact that you can really never have too thick a skewer, and the more intense the heat source, the thicker and sturdier the skewer should be. That means that if you want to cook over really high heat, like on a wood fire, metal skewers are your best friends. On the other hand, if you're camping, bamboo or wood skewers are good because you can toss them in the fire after you eat and have one less thing you have to carry out with you. (If you use wood or bamboo, remember to soak them for at least an hour before using them or they risk catching on fire.) Double skewering—you can even buy two-pronged skewers—prevents ingredients from swiveling on the kebabs when you turn them. They're also good for softer ingredients that might get a little loose on a single skewer, such as mushrooms or zucchini. Finally, I recommend you do yourself a favor and invest in some wood-handled, extra-long skewers (I'm talkin' 2 feet long here) so that you skewer a lot more often. Your family and your wallet will thank you.

The peel, skin, and shells are your friends. For the skewer to have a nice, secure grip on ingredients, it helps to have a little something extra to hold on to, so try to use skin-on vegetables, tail-on shrimp, and pieces of meat that have some connective tissue, fat, or skin on them. And push the skewer through the thickest part of whatever piece you're threading; this helps ensure that you get the skewer all the way through without tearing the piece.

Cut even and uniform pieces. The size you cut each separate ingredient will determine how well it cooks. If the mushrooms are cut small and the onions are big, well, now you've got mushy mushrooms and raw onions. Yuck. So keep in mind that uniformity and consistency are key. No one likes undercooked or overcooked food, and especially if you want a nice crust on medium-rare meat, like I'll talk more about just below, the pieces have to be uniform so they can all touch the grill. Also, pair ingredients that have similar cook times on the kebabs.

Give 'em some elbow room. When making chicken, pork, and vegetable kebabs, make sure you don't squash the ingredients together super tight and close. Spread out the ingredients a little bit, spacing them somewhere between only barely touching and 1/8 inch apart so that the heat can get in between the items and cook them all the way through. Beef and lamb are exceptions (there are *always* exceptions, aren't there?), because you want a good, brown, caramelized outer crust but you also want medium-rare meat. So you can let these be flush up against other ingredients. But in order for this to work the way it's supposed to, you've gotta remember the last rule and cut the pieces the same size.

Don't overload your skewer. Especially when you're working with wood or bamboo skewers, if you put too much weight on them, they'll break. Plus, it's easier to handle a skewer with fewer items than a skewer that's so full it wobbles when you lift it.

The broiler is a viable backup plan. There are all sorts of reasons that a grill might not be feasible for you—whether all the time or just tonight because your spouse forgot to buy the charcoal/wood/gas—but that should not by any means stop you from kebabing. Put the rack about 6 inches from the heat source and turn that broiler on high. Place a rack on a baking sheet and line those skewers up on it, making sure they don't touch one another. The rack is necessary because for perfectly cooked skewers it's important that the hot oven air can circulate all around them. Broil until browned on one side, then flip and finish off on the other side.

Shrimp and Hot Links Kebabs
with Lemon Garlic Butter

One of my golden rules for grilling shrimp is that the larger the shrimp, the better they will survive on the grill, withstanding the high heat without overcooking. I find that the perfect size is tail-on 16/20 shrimp (the number signifies how many shrimp are in 1 pound). Also, be sure to flip or pull 'em as soon as you get a nice pink color on the grilled side, so that they don't turn leathery.

***MAKES* 4 to 6 servings • *TIME* 45 minutes**

Twelve 12-inch bamboo or metal skewers

2 pounds tail-on 16/20 (extra jumbo) shrimp, peeled and deveined

1 pound precooked hot links, cut into ½-inch-thick rounds

2 teaspoons kosher salt

½ teaspoon freshly ground black pepper

¼ pound (1 stick) unsalted butter, cut into several pieces

Juice of 2 lemons

6 garlic cloves, minced

2 teaspoons smoked Spanish paprika

¼ cup finely sliced chives, for garnish

I like to call this a "brush."

1 If using bamboo skewers, place them in a shallow dish and cover completely with water. Soak for at least 1 hour.

2 Drain the skewers if necessary. Thread a skewer through the tail of a shrimp, then crosswise through a hot link, and then through the top (head) part of the shrimp, so that the shrimp is "hugging" the hot link. Repeat so that each skewer has 4 shrimp-and-hot-link combos, leaving 2 inches at the base and placing the kebabs on a baking sheet as you go. Season the kebabs with half the salt and pepper.

3 Preheat a grill to medium-high.

4 In a medium skillet over medium-high heat, melt the butter, then add the lemon juice, garlic, smoked paprika, and remaining salt and pepper. Cook just until the garlic is fragrant, 2 to 3 minutes. Remove the brush from the heat and set aside.

5 Grill the shrimp kebabs until the shrimp turn evenly pink and are slightly charred on one side, 4 to 5 minutes. Brush with the lemon garlic butter and flip the skewers over. Cook for 4 to 5 minutes more, brushing several times. Remove from the grill.

6 Stack the shrimp kebabs on a large serving platter. Garnish with the chives. Serve.

Hawaiian Pineapple Chicken Teriyaki Kebabs

Here we've got charred luscious pineapple and chicken, but you've gotta keep your eye on one thing to make sure it turns out that way: Don't let the chicken sit too close to the pineapple. The enzymes from the pineapple will break down the chicken and make it mealy. And make sure you use cured Spanish chorizo here; raw (Mexican) chorizo won't work.

MAKES 4 to 6 servings • TIME 1 hour, plus 30 minutes for marinating

Twelve 12-inch bamboo or metal skewers

Teriyaki marinade and sauce

1/2 cup low-sodium teriyaki sauce

1/2 cup low-sodium soy sauce

1/2 cup pineapple juice

1/2 cup mirin (Japanese rice wine)*

1/4 cup lightly packed light brown sugar

2 tablespoons grated ginger

1/2 cup finely sliced green onions (white and light green parts)

5 to 6 turns freshly ground black pepper

1/2 teaspoon red chili flakes

2 tablespoons cornstarch

Kebabs

2 pounds boneless, skinless chicken breast, cut into 1-inch pieces

1 pound cured Spanish chorizo, cut into 1/2-inch-thick rounds

1/2 pineapple, peeled, cored, and cut into 1-inch cubes (about 2 cups)

1 If using bamboo skewers, place them in a shallow dish and cover completely with water. Soak for at least 1 hour.

2 To make the marinade and sauce, in a large bowl, combine all the ingredients except for the cornstarch. Whisk to combine.

3 Transfer one-third of the marinade to a small saucepan and whisk in the cornstarch (leave the remaining marinade in the large bowl). Bring to a simmer over medium-high heat and simmer until thickened and clear, 2 to 3 minutes. Remove the teriyaki sauce from the heat and set aside.

4 To make the kebabs, add the chicken to the bowl with the marinade. Mix well to coat thoroughly. Cover and refrigerate for at least 30 minutes and up to 1 hour.

5 Preheat a grill to medium-high.

6 Remove the chicken from the refrigerator and drain the skewers if necessary. Thread a skewer in this order: chicken, chorizo, pineapple, and each color of bell pepper, keeping a very small gap between ingredients so they cook evenly. Repeat three times on the same skewer, leaving 2 inches at the base of the skewer. Repeat to make the rest of the skewers. Sprinkle with the salt and black pepper.

For a quicker preparation you might be tempted to use canned pineapple, but please don't! It's too soft and will fall off the skewers. Instead, look for diced fresh pineapple in the produce section.

1 red bell pepper, seeded and cut into 1-inch dice

1 green bell pepper, seeded and cut into 1-inch dice

1 yellow bell pepper, seeded and cut into 1-inch dice

1 teaspoon kosher salt

5 or 6 turns freshly ground black pepper

¼ cup finely sliced green onions (white and light green parts), for garnish

*Mirin, or Japanese rice wine, adds both acidity and a little sweetness to the teriyaki sauce. You can find it in Asian supermarkets, and it's worth having a bottle around for times like these. Or use ½ cup dry white wine and ½ teaspoon sugar in its place.

7 Grill the kebabs until the chicken is light brown and crispy, 5 to 6 minutes. Flip and grill until the chorizo is crispy and the vegetables are charred and tender, another 3 to 4 minutes. Transfer to a plate to rest.

8 Stack the kebabs on a large serving platter. Drizzle with the teriyaki sauce and garnish with green onions. Serve.

Tip: For a quicker preparation you might be tempted to use canned pineapple, but please don't! It's too soft and will fall off the skewers. Instead, look for diced fresh pineapple in the produce section.

Mediterranean Lamb Kebabs

with Tzatziki Sauce and Feta Olive Tapenade

Marinating boneless leg of lamb in a tangy mixture that includes olives, capers, and vinegar tenderizes it and adds incredible flavor. The longer you can let it marinate, the better it'll be. Grilling a lemon wedge on the kebab right along with the lamb is a simple step that gives big payback. It really brings out the lemon's juices and seems to make them more concentrated and even a bit sweeter. So make sure you remind everyone to squeeze that grilled wedge over the lamb once the skewers are on their plates.

MAKES **4 to 6 servings** • *TIME* **1 hour, plus 1 hour for marinating**

Twelve 8-inch bamboo or metal skewers

Tzatziki sauce

2 cups plain Greek yogurt

2 teaspoons minced garlic

1/4 cup minced onion

1/4 cup grated seeded cucumber

1 tablespoon minced flat-leaf parsley

1 tablespoon minced dill

Juice and grated zest of 1 lemon

2 tablespoons extra-virgin olive oil

1 1/2 teaspoons kosher salt

1/2 teaspoon freshly ground black pepper

Feta olive tapenade

1/4 pound feta cheese, cut into small dice (about 1 cup)

1/2 pound pitted mixed olives, drained and chopped (about 1 1/2 cups)

2 tablespoons chopped oregano

2 tablespoons extra-virgin olive oil

1 If using bamboo skewers, place them in a shallow dish and cover completely with water. Soak for at least 1 hour.

2 To make the tzatziki sauce, in a medium bowl, whisk all the ingredients until well combined. Cover and refrigerate for at least 30 minutes and up to 2 days.

3 To make the tapenade, in a medium bowl, mix all the ingredients until well combined. Cover and set aside.

4 To prepare the kebabs, in a large bowl, combine the olives, capers, oregano, garlic, salt, black pepper, chili flakes, olive oil, and vinegar and whisk to combine. Add the lamb and mix to coat thoroughly. Cover and refrigerate for at least 1 hour and up to overnight.

5 Preheat a grill to medium-high.

6 Remove the lamb from the refrigerator and drain the skewers if necessary. Thread a skewer in this order: a lemon wedge, then 5 chunks of lamb, pressing the chunks against one another. Leave 2 inches at the base of the skewer. Repeat to make the rest of the skewers.

4 or 5 turns freshly ground black pepper

1/4 teaspoon red chili flakes

Kebabs

1/4 cup minced pitted Kalamata olives

2 tablespoons drained capers, minced

2 tablespoons chopped oregano

4 garlic cloves, minced

1 teaspoon kosher salt

1/2 teaspoon freshly ground black pepper

1/2 teaspoon red chili flakes

1/4 cup extra-virgin olive oil

2 tablespoons red wine vinegar

2 pounds boneless leg of lamb, cut into 1-inch cubes

3 lemons, quartered

7 Grill the kebabs until the lamb is browned and crispy outside and pink in the middle, 3 to 4 minutes on each side, turning once. Transfer to a plate to rest.

8 Stack the lamb kebabs on a large serving platter, drizzle with tzatziki sauce, and serve with the feta olive tapenade.

Sirloin Kebabs
with Cremini Mushroom Pan Sauce

This brings the classic combination of steak, onions, and mushrooms to a whole other level.

MAKES **4 to 6 servings •** ***TIME*** **1½ hours, plus at least 1 hour for marinating**

Twelve 12-inch bamboo skewers

Kebabs

2 medium shallots, minced

2 garlic cloves, minced

½ cup dry red wine

¼ cup balsamic vinegar

¼ cup extra-virgin olive oil

Needles from 4 rosemary sprigs

2 teaspoons kosher salt

1 teaspoon freshly ground black pepper

2 pounds sirloin steak, cut into 1-inch cubes

18 cipollini onions

18 cremini mushrooms

¼ cup chopped flat-leaf parsley, for garnish

Cremini mushroom pan sauce

2 tablespoons extra-virgin olive oil

2 medium shallots, thinly sliced

1 teaspoon kosher salt

2 garlic cloves, minced

1 pound cremini mushrooms, coarsely chopped

1 tablespoon all-purpose flour

1 Place the skewers in a shallow dish and cover completely with water. Soak for at least 1 hour.

2 To prepare the kebabs, in a large bowl, whisk together the shallots, garlic, wine, vinegar, olive oil, rosemary, 1 teaspoon of the salt, and ½ teaspoon of the pepper. Add the beef cubes and mix well to coat thoroughly. Cover and refrigerate for at least 1 hour and up to overnight.

3 To peel the cipollini onions, bring a large saucepan of water to a boil and set a large bowl of ice water on the counter. Submerge the onions in the boiling water for 10 seconds, then remove with a spider or large slotted spoon and immediately transfer to the ice water. Trim the ends and remove the peels. The peels should slip off with minimal trouble; if they don't, repeat the process. Set aside.

4 To prepare the pan sauce, heat the olive oil in a large sauté pan over medium-high heat. Add the shallots and salt and sauté until the shallots are lightly browned, 6 to 7 minutes. Add the garlic and mushrooms and sauté until the mushrooms have sweated down and lost their water, 5 to 6 minutes.

5 Add the flour and stir to coat the mushroom mixture. Deglaze the pan by adding the beef stock and scraping up the browned bits from the bottom of the pan. Bring to a boil, then reduce the heat and simmer the sauce until reduced by one-third, 7 to 8 minutes.

1 cup Beef Stock (page 226 or low-sodium store-bought)

3 tablespoons unsalted butter

2 tablespoons minced chives

½ teaspoon freshly ground black pepper

6 Stir in the butter and chives. Season with the pepper. Remove from the heat and set aside.

7 Preheat a grill to medium-high.

8 Remove the beef from the refrigerator and drain the skewers if necessary. Thread a skewer in this order: sirloin chunk, onion, sirloin chunk, mushroom, pressing all the ingredients close to one another. Repeat two more times, leaving 2 inches at the base. Repeat to make the remaining skewers.

9 Grill the kebabs until the steak is crispy and browned on the outside and pink on the inside, and the onions and mushrooms are charred, 5 to 6 minutes on each side, turning once. Transfer to a plate to rest.

10 Rewarm the cremini mushroom pan sauce if necessary. Stack the sirloin kebabs on a large serving platter. Spoon the sauce over the top and garnish with parsley. Serve.

I wish they always got along like this (lol).

Taco Bar Night

When I was a kid, I thought that **taco night was one of the greatest nights in the world,** because it meant meat (we didn't eat it as often as I wanted it)—and I got to make my own food! We had a lazy Susan in the middle of our dining table and we'd overload it with all the glass bowls it could hold, each one filled to the brim with taco makings: grated cheese, beans, olives, fresh tomato salsa, smashed avocado, sliced green onions, the aforementioned meat, and, of course, fresh corn tortillas. We'd spin that thing back and forth so fast you'd get dizzy if you looked at it too long. And here's the thing that got me every single taco night: By the time we had sent that lazy Susan around enough for me, my mom, and my sister to make our first taco, my dad had already *made and eaten* at least **two whole tacos**! It was an ongoing joke for my sister to say each time, "So, Dad, how many have you had already?" But then, as quickly as he'd begun, he'd suddenly just . . . stop. Of course by this time Dad had probably scarfed down five or six tacos in all, but so fast and sly you didn't realize you were being outpaced two to one. Sometimes I'd tease him by asking, "Dad, why aren't you having any more? Aren't you still hungry?" And he'd reply, all Zen and Yoda-like, "It doesn't have to do with whether I'm still hungry or not. I just don't need any more."

Whaaa? What does that even mean? You eat this stuff until you pass out! Just take a look at these recipes and tell me if *you* can practice any restraint.

This spread looks similar to the one we put out on those taco nights when I was a kid, but there are certainly a few updates. The Parm tortillas, for instance, are definitely my spin, and they are a twenty-first-century Fieri family fave. If you're doing this on a busy weeknight, go ahead and streamline by picking just one filling and a few toppings. No matter what night it is, there's stuff here for even the smallest hands to do—most kids I know are stoked to do things like smash avocados and crumble cheese.

The Taco Bar Setup

MAKES **8 to 10 servings** • ***TIME*** **2½ hours**

Turkey Taco Meat (page 182)

Black Beans and Chorizo (page 182)

Spanish Rice (page 183)

Mexican Slaw (page 183)

Parmesan Tortillas (page 184)

Smashed Avocados (page 184)

Pico de Gallo (page 290)

Roasted Tomatillo Salsa (page 289)

Salsa Rojo (page 291)

2 ounces Cotija cheese, crumbled (about ½ cup), for serving

Place all the dishes in individual bowls and platters and arrange on the table. Then call in the cavalry!

Turkey Taco Meat

MAKES **about 4 cups**

2 tablespoons extra-virgin olive oil
1 small sweet onion, minced
1 red bell pepper, seeded and diced
1 poblano pepper, seeded and diced
1 jalapeño, seeded and minced
1 small zucchini, diced
1 small carrot, diced
2 teaspoons kosher salt
2 garlic cloves, minced
2 pounds ground lean turkey
1 cup canned tomato sauce
2 teaspoons Mexican oregano
1 teaspoon ground cumin
½ teaspoon ground coriander

1 In a large sauté pan, heat the olive oil over medium-high heat until shimmering. Add the onion, bell pepper, poblano, jalapeño, zucchini, carrot, and salt. Sauté until the onion is translucent, 7 to 8 minutes. Add the garlic and cook for 1 minute, until fragrant.

2 Add the turkey and cook, breaking up the meat with a wooden spoon, until cooked through and browned, 8 to 10 minutes.

3 Add the tomato sauce, oregano, cumin, and coriander and mix well. Bring to a boil, then reduce the heat and simmer, stirring occasionally, until the carrots are tender and the spices are well blended, 18 to 20 minutes. Remove from the heat and set aside.

Black Beans and Chorizo

MAKES **about 4 cups**

1 tablespoon extra-virgin olive oil
One 4-ounce uncooked (Mexican) chorizo sausage link, casing removed
1 medium sweet onion, minced
2 garlic cloves, minced
1 teaspoon dried Mexican oregano
Two 15-ounce cans black beans, rinsed and drained
2 teaspoons kosher salt

1 Heat the olive oil over medium-high heat in a medium, heavy-bottomed saucepan. Add the chorizo and sauté until the fat is well rendered, 5 to 6 minutes. Stir in the onion, garlic, and oregano and cook until softened, 1 to 2 minutes. Add the beans, salt, and 2 cups water. Bring to a boil, then reduce the heat and simmer for 15 to 20 minutes.

2 Remove about one-quarter of the beans and transfer to a bowl. Mash them using a wooden spoon or potato masher. Stir the mashed beans back into the pot. Cover and set aside to keep warm. (You can store the beans in an airtight container in the refrigerator for 3 to 4 days.)

This will thicken the remaining liquid.

Spanish Rice

MAKES **about 8 cups**

2 cups uncooked parboiled white rice
3 tablespoons canola oil
1 medium sweet onion, finely chopped
2 green bell peppers, seeded and finely chopped
1 red bell pepper, seeded and finely chopped
½ jalapeño, seeded and minced
¾ cup (half a 12-ounce bottle) Mexican beer
2½ cups Chicken Stock (page 228 or low-sodium store-bought)
1 cup canned tomato sauce
3 tablespoons fresh lemon juice
2 teaspoons dried Mexican oregano
1 teaspoon ground cumin
1 teaspoon kosher salt
½ cup chopped cilantro

1 Preheat the oven to 350°F.

2 Spread the rice evenly on a rimmed baking sheet and bake until evenly toasted and nutty smelling, 5 to 7 minutes. Let the rice cool on the baking sheet.

3 In a medium saucepan, combine the canola oil, onion, bell peppers, and jalapeño and cook over medium-high heat, stirring, until the onion is translucent, 5 to 6 minutes.

4 Stir in the toasted rice and cook stirring, for 2 to 3 minutes. Deglaze the pan by adding the beer and scraping up the browned bits from the bottom of the pan.

5 Add the chicken stock, tomato sauce, lemon juice, oregano, cumin, and salt and stir well to combine. Bring to a boil, then reduce the heat and simmer, uncovered, for 5 to 6 minutes.

6 Stir, cover, and simmer until the rice is tender and the liquid has been absorbed, about 25 minutes. Remove from the heat. Stir in the cilantro and keep warm.

Mexican Slaw

MAKES **about 6 cups**

1 small cabbage, thinly sliced
1 teaspoon kosher salt
½ cup sour cream
Juice of 2 limes
¼ cup chopped cilantro
2 garlic cloves, minced
1 teaspoon ground cumin
3 or 4 turns freshly ground black pepper

1 In a large bowl, combine the cabbage and salt and stir. Let stand for about 15 minutes, or until the cabbage is slightly wilted.

2 Add the sour cream, lime juice, cilantro, garlic, cumin, and pepper and stir well to combine. Use at once or store in an airtight container in the refrigerator for up to 2 days.

Parmesan Tortillas

MAKES **12 tortillas**

1 tablespoon extra-virgin olive oil
Twelve good-quality 6-inch corn tortillas
1¾ ounces Parmesan cheese, finely grated (about ½ cup)

1 Lightly brush a large, nonstick skillet or griddle with olive oil and heat over medium-high heat. Warm a tortilla for about 15 seconds on each side.

2 Lightly coat one side with a couple teaspoons of Parmesan. Warm through, and then flip it so it's cheese side down in the pan. Cook until the cheese is browned and crisp (it will stick to the tortilla), about 15 seconds. Remove from the pan.

3 Repeat with the remaining tortillas and cheese, brushing the pan with oil as needed. Set aside, covered with a clean kitchen towel.

Smashed Avocados

MAKES **about 5 cups**

4 ripe Hass avocados, halved and pitted
½ cup Pico de Gallo (page 290)
1 tablespoon extra-virgin olive oil
1 teaspoon kosher salt
3 or 4 turns freshly ground black pepper

1 Scoop out the avocado flesh into a medium bowl. Smash with a fork.

2 Add the pico de gallo, olive oil, salt, and pepper and stir well to combine. Cover flush with plastic wrap (to prevent the top of the guacamole from turning brown) and set aside. This is best eaten soon after making it, but you can refrigerate it overnight if necessary.

Pizza Night

Most people don't make pizza at home because they think the dough is tough to make. It really doesn't have to be, and the recipe on page 190 is easy and foolproof. But I get it—we have to choose our battles when it comes to spending time in the kitchen. So if you'd rather focus on getting all hands on deck for *topping* the pizza, *and* if the idea of making the dough from scratch is about to make you turn the page to find the next series of recipes—wait! Grab a ball of dough from the grocery store, or even go to your favorite local pizza joint and ask if they'll sell you some. In either case, all you need to do is bring it home, roll it out, and call in the troops to put on their favorite toppings. You'll have so much fun that next time you'll want to try your hand at the dough, too.

So let's get on with this pizza party. And let's start with what kind of pizza I'm talkin' about when I'm talkin' about pizza. With most American pizza—how can I put this nicely?—the dough is too thick for me and the sauce and cheese are way overdone. It's basically overburdened, soggy bread posing as pizza. What *I* mean by pizza is the true Neapolitan, with a thin crust and a light touch with the sauce and cheese. Of course I know that not everyone is such a purist, and I promise that I'm more than willing to bend my own rules about what constitutes a true pizza in order to please the masses . . . or at least the kids. For proof, you don't need to look any further than the recipes that follow.

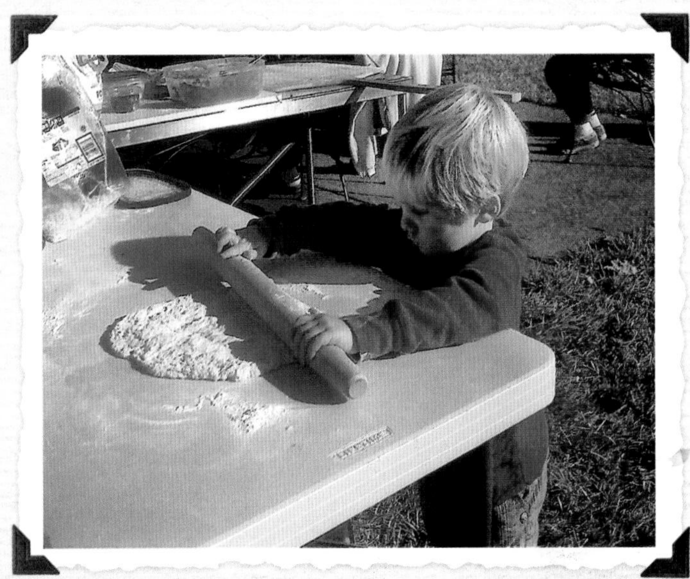

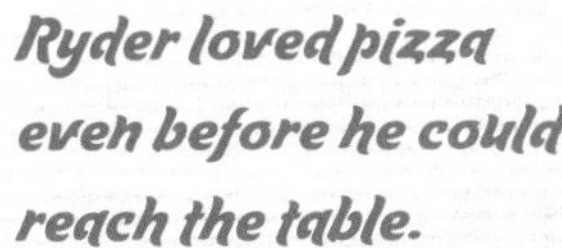

Ryder loved pizza even before he could reach the table.

Home-Baked Pizza 101

Whether you go for the pure "just enough" model of pizza or prefer the pile-it-all-on special, pay close attention to how you cook the pizza for best results. To begin, I feel the ideal way to cook pizza is in a wood-fired pizza oven.

Okay, okay, are you done laughing? *I know* you're working with the oven in your kitchen right now, so I'm gonna tell you how to turn it into the next best thing to that ideal. First, we've gotta understand that the keys to creating a good crust in a regular oven are to crank the heat as high as possible and ensure that the pizza is as evenly exposed to that heat as possible. You'll need two tools to make this happen: a pizza stone on which to bake the pizza and a peel to get the pizza onto and off the stone. Some recipes suggest that you can use, say, a rimless baking sheet to do this transferring, but there's really no replacement for a peel—they're not expensive. I prefer wood peels because those made of metal are very susceptible to the high temperatures of the oven; if the peel gets hot while the pizza is on it, the pizza is much more likely to stick. Pizza stones are typically made of ceramic or stoneware. You don't need anything fancy, so just go with what's within your budget, and once you have a pizza stone and pizza peel in your house, family pizza nights will be a once-a-week event, at minimum.

Place the pizza stone on the center rack of the oven and preheat the oven as hot as it will go. (I say 500°F in the recipes here so that I can provide some idea of timing, but if your oven goes higher, by all means crank it and adjust the cooking time downward a little.) Also, preheat that baby for as long as you can, ideally at least an hour, so that the stone gets as hot as possible. If you're baking more than one pizza, give the stone a 15-minute break between pizzas so that it can get hot again and you can get that really good crust on each one.

After you roll out the dough and before you top it, lightly coat the peel with cornmeal or flour (or equal amounts of each); you need just enough to act as ball bearings and keep the dough from sticking to the peel—don't add too much because it has a tendency to burn. Carefully transfer the rolled-out dough onto the floured peel and before you add a single topping, shake it gently back and forth on the peel; it should move freely. If it doesn't, sneak a little more flour or cornmeal under the side that's sticking. As soon as you've confirmed that it's not sticking, go ahead and top it and bake it.

To get an evenly baked crust, we have to compensate for the fact that oven temperature usually varies slightly from the front to the rear. So halfway through baking, use the pizza peel to spin the pizza 180 degrees so that the half that was in front is now in back. But don't turn it until the dough sets up or you'll tear it. And while you're in there, pop any air bubbles on the dough with the tip of a sharp knife.

Note that these baking instructions don't apply to frozen pizzas or to pizza made using prebaked dough. Often the intense heat of the pizza stone will cause these to burn.

The recipes here are for 1 pizza each, but of course everything can be easily multiplied according to how many people you've got eating. If you're setting up a toppings bar so that many hands can do the saucing and adorning, you can either keep each pizza's suggested toppings together or let people concoct their own creations. If you go that route, make sure you warn everyone against overloading the dough, and give it a little shake from time to time so that it doesn't stick to the peel.

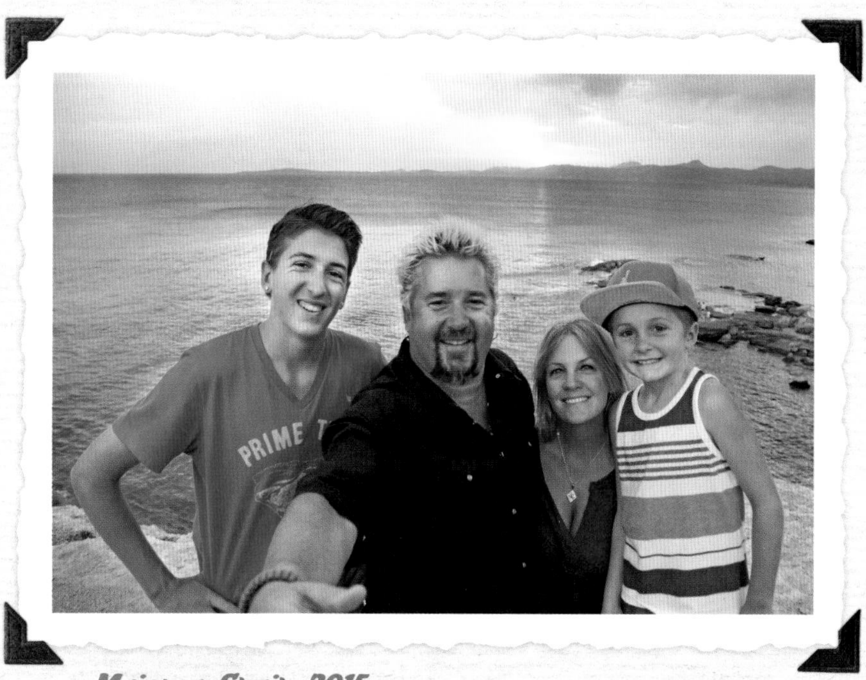

Majorca, Spain, 2015.

Pizza Dough

Using all-purpose flour here gives you a chewy, substantial crust. For a lighter, crispier crust, use "00" flour. This flour is as finely ground as you can buy and has a lower gluten content than regular, all-purpose flour, so the dough won't develop too much chewiness even with a fair amount of kneading. The easiest way to roll out the dough is on a cool, flat, lightly floured surface using a rolling pin. Specific directions on rolling are in the individual pizza recipes.

MAKES **enough dough for one 12-inch pizza** • ***TIME*** **45 minutes, plus 1 hour 45 minutes rising time**

1 teaspoon sugar

1 cup warm (110°F to 115°F) water

1 tablespoon active dry yeast

3 tablespoons extra-virgin olive oil

1 teaspoon kosher salt

2½ cups all-purpose flour, plus more for dusting

Tip: This recipe doubles well if you want to make more than one at a time, or if you want to store one for another night. To store the dough, prepare it through step 6. Wrap the dough tightly in plastic wrap and freeze for up to 3 months. When ready to use, thaw overnight in the refrigerator, then set it out at room temperature for 1 hour (this takes the place of step 7).

1 In the bowl of a stand mixer fitted with the dough hook, dissolve the sugar in the warm water. Sprinkle the yeast on top and let stand until foamy, about 10 minutes.

2 Add 2 tablespoons of the olive oil, the salt, and the flour. Turn the mixer on low speed and gently beat until the dough starts to come together and the flour is completely incorporated, 3 to 4 minutes.

3 Increase the speed to medium and knead the dough until it pulls away from the side of the bowl and is smooth, 6 to 8 minutes.

4 Transfer the dough to a floured board and knead by hand for 2 to 3 minutes, until the dough is smooth and has a good amount of elasticity.

5 Rub a large bowl with the remaining 1 tablespoon olive oil. Place the dough in the bowl and turn it to coat it all over with oil. Cover the bowl with plastic wrap. Let rise in a warm place until it has doubled in size, about 1 hour.

6 Remove the dough from the bowl and place it on a lightly floured surface. Divide the dough in half for 2 small pizzas, or keep whole for 1 large pizza. Punch the dough down with the palms of your hands and form it into a smooth, tight ball.

7 Cover loosely with plastic wrap and set in a warm place to rise again and double in volume once more, 30 to 45 minutes.

8 Proceed as directed in pizza recipes to shape, top, and bake the pizza(s).

Monday Night Pan Pizza

No one likes Mondays . . . except when there's Monday Night Football. But they're especially hard when you come home to a fridge full of leftovers and no plan for dinner. Here's how you cheer up the crew on Monday night, while using up all the odds and ends from the weekend (pork chops, pot roast, whatever you have that's already cooked—or cook off some sausage and let it cool before using it). Forget about rolling the dough and using the peel and stone—there's no time even for that tonight—just roll it lightly and then press it into a rimmed baking sheet, then top with red sauce, cheese, and those leftovers. Or, if you need some more specific guidelines, just follow this recipe and you and your brood will be chasing away those Monday blues in no time.

MAKES **one 9 x 13-inch pizza** • ***TIME*** **45 minutes**

2 tablespoons extra-virgin olive oil

1 Pizza Dough (opposite, or use store-bought)

All-purpose flour, for rolling the dough

4 to 5 ounces (1/2 to 2/3 cup) Pizza Sauce (page 295)

6 ounces mozzarella cheese, sliced 1/4 inch thick

1 pound sweet fennel sausage, cooked and crumbled

1/4 pound thinly sliced Genoa salami

1 cup sliced fire-roasted bell pepper (see page 32)

1/2 pound (about 1 1/2 cups) pulled pork from Slow-Roasted Pork Shoulder (page 83)

1 cup crushed San Marzano tomatoes

1/4 pound Provolone cheese, grated (about 1 cup)

1/4 cup chopped drained oil-packed Calabrian chiles or any mild chiles

1/4 cup torn basil leaves, for garnish

1 Preheat the oven to 350°F. Brush a rimmed 9 x 13-inch baking sheet with the olive oil.

2 Place the dough on a lightly floured work surface and use your fingers to gently shape it into a flat rectangle, then use a rolling pin to gently roll it into a rough rectangle shape. Place it on the prepared baking sheet. Stretch and press the dough with your fingers into the bottom and three-quarters of the way up the sides of the pan. With a fork, poke holes in the dough on the bottom of the pan.

3 Spread the pizza sauce across the dough, leaving a 1/2-inch border. Layer the sliced mozzarella evenly on top. Sprinkle the sausage over the mozzarella, spreading it out to the edges. Shingle the salami evenly over the sausage. Top with the roasted bell peppers and shredded pork. Spoon the tomatoes evenly over the pork. Top with the Provolone and chiles.

4 Bake until the crust is golden brown and crispy, 18 to 20 minutes, rotating the pan halfway through baking. Puncture any large bubbles that have formed with the tip of a thin-bladed knife.

5 Garnish with the basil, slice, and serve.

Mac 'n' Cheese Burger Pizza

Do I even need to say out loud that your kids will *loooove* this?

MAKES **one 12-inch pizza** • ***TIME*** **45 minutes**

1 tablespoon extra-virgin olive oil

1 pound ground beef (80% lean)

1 tablespoon kosher salt

4 or 5 turns freshly ground black pepper

3/4 cup Cheese Sauce (page 296)

1 cup dry elbow macaroni, cooked al dente

1 Pizza Dough (page 190, or use store-bought)

All-purpose flour, for rolling the dough and dusting the peel (cornmeal or a 50/50 blend can be used for the peel)

3/4 cup Pizza Sauce (page 295)

1 Set a pizza stone directly on the center rack of the oven. Preheat the oven to 500°F.

2 Heat the olive oil in a large sauté pan set over medium-high heat until hot. Add the ground beef and season with the salt and pepper, breaking up the meat with a wooden spoon, until well browned, 8 to 9 minutes. Remove from the heat and set aside to cool.

3 Combine the cheese sauce with the cooked macaroni. Set aside.

4 Place the dough on a lightly floured surface and use your hands to gently stretch it into a flat round, then use a rolling pin to roll it into a 12-inch round, gradually working it out from the center and gently spinning the dough after every couple of rolls. Lightly flour the work surface as necessary to keep the dough from sticking. Sprinkle a pizza peel lightly with flour and place the dough round on it.

5 Spread the pizza sauce evenly over the rolled dough, leaving a 1/2-inch border. Sprinkle generously with the cooked ground beef. Top with the mac 'n' cheese mixture.

6 Slide the pizza from the peel onto the hot stone. Bake until the crust is crispy and golden brown around the edges, 8 to 12 minutes, rotating the pizza halfway through baking (but only after the crust is set enough that it won't stick to the pizza stone). Puncture any large bubbles that have formed with the tip of a thin-bladed knife.

7 Keep the pizza on the peel or transfer it to a flat platter. Slice as desired and serve.

Mediterranean Pizza

This is like a cross between hot 'n' chewy flatbread and a zesty Greek pita.

MAKES **one 12-inch pizza •** ***TIME*** **45 minutes**

- 1 Pizza Dough (page 190, or use store-bought)
- All-purpose flour, for rolling the dough and dusting the peel (cornmeal or a 50/50 blend can be used for the peel)
- 2 tablespoons extra-virgin olive oil
- 1 tablespoon thyme leaves
- 3/4 ounce Parmesan cheese, grated (about 1/4 cup)
- 1 teaspoon kosher salt
- 1 1/2 cups store-bought hummus
- 1 small seedless cucumber, thinly sliced
- 2 cups lightly packed baby arugula, coarsely chopped
- 1/4 cup chopped pitted Kalamata olives
- 2 tablespoons slivered red onion
- 1/2 cup halved cherry tomatoes
- 1 ounce feta cheese, crumbled (about 1/4 cup)
- 1 tablespoon za'atar seasoning

1 Set a pizza stone directly on the center rack of the oven. Preheat the oven to 500°F.

2 Place the dough on a lightly floured surface and use your hands to gently stretch it into a flat round, then use a rolling pin to roll it into a 12-inch round, gradually working it out from the center and gently spinning the dough after every couple of rolls. Lightly flour the work surface as necessary to keep the dough from sticking. Sprinkle a pizza peel lightly with flour and place the dough round on it.

3 Brush the olive oil over the pizza dough, leaving a 1/2-inch border. Sprinkle the thyme, Parmesan, and salt evenly over the olive oil. Slide the dough from the peel onto the hot stone. Bake until the crust is crispy and golden brown around the edges, 8 to 12 minutes, rotating the pizza halfway through baking (but only after the crust is set enough that it won't stick to the pizza stone). Puncture any large bubbles that have formed with the tip of a thin-bladed knife.

4 Keep the pizza on the peel or transfer it to a flat platter. Spread the hummus over the warm crust. Top with the cucumber, arugula, olives, red onion, tomatoes, and feta and sprinkle with the za'atar seasoning.

5 Slice as desired and serve.

Chicken Bacon Ranch Pizza

Among the best parts of this pizza, which has many best parts, is the contrast between the hot bacon, cheese, and chicken topping and the fresh garnish of sliced green onions, grated Parm, and cool ranch dressing.

MAKES **one 12-inch pizza •** ***TIME*** **45 minutes**

3/4 cup Ranch Dressing (page 292)

1/4 cup buttermilk

1 Pizza Dough (page 190, or use store-bought)

All-purpose flour, for rolling the dough and dusting the peel (cornmeal or a 50/50 blend can be used for the peel)

2 ounces mozzarella cheese, grated (about 1/2 cup)

2 ounces Jack cheese, grated (about 1/2 cup)

1 cup shredded Oven Roasted Chicken (page 71) or rotisserie chicken

6 slices applewood bacon, cooked and chopped

2 tablespoons thinly sliced green onions (white and light green parts), for garnish

2 tablespoons grated Parmesan cheese, for garnish

1 Set a pizza stone directly on the center rack of the oven. Preheat the oven to 500°F.

2 Whisk the ranch dressing and the buttermilk in a medium bowl. Set aside.

3 Place the dough on a lightly floured surface and use your hands to gently stretch it into a flat round, then use a rolling pin to roll it into a 12-inch round, gradually working it out from the center and gently spinning the dough after every couple of rolls. Lightly flour the work surface as necessary to keep the dough from sticking. Sprinkle a pizza peel lightly with flour and place the dough round on it.

4 Spread 1/4 cup of the dressing over the pizza dough, leaving a 1/2-inch border. Top with the cheeses, chicken, and bacon.

5 Slide the dough from the peel onto the hot stone. Bake until the crust is crispy and golden brown around the edges, 8 to 12 minutes, rotating the pizza halfway through baking (but only after the crust is set enough that it won't stick to the pizza stone). Puncture any large bubbles that have formed with the tip of a thin-bladed knife.

6 Keep the pizza on the peel or transfer it to a flat platter. Garnish with the green onions and Parmesan and a swirl of the dressing. Slice as desired and serve.

All Fieris are known for tellin' great jokes and wild stories.

The Chili Bar

I know I get a lot of attention for some of my more outta-bounds sayings and doings, but I'll tell ya', I've got nothin' on my dad, Jim (or Jamps, as he's been known to just about everyone since Hunter learned to talk and renamed him). And the year he and his buddy Wes crashed the annual chili contest at the town fair in Ferndale, California, is not only a perfect example of the craziness that guy is capable of but also goes to show that whatever culinary chops I got have their roots in him.

When I was a kid the Humboldt County Fair happened every year in August. Early on the morning of the annual chili cook-off, when I was about twelve years old, I was set up at the fair minding my hot pretzel business ("The Awesome Pretzel") with a clear view of all the activity. Probably about a dozen different competitors were there unloading their tents and portable stoves and chili makings. It was at least a couple of hours before they could start cooking (there are strict rules around these sorts of contests), and there was a lot for them to get done before the starting bell clanged.

All at once my dad and his buddy Wes ride up on their horses. I watched them tie off the horses right in the center of the park and start unloading from their saddle bags all sorts of cooking gear: pots, pans, spoons, spatulas, rocks, wood, you name it. Soon they had built a good-size fire **right there in the middle of the fairgrounds.** Then—from I don't know where—they pulled out a hubcap. They threw it in the middle of the fire, heated a big cast-iron skillet, and started cooking! The chili judges came tearing over and started barking at them, "This is a technical foul! You can't be starting your chili now!" Dad just looked at those flustered judges and said, "We are *not* making chili. We're trying to make our damn breakfast!" And soon enough they had sausage, bacon, potatoes, eggs—a real horseman's meal (did I mention the beer?)—coming off that fire for anyone who wanted some. Competitors, judges, passersby, **anyone who asked was welcome to share.**

Of course breakfast service wasn't *really* what Jamps and Wes had in mind that morning. Soon enough they pulled out the kicker—and I mean that literally. A full hindquarter of bear leg came out of one of those saddlebags (don't ask me how) and they strung it up in a tree right there in the center of that park. The minute the clock struck 10:00 A.M.—the official start time of the cook-off—I'll be damned if they didn't start slicing the fat off it and rendering it for the chili they were setting to make! Before long the smell of sizzling bear meat was drifting across the whole fairgrounds while Jamps and Wes shared their beers equally between themselves and the pot of chili they were soon tending. They threw some flour tortillas on the hot hubcap and anyone who wanted a taste could tear off a bit of warm tortilla and scoop out some of that fragrant bear-and-beer chili. Even my mom got in on the act, coming out with Wes's wife dressed like cheerleaders to cheer them on.

Of course they couldn't win the official competition because they were disqualified a million ways to Sunday, but **that was one unbelievable chili.** And my twelve-year-old self learned some pretty amazing lessons about how to bring everyone around you in on whatever fun you're cooking up. To the surprise of absolutely no one, they crushed it in the "People's Choice" award. Jamps always has known how to put on a show.

Thankfully, you don't need an open fire hubcap stove *or* a bear leg to put on your own chili show. Just set out the chili bar we've got going on here.

The Chili Bar Setup

MAKES **8 to 10 servings** • ***TIME*** **2½ hours**

Texas Chili (opposite)

Turkey Chili with Cannellini Beans (page 200)

For serving

Lime Crema (page 201)

Fried Potato Straws (page 201)

½ pound sharp cheddar cheese, grated (about 2 cups)

½ pound Jack cheese, grated (about 2 cups)

½ cabbage head, cored and finely shredded

1 large sweet onion, diced

1 cup finely chopped cilantro

1 cup finely sliced green onions (white and light green parts)

2 jalapeños, seeded and sliced into fine rings

2 Fresno chiles (or use jalapeño or serrano), seeded and sliced into fine rings

Twelve good-quality 6-inch corn tortillas, warmed

1 pound spaghetti, cooked until al dente, kept warm

To make the chili bar, place the two kinds of chili in large serving bowls. Arrange the accompaniments in separate bowls and set them all on the counter or table around the chili and invite everyone to garnish their own bowls as they please!

Texas Chili

Real Texas chili is made from not much more than beef and homemade red chili sauce. Texans call it a "bowl of red," and with no beans, tomatoes, or other distractions, what you see is what you taste—primarily the two main ingredients—so it's important that they're done right. Start with a good mix of dried and fresh chiles and use two kinds of beef, and you'll be halfway to Texas without even leaving your house.

MAKES **about 3 quarts** • ***TIME*** **2½ hours**

2 dried chiles de árbol

2 dried ancho chiles

2 dried guajillo chiles

1 cup hot tap water, or as needed

2 tablespoons extra-virgin olive oil

1 medium sweet onion, diced

4 garlic cloves, minced

1 red bell pepper, seeded and diced

1 Fresno chile, seeded and minced

2 Anaheim chiles, seeded and diced

1½ pounds chuck roast, cut into ½-inch cubes

1½ pounds ground beef (80% lean)

2 tablespoons all-purpose flour

3 tablespoons chili powder

2 tablespoons ground cumin

½ teaspoon freshly ground black pepper

Pinch of cayenne pepper

One 12-ounce bottle Mexican beer

1½ quarts Beef Stock (page 226 or low-sodium store-bought)

1½ tablespoons kosher salt

¼ cup chopped cilantro

1 Remove the stems and seeds from the dried chiles and tear them into large pieces. Toast the chiles in a large skillet over medium-high heat until they start to change color, about 2 minutes. Transfer to a small bowl and add hot water to just cover the chiles. Cover and let steam for 15 minutes. Place the chiles and soaking liquid in a blender and puree until smooth. Set aside.

2 In a large Dutch oven over medium-high heat, combine the olive oil, onion, garlic, bell pepper, Fresno chile, and Anaheim chiles and sauté until the onion is translucent, 6 to 7 minutes. Add both kinds of beef and cook until browned and cooked through, 7 to 8 minutes.

3 Add the flour, chili powder, cumin, black pepper, and cayenne and sauté until fragrant, about 2 minutes. Deglaze the pan by adding the beer and scraping up the browned bits from the bottom of the pan. Add the beef stock, salt, and blended chiles and bring to a boil, then reduce the heat to a low simmer.

4 Partially cover the pan and simmer until the beef is tender and the chili has thickened, about 2 hours.

5 Remove from the heat. Stir in the cilantro, cover, and keep warm until serving.

Turkey Chili with Cannellini Beans

Ground turkey is at the base of this wholesome chili. Using a blend of light meat and richer dark meat and a bunch of fire-roasted fresh chiles and bold spices ensures that it's not only healthy, it's also packed with awesome flavor.

MAKES **about 3 quarts •** ***TIME*** **1½ hours**

8 Hatch chiles, fire-roasted (see page 32)

¼ bunch cilantro, chopped

¼ cup extra-virgin olive oil

1 large sweet onion, diced

4 garlic cloves, minced

2 teaspoons kosher salt

3 pounds ground turkey (50/50 light and dark meat)

¼ cup all-purpose flour

¼ cup chili powder

3 tablespoons ground cumin

½ teaspoon freshly ground black pepper

Pinch of cayenne pepper

4 cups Chicken Stock (page 228 or low-sodium store-bought)

Two 15-ounce cans cannellini beans, with liquid

1 In a blender or food processor, puree the Hatch chiles and cilantro until smooth. Set aside.

2 In a large Dutch oven over medium-high heat, combine the olive oil, onion, garlic, and salt. Cook until the onion is translucent, 5 to 6 minutes. Add the turkey and cook until browned and cooked through, breaking it up with a wooden spoon, 7 to 8 minutes.

3 Add the flour, chili powder, cumin, black pepper, and cayenne and sauté until fragrant, about 2 minutes. Deglaze the pan by adding the chicken stock and scraping up the browned bits from the bottom of the pan. Add the reserved pureed chiles and cilantro. Bring to a boil, then reduce the heat to a low simmer.

4 Add the beans and simmer, partially covered, until the turkey is tender and the chili has thickened, about 1 hour. Remove from the heat, cover, and keep warm until serving.

Lime Crema

MAKES **1¼ cups**

1 cup sour cream
¼ cup heavy cream
Juice and grated zest of 1 lime
1 teaspoon kosher salt

In a small mixing bowl, combine all the ingredients and whisk until well blended and creamy. Use at once or cover and refrigerate for up to 2 days.

Fried Potato Straws

MAKES **about 3 cups**

Canola oil, for frying
2 russet potatoes
1 teaspoon kosher salt
4 or 5 turns freshly ground black pepper

1 Pour canola oil into a deep cast-iron skillet to a depth of 2 inches. Heat over high heat to 350°F. Line a plate with paper towels.

2 While the oil is heating, lightly scrub the potatoes with a firm brush under running water. Use the fine julienne blade on a mandoline to cut the potatoes. (Alternatively, very thinly slice the potatoes lengthwise. Stack the slices and very thinly slice them lengthwise to make long, thin straws.) Rinse the potato straws under cold running water. Pat dry on paper towels.

This rinses off the starch and makes the straws nice 'n' crispy.

3 Working in batches, fry the potatoes in the oil until golden brown and crispy, about 2 minutes. With a slotted spoon or spider, transfer the straws to the paper-towel-lined plate. Season with salt and pepper immediately and serve.

UNDER PRESSURE

My homage to A Christmas Story. . . .
We love that movie.

The Fastest Kitchen Tool in the West (also the East, North, and South)

When I was a kid my mom was always cooking something in the pressure cooker, and man, it freaked me out. She'd get it going and I'd think, *Holy cow, what is she doing? This thing sounds angry,* and run the other way. I mean, who can trust a cooking utensil that doesn't let you check your food while it's cooking, and that rattles and hisses like an angry cat? Then, about ten years ago—when I was finally able to recognize that my mother probably wasn't trying to kill us with that fizzing pot all those years ago—I decided it was time to conquer the pressure cooker. I began cooking anything and everything I could in it. What I discovered (and what Mom has clearly always known) is that the pressure cooker is, hands down, one of the most useful, most efficient, most economical kitchen tools there is. But here's what's weird. There's a handful of tools that I think are underutilized in the kitchen (a shout-out here to the wok, mandoline, and citrus zester), but you could add them all together and they'd *still* not match how underutilized the pressure cooker is. **I just don't get why there aren't more people riding the pressure cooker bandwagon.**

It's not just home cooks who are intimidated by it; professional chefs are, too. On *Guy's Grocery Games,* I never want anyone to be debilitated by not having a tool they want or need, so I always make sure there's a pressure cooker available. Out of all the *GGG* shows we've shot, I think we've seen no more than five or ten chefs ever use it! The pressure cooker actually cuts down cooking time to a fraction of what it would take ordinarily. So either the *GGG* chefs don't understand that *speed* is a factor in the *Grocery Games* or they're as wary of it as I once was.

People, hear this: **The pressure cooker is perfectly safe, and its beauty is its incredible speed.** I know someone out there reading this right now is thinking, "Uh-uh, Guy, the most time-saving tool in *my* kitchen is the slow cooker." But tell me, how is cooking a pork shoulder for 8 hours more efficient than cooking it for 45 minutes? Then consider the added bonus that you can cook the vegetables and sear the meat all in the same pot (try *that* in your slow cooker). Now are you ready to hop on the bandwagon? **I sure hope so, 'cause we're headed straight to Flavortown.**

Pressure Cooking 101

Picture those nights when you come home from a long day, the crew is clamoring for dinner, and you need something fast. If this makes you think of boneless, skinless chicken breasts—a very popular go-to for fast cooking—you're not alone, but you *are* missing out. Chicken breast has gotta be one of the least flavorful, least texturally interesting pieces of meat there is. For depth of flavor you need skin, cartilage, some nice fat, maybe even bones. All this good stuff makes items like chicken thighs, pork shoulder, lamb shanks, and brisket take longer to cook—and potential nonstarters on a busy weeknight. Well, that's where the pressure cooker comes in, because it makes it possible to cook in a fraction of the time it would take in a regular pot, and you get killer flavor and texture.

It does this thanks to an almost brilliantly simple concept. When you put the lid on top and twist it into place, it forms an airtight seal. Under heat, pressure builds inside the pot, usually to 15 pounds per square inch (psi), which raises the boiling point of water from the sea-level standard 212°F to 250°F. (Some models can stay at a lower pressure in addition to this standard, but for the recipes here, 15 psi is all you'll need.) This means the environment in the pot is significantly hotter than in a regular pot, so food cooks much faster.

That's all there is to it, and there are only a few keys you need to know for successful pressure cooking.

- You must have liquid in the pot, and in most cases it should just barely cover the food you're cooking. This'll often be around 2 cups, but it can vary depending on the depth and width of your pot. Be sure to read the manual that comes with your cooker and follow the directions in the recipes.
- Don't fill the pressure cooker beyond two-thirds full for the recipes here. When cooking foods like dry beans and rice that expand a lot, don't fill more than half full. Most cookers are marked to indicate these maximum "fill to" points. Going over these lines risks clogging the release valve or creating excessive pressure.
- Standard pressure cookers run in sizes from 4 quarts to 8 quarts. The recipes in this chapter are based on a 6-quart cooker. If you're using

an 8-quart pressure cooker, you may increase the ingredients by half, although you don't have to. If using a 4-quart pot, decrease the ingredients by half. Be sure not to overfill the pressure cooker.

- You'll know the cooker has reached full pressure because (in newer models) an indicator will tell you or (in older models) the weighted jiggler valve on top wobbles and whistles like crazy. When you get to this point, reduce the heat to a simmer to keep pressure steady but not going at full throttle; stuff in there *can* burn if you let all the liquid steam away.
- Start timing only after the pressure cooker has come to pressure. When the time is reached, remove the pressure cooker from the heat. Don't try to open it as it'll still be sealed. The recipes here are written with every kind of cooker in mind, including the no-frills models, and they instruct you to let the cooker sit off the heat to cool and slowly release most of its pressure. Some modern cookers have a dedicated pressure release feature. After the cooling time indicated in the recipe, you can carefully engage this "steam release" feature to discharge the rest of the gentle pressure. If you don't have this feature on your cooker, wait until the cover lock has released; this is the indication that the pressure is discharged. Then remove the top pressure regulator cap and let the pot stand a few more minutes for the remaining pressure to release. Then you can unlock and remove the lid.
- Although none of the recipes here fall into this category, you'll see elsewhere that some recipes and foods that need very short or precise cooking will sometimes call for a "quick release." If your cooker has the release valve, you may use it and discharge the steam immediately. Or, for no-frills models, use the ice water method: Fill the sink with ice and water. When the cooking time is reached, place the cooker directly into the sink and let it stand until the pressure has released; it'll happen more quickly this way than simply letting the pressure release naturally.
- Read your manual! There are lots of different kinds of pressure cookers out there—from simple to digital and electric models with more bells and whistles. They all work beautifully, but these general directions might need to be tweaked for your specific model.

Balsamic BBQ Short Ribs

One of my favorite mealtimes is the Friday night after a week of filming *Guy's Grocery Games*. We run *GGG* like a real grocery store, and at the end of the week everything that's perishable in the "store" has to be cleared out. We give most of it to local food banks, but there are always a few odds and ends that come home with the staff or me—and since there are often a few of my chef buddies in town for shooting, they come home with me, too.

So one night I get back to our house at around seven or eight with a bunch of hungry guys and bunch of short ribs. I declare that I'm barbecuing those ribs and **the guys go nuts razzing me.** They say (with more than a little worry) that there's no way I can do full-on BBQ ribs before at least one or two of them pass out from hunger. But you already know where this is going, right? I pressure-cook those babies for 30 minutes, then I slap 'em on the grill for a few minutes to crisp up and get nice and glazed. A little while later those guys are eatin' their words right along with the falling-off-the-bone BBQ short ribs. **It's a good thing I saved the recipe.**

MAKES **4 to 6 servings •** ***TIME*** **2 hours, plus chilling time**

- **4½ pounds bone-in short ribs**
- **2 teaspoons kosher salt, plus a pinch to season the vegetables**
- **2 teaspoons freshly ground black pepper**
- **2 tablespoons extra-virgin olive oil**
- **2 medium onions, cut into ¼-inch dice**
- **2 large celery stalks, cut into ¼-inch dice**
- **2 large carrots, cut into ¼-inch dice**
- **4 garlic cloves, minced**
- **2 cups full-bodied red wine**
- **2 cups Beef Stock (page 226 or low-sodium store-bought)**
- **4 rosemary sprigs**
- **6 thyme sprigs**
- **½ cup balsamic vinegar**
- **½ cup BBQ sauce**
- **¼ cup molasses**

1 Season the short ribs with 1 teaspoon each of the salt and black pepper. Heat the olive oil in a pressure cooker over high heat until hot. Add the ribs and sear well on all sides until nice and brown, 8 to 10 minutes total. Transfer to a plate and set aside.

2 Reduce the heat to medium-high and add the onions, celery, carrots, and a pinch of salt. Sauté the vegetables until lightly browned, 7 to 8 minutes. Add the garlic and cook for 1 minute, until fragrant. Deglaze the pan by adding the wine and beef stock and scraping up the browned bits from the bottom of the pan.

3 Tie the rosemary and thyme together tightly with kitchen twine and add them to the pot along with the vinegar, BBQ sauce, molasses, brown sugar, and chili flakes. Stir well to combine and make sure the sauce just covers the short ribs; add a little water if necessary.

RECIPE CONTINUES →

Game changer!

RECIPE CONTINUED FROM PAGE 207

1/4 cup lightly packed brown sugar

1/2 teaspoon red chili flakes

1/4 cup minced chives, for garnish

4 Cover with the pressure cooker lid and securely lock it in place according to your pressure cooker's directions. Increase the heat to high and bring the cooker to high pressure; you can tell it's there by the steam escaping from the valve or a high-pitched whistling noise. Reduce the heat to medium and cook for 30 minutes, adjusting the heat as necessary to maintain a steady, consistent pressure.

5 Remove the pressure cooker from the heat and let the pressure come down for 10 minutes. If the cooker has a dedicated steam or pressure release valve, carefully discharge any remaining gentle pressure by releasing it. If the cooker has just the top pressure regulator, wait for the cover lock to release, then carefully remove the regulator cap. Let the pot stand for 3 to 4 minutes. Unlock and remove the lid.

6 Transfer the short ribs to a tray, taking care to keep the meat and bones attached (they will be tender and can fall off if not handled gently). Let cool completely, then refrigerate until well chilled.

7 Meanwhile, place the pressure cooker over medium-high heat and cook the sauce, uncovered, over medium-high heat until thick and syrupy, 5 to 6 minutes. Remove and discard the herb bundle. Remove the balsamic BBQ sauce from the heat and set aside.

8 Preheat a grill to medium-high.

9 Remove the ribs from the refrigerator and season with the remaining 1 teaspoon each salt and black pepper. Grill the ribs meat side down until lightly crisped and brown, 3 to 4 minutes. Turn the ribs over, then baste with the balsamic BBQ sauce. Cook for 1 minute, then turn and baste rapidly two or three more times until the sauce has coated the ribs and is thick and sticky but not burned. Transfer to a serving platter when completely glazed.

10 Garnish with the chives and serve with extra sauce on the side.

Pork Shoulder
with Italian Gravy

Italian American grandmothers and their families still lovingly refer to "Sunday gravy," which is a tradition as much as it is a recipe: a tomato-and-meat sauce that simmers for hours and is served with pasta when the full extended family comes for Sunday dinner. Unfortunately, not too many of us are able to tend a pot of simmering sauce all day long, even on a weekend. The pressure cooker means we don't have to. It lets us deliver real-deal Italian gravy with meatballs and tender pork shoulder in about an hour. **Now, *that's* what I'm talkin' about: a tradition even the busiest modern family can embrace.**

MAKES **4 to 6 servings** • *TIME* **1½ hours**

Meatballs

2 thick slices white bread, crusts removed, cut into small cubes

⅓ cup whole milk

1 pound sweet Italian pork sausage

1 pound ground beef (80% lean)

1 onion, minced

1 garlic clove, minced

3 tablespoons finely chopped basil

1 teaspoon Italian seasoning

1 egg, beaten

1 teaspoon kosher salt

4 or 5 turns freshly ground black pepper

Pork and gravy

One 3-pound boneless pork shoulder, cut into 1½-inch cubes

2 tablespoons kosher salt

1 teaspoon freshly ground black pepper

3 tablespoons extra-virgin olive oil

1 To prepare the meatballs, combine the bread cubes and milk in a large bowl and mix well so that the bread is completely soaked through, about 5 minutes. Add the sausage, ground beef, onion, garlic, basil, Italian seasoning, egg, salt, and pepper and mix until well combined. Form into golf-ball-size meatballs (about 2 ounces each) and place on a rimmed baking sheet. Refrigerate to chill and firm up, about 20 minutes.

2 Meanwhile, season the pork with 1 tablespoon of the salt and ½ teaspoon of the pepper. Heat the oil in a pressure cooker over medium-high heat until hot. Add the pork and brown on all sides, 8 to 10 minutes total. Transfer to a plate and set aside.

3 Add the meatballs to the pot in batches to brown all over, 3 to 4 minutes per side. Transfer to a plate and set aside.

4 Add the onion, celery, and carrots to the pot and sauté until the onion is translucent, 4 to 5 minutes, scraping up the browned bits on the bottom of the pot. Add the garlic, thyme, basil, and fennel seeds and cook for 1 minute, until fragrant. Add the tomato paste and cook for 1 minute. Deglaze the pot by adding the wine and scraping up the

1 large sweet onion, diced

2 celery stalks, diced

2 carrots, diced

4 garlic cloves, minced

4 thyme sprigs

1/4 cup torn basil

1 teaspoon fennel seeds

2 tablespoons tomato paste

1 cup full-bodied red wine

Two 28-ounce cans whole San Marzano tomatoes, with their juice

1/4 cup chopped flat-leaf parsley, for garnish

1 3/4 ounces Parmesan cheese, grated (about 1/2 cup), for garnish

1 pound spaghetti or penne rigate pasta, cooked al dente, for serving

browned bits from the bottom of the pan. Cook for 2 to 3 minutes, until the liquid has slightly reduced. Add the tomatoes. Bring to a simmer, breaking up the tomatoes with the back of a wooden spoon.

5 Return the pork and meatballs to the pot and arrange them so they are just covered with the sauce; add water if necessary.

6 Cover with the pressure cooker lid and securely lock it in place according to the manufacturer's directions. Increase the heat to high and bring the cooker to high pressure; you can tell it's there by the steam escaping from the valve or a high-pitched whistling noise. Reduce the heat to medium and cook for 30 minutes, adjusting the heat as necessary to maintain a steady, consistent pressure.

7 Remove the pressure cooker from the heat and let the pressure come down for 10 minutes. If the cooker has a dedicated steam or pressure release valve, carefully discharge any remaining gentle pressure by releasing it. If the cooker has just the top pressure regulator, wait for the cover lock to release, then carefully remove the regulator cap. Let the pot stand for 3 to 4 minutes. Unlock and remove the lid. Skim off and discard any fat on the surface and remove and discard the thyme sprigs.

8 Garnish with the parsley and grated Parmesan. Serve with the pasta on the side.

Lamb Shanks
with Cannellini Beans and Artichokes

I often see people dredge meat in flour before browning it for a braise or stew. I'm not a big fan of that technique. You end up with browned flour that just falls off the meat anyway. Instead, brown the seasoned meat and really build that flavor. Then add some flour separately to the pot so that it can do its thickening thing. It doesn't add any extra time and it makes a big difference in the big flavor you'll get.

MAKES **4 to 6 servings •** ***TIME*** **1 hour**

Four 18- to 20-ounce lamb shanks (5 pounds total)

3 teaspoons kosher salt

1 teaspoon freshly ground black pepper

¼ cup extra-virgin olive oil

1 medium onion, cut into ½-inch dice

2 large celery stalks, cut into ½-inch dice

2 large carrots, cut into ½-inch-thick slices

2 garlic cloves, minced

2 tablespoons all-purpose flour

1 quart Chicken Stock (page 228 or low-sodium store-bought)

6 thyme sprigs

2 bay leaves

One 15-ounce can artichoke hearts, drained and quartered

One 15-ounce can cannellini beans, drained

Juice and grated zest of 1 lemon

1 Season the lamb shanks with 2 teaspoons of the salt and ½ teaspoon of the pepper. Heat the olive oil in a pressure cooker over medium-high heat until hot. Add the lamb shanks and brown on all sides, 7 to 8 minutes total. Transfer to a plate and set aside.

2 Add the onion, celery, carrots, and remaining 1 teaspoon salt. Sauté until the onion is translucent, 4 to 5 minutes. Add the garlic and cook for 1 minute, until fragrant. Dust with the flour and mix well to coat the vegetables. Deglaze the pan by adding the chicken stock and scraping up the browned bits from the bottom of the pan.

3 Return the lamb shanks to the pot and add the thyme and bay leaves. Make sure the liquid just covers the lamb shanks; add water if necessary. Stir well.

4 Cover with the pressure cooker lid and securely lock it in place according to the manufacturer's directions. Increase the heat to high and bring the cooker to high pressure; you can tell it's there by the steam escaping from the valve or a high-pitched whistling noise. Reduce the heat to medium and cook for 30 minutes, adjusting the heat as necessary to maintain a steady, consistent pressure.

RECIPE CONTINUES →

This pressure cooker has been through it all!

← RECIPE CONTINUED FROM PAGE 212

5 Remove the pressure cooker from the heat and let the pressure come down for 10 minutes. If the cooker has a dedicated steam or pressure release valve, carefully discharge any remaining gentle pressure by releasing it. If the cooker has just the top pressure regulator, wait for the cover lock to release, then carefully remove the regulator cap. Let the pot stand for 3 to 4 minutes. Unlock and remove the lid. Skim off and discard any fat on the surface and remove and discard the thyme sprigs and bay leaves.

6 Set the pressure cooker over medium-high heat and gently mix in the artichoke hearts and beans. Simmer until the artichokes and beans are tender, 8 to 9 minutes.

7 Stir in the lemon juice and zest. Serve.

Chicken Cacciatore
with Parmesan Polenta

The Italian name for this hearty dish translates to "hunter-style" stew. (We should have named our son Hunter "Cacciatore.") The ingredients and the pressure cooker translate to huge flavor in less than an hour, no hunting license required. If you happen to have one, though, cacciatore is also great when made with wild rabbit instead of chicken.

MAKES **4 to 6 servings** • *TIME* **1 hour 15 minutes**

Chicken cacciatore

One 3- to 4-pound whole chicken

3 teaspoons kosher salt

½ teaspoon freshly ground black pepper

¼ cup extra-virgin olive oil

1 large sweet onion, finely chopped

1 red bell pepper, seeded and cut into ½-inch dice

1 yellow bell pepper, seeded and cut into ½-inch dice

1 orange bell pepper, seeded and cut into ½-inch dice

1 pound cremini mushrooms, quartered

4 garlic cloves, minced

½ teaspoon dried oregano

¼ teaspoon red chili flakes

3 tablespoons drained capers

1 cup dry white wine

2 cups Chicken Stock (page 228 or low-sodium store-bought)

One 28-ounce can crushed San Marzano tomatoes, with their juice

1 To make the chicken cacciatore, place the chicken breast side up on a clean, dry cutting board. Pull a leg away from the body and cut the skin between the thigh and body. Bend the leg back and rotate it until the hip joint pops out of the socket. Cut between and below the joint, close to the body, to remove the whole leg and thigh. Repeat on the other side.

2 Using kitchen shears, remove the backbone by cutting down from the neck on both sides. Cut around the wishbone at the top of the breast beneath the neck and remove it. (Save these parts in the freezer to make Chicken Stock, page 228). Remove the wings from the breasts and set aside.

3 Flip the chicken breast side down and cut lengthwise straight through the breast plate to separate the breast halves. Cut each breast half crosswise in half again.

4 Pat the eight chicken pieces dry with paper towels. Season on both sides with 1½ teaspoons of the salt and ¼ teaspoon of the black pepper. Heat the olive oil in a pressure cooker over medium-high heat until hot. Working in batches as needed, add the chicken pieces skin side down and brown, 5 to 7 minutes. Turn the pieces over and brown on the second side, about 5 minutes. Transfer to a plate and set aside.

RECIPE CONTINUES →

It didn't look like this for long.
We devoured it!

← RECIPE CONTINUED FROM PAGE 215

Parmesan polenta

1½ teaspoons kosher salt

2 cups stone-ground cornmeal

7 ounces Parmesan cheese, grated (about 2 cups)

2 tablespoons unsalted butter

3 to 4 turns freshly ground black pepper

¼ cup chopped flat-leaf parsley, for garnish

1¾ ounces Parmesan cheese, grated (about ½ cup), for garnish

5 Add the onion, bell peppers, and mushrooms to the pot and sauté until the onion is translucent, 4 to 5 minutes, scraping up the browned bits on the bottom of the pot. Add the garlic, oregano, and chili flakes and cook for 1 minute, until fragrant. Add the capers and cook for 1 minute. Deglaze the pot by adding the wine and scraping up the browned bits from the bottom. Cook the wine for 3 to 4 minutes, until slightly reduced. Add the chicken stock, tomatoes, and remaining 1½ teaspoons salt and ¼ teaspoon black pepper and bring to a simmer, breaking up the tomatoes with the back of a wooden spoon.

6 Return the chicken to the pot and nestle in the pieces so that they are just covered with liquid; add water if necessary.

7 Cover with the pressure cooker lid and securely lock it in place according to the manufacturer's directions. Increase the heat to high and bring the cooker to high pressure; you can tell it's there by the steam escaping from the valve or a high-pitched whistling noise. Reduce the heat to medium and cook for 20 minutes, adjusting the heat as necessary to maintain a steady, consistent pressure.

8 Remove the pressure cooker from the heat and let the pressure come down for 10 minutes. If the cooker has a dedicated steam or pressure release valve, carefully discharge any remaining gentle pressure by releasing it. If the cooker has just the top pressure regulator, wait for the cover lock to release, then carefully remove the regulator cap. Let the pot stand for 3 to 4 minutes. Unlock and remove the lid.

9 Using a slotted spoon, transfer the chicken to a plate; set aside. Place the pressure cooker over medium-high heat and cook, stirring often, until the sauce has reduced and thickened, 4 to 5 minutes. Return the chicken to the pot and spoon the sauce over the top to baste.

RECIPE CONTINUES →

RECIPE CONTINUED FROM PREVIOUS PAGE

10 Meanwhile, to make the polenta (this can be done while the chicken is cooking), in a large, heavy-bottomed saucepan, bring 8 cups water and 1 teaspoon of the salt to a boil over medium-high heat. Whisk the cornmeal into the boiling water in a steady stream and continue whisking until fully incorporated. Reduce the heat to medium-low and simmer, stirring continuously, for 2 to 3 minutes.

11 Cook the polenta until it is thick, glossy, and pulling away from the sides of the pan, 35 to 40 minutes, stirring every few minutes and scraping the bottom of the pan to prevent sticking.

12 Add the Parmesan and butter, stirring quickly to incorporate. Season with the remaining ½ teaspoon salt and the pepper and stir. Remove from the heat. Cover and keep warm if necessary.

13 Transfer the polenta to a large serving platter. Spoon the chicken and sauce over the polenta. Garnish with the parsley and Parmesan. Serve.

My favorite picture of Hunter.

Pressure Cooker Chicken Thigh "Tagine"

Tagine is the name for an earthenware cooking pot with a domed lid as well as the Moroccan dish that's traditionally slow cooked in it. This recipe proves that you don't need the special pot or half a day to get the big, bold flavor of the classic version. You do need chicken *thighs,* however; don't try replacing them with chicken breasts. Only the thighs have what it takes to stand up to the pressure of the pot, and they will absorb all those spices and flavors without becoming dried out and stringy.

MAKES 4 to 6 servings • TIME 1 hour

2 tablespoons ground coriander

1½ tablespoons ground turmeric

1½ tablespoons sweet paprika

1 teaspoon ground allspice

Pinch of ground cinnamon

3 pounds bone-in, skin-on chicken thighs, trimmed

1 tablespoon kosher salt

6 or 7 turns freshly ground black pepper

2 tablespoons extra-virgin olive oil, plus more if needed

1 medium sweet onion, minced

4 Roma tomatoes, cored, seeded, and coarsely chopped

6 garlic cloves, minced

1 tablespoon grated ginger

1 cup sliced pitted green olives

½ cup golden raisins

2 tablespoons tomato paste

1 In a dry skillet over medium heat, gently toast the coriander, turmeric, paprika, allspice, and cinnamon until fragrant, about 2 minutes. Transfer to a bowl and set aside.

2 Pat the chicken thighs dry with paper towels. Season on all sides with half of the salt and pepper and the toasted spices. In a pressure cooker over medium-high heat, heat the olive oil until hot. Working in batches, add the chicken pieces skin side down and brown, 4 to 5 minutes. Turn the chicken and brown the other side, about 4 minutes. Transfer to a plate and set aside; repeat with the remaining chicken, adding a little more oil to the pan if necessary.

3 Add the onion and tomatoes to the pot and sauté until the onion is translucent, 4 to 5 minutes. Add the garlic and ginger and cook for 1 minute, until fragrant. Add the olives, raisins, and tomato paste and cook for 1 minute. Deglaze the pan by adding the chicken stock and scraping up the browned bits from the bottom of the pan.

4 Bring to a simmer and return the chicken to the pot. Mix well so that it is just covered with liquid; add water if necessary.

RECIPE CONTINUES 

RECIPE CONTINUED FROM PREVIOUS PAGE

1 quart Chicken Stock (page 228 or low-sodium store-bought)

¼ cup chopped cilantro, for garnish

Grated zest of 1 lemon, for garnish

5 Cover with the pressure cooker lid and securely lock it in place according to the manufacturer's directions. Increase the heat to high and bring the cooker to high pressure; you can tell it's there by the steam escaping from the valve or a high-pitched whistling noise. Reduce the heat to medium and cook for 20 minutes, adjusting the heat as necessary to maintain a steady, consistent pressure.

6 Remove the pressure cooker from the heat and let the pressure come down for 10 minutes. If the cooker has a dedicated steam or pressure release valve, carefully discharge any remaining gentle pressure by releasing it. If the cooker has just the top pressure regulator, wait for the cover lock to release, then carefully remove the regulator cap. Let the pot stand for 3 to 4 minutes. Unlock and remove the lid.

7 Return the pot to high heat and simmer, uncovered, for 5 to 7 minutes to reduce the braising liquid.

8 Transfer the chicken thighs and sauce to a serving platter. Garnish with the cilantro and lemon zest. Serve.

Quick BBQ Brisket

This is killer on its own and it makes double-killer brisket sandwiches the next day. Just make sure you get what's called the second, or deckle, cut of brisket. It has the amount of fat we need for the smokin' flavor we want. The pressure cooker cuts the braising time down to a fraction of what it takes in a regular pot, but for righteous results you've still gotta let the spice rub soak in for at least a couple of hours before cooking.

MAKES 4 to 6 servings • TIME 1 hour 15 minutes, plus at least 2 hours for the brisket rub

Brisket rub

2 tablespoons paprika

2 tablespoons granulated garlic

1 tablespoon granulated onion

1 tablespoon chili powder

½ teaspoon cayenne pepper

1 tablespoon kosher salt

2 teaspoons freshly ground black pepper

4 pounds second-cut (deckle) beef brisket, cut into 3 equal pieces

BBQ sauce

2 cups Beef Stock (page 226 or low-sodium store-bought)

1 cup BBQ sauce, such as Guy Fieri Bourbon Brown Sugar BBQ sauce

½ cup ketchup

¼ cup yellow mustard

2 tablespoons Worcestershire sauce

2 tablespoons apple cider vinegar

1 teaspoon liquid smoke (see sidebar, page 224)

¼ teaspoon red chili flakes

2 tablespoons canola oil

1 large yellow onion, sliced ½ inch thick

1 To prepare the brisket rub, combine all the ingredients in a small bowl. Rub into and all over the brisket pieces. Wrap with plastic wrap and place in the refrigerator on a baking sheet for at least 2 hours and up to overnight.

2 To make the BBQ sauce, combine all the ingredients in a large bowl and whisk well to combine. Cover and set aside.

3 In a pressure cooker over medium-high heat, heat the canola oil until hot. Add the brisket pieces and cook for 6 to 7 minutes on each side, until well browned. Add the onion and bell peppers to the pot and cook, stirring, until browned, 1 to 2 minutes.

4 Pour in the reserved BBQ sauce and the beer. Add enough water to come just three-quarters of the way up the sides of the beef in the pot. Bring to a simmer.

5 Cover with the pressure cooker lid and securely lock it in place according to the manufacturer's directions. Increase the heat to high and bring the cooker to high pressure; you can tell it's there by the steam escaping from the valve or a high-pitched whistling noise. Reduce the heat to medium and cook for 45 minutes, adjusting the heat as necessary to maintain a steady, consistent pressure.

RECIPE CONTINUES →

RECIPE CONTINUED FROM PREVIOUS PAGE

1 red bell pepper, seeded and cut into ½-inch slices

1 green bell pepper, seeded and cut into ½-inch slices

One 12-ounce bottle lager beer

¼ cup thinly bias-sliced green onions (white and light green parts), for garnish

Kosher salt, for finishing the meat

6 Remove the pressure cooker from the heat and let the pressure come down for 10 minutes. If the cooker has a dedicated steam or pressure release valve, carefully discharge any remaining gentle pressure by releasing it. If the cooker has just the top pressure regulator, wait for the cover lock to release, then carefully remove the regulator cap. Let the pot stand for 3 to 4 minutes. Unlock and remove the lid.

7 Using tongs, transfer the brisket to a plate and set aside. Place the pot with the braising liquid over high heat and simmer the sauce until reduced and slightly thickened.

8 Slice the brisket against the grain, arrange it on a serving platter, and spoon the sauce, onion, and bell peppers on top. Garnish with the green onions and finish with a sprinkle of salt. Serve.

Liquid Smoke

I've gotta take a moment to dispel a rumor I still hear around from time to time. Liquid smoke is *not* a synthetic chemical cocktail. The good stuff is made by capturing the condensation (liquid) that comes from burning wood (smoke). There are some producers that add extra flavorings and junk you don't want in there, so read the label to avoid those.

Spicy Lamb and Chickpea Curry

You want lamb curry in a hurry? When the pressure cooker is fired, you're in business.

***MAKES* 6 servings • *TIME* 1 hour**

3 pounds boneless lamb shoulder, cubed

2 tablespoons curry powder

3 teaspoons kosher salt

5 or 6 turns freshly ground black pepper

4 tablespoons extra-virgin olive oil

1 large sweet onion, cut into ½-inch dice

2 tablespoons grated ginger

6 garlic cloves, minced

1 serrano chile, seeded and minced

2 teaspoons cumin seeds

1 teaspoon coriander seeds, crushed in a mortar and pestle

1 teaspoon ground turmeric

1 tablespoon tomato paste

1 large russet potato, peeled and cut into 1-inch cubes

3 cups Chicken Stock (page 228 or low-sodium store-bought)

Two 15-ounce cans chickpeas, rinsed and drained

½ cup plain Greek yogurt

½ cup chopped cilantro

1 Season the lamb with the curry powder, 1½ teaspoons of the salt, and a few turns of pepper. Mix well to coat the lamb evenly and set aside.

2 In a pressure cooker over medium heat, heat 2 tablespoons of the olive oil until hot. Add the onion, ginger, garlic, and serrano and cook until the onion is softened, 5 to 6 minutes, stirring and using a wooden spoon to mash the mixture into a paste. Transfer to a dish and set aside.

3 Increase the heat to high and heat the remaining 2 tablespoons olive oil until hot. Add the lamb and brown all over, 8 to 10 minutes total. Stir in the cumin seeds, coriander, and turmeric and toast until fragrant, 30 to 40 seconds. Add the tomato paste and the reserved onion-chile paste and mix well. Add the potato and stock to the pot and season with the remaining 1½ teaspoons salt and a few turns of pepper. Stir well so that the lamb is just covered with liquid; add water if necessary. Bring to a simmer.

4 Lock the pressure cooker lid in place according to the manufacturer's directions. Bring the cooker to high pressure over high heat; you can tell it's there by the steam escaping from the valve or a high-pitched whistling noise. Reduce the heat to medium and cook for 20 minutes, adjusting the heat as necessary to maintain a steady, consistent pressure.

5 Remove from the heat and let stand for 10 minutes. If the cooker has a dedicated release valve, carefully discharge any remaining gentle pressure by releasing it. If the cooker has just the top pressure regulator, wait for the cover lock to release, then carefully remove the regulator cap. Let the pot stand for 2 to 3 minutes. Unlock and remove the lid. Stir in the chickpeas. Cook over high heat, stirring occasionally, until the sauce has reduced slightly, about 10 minutes. Reduce the heat to medium and stir in the yogurt. Fold in the cilantro. Serve.

Pressure Cooker Stocks

I hear all the time from people who think making their own stock is too time consuming. But when there's a pressure cooker on board, the cooking time is cut to a fraction. Which means . . . no more excuses! Seriously, I can't think of a better place to economize on money and time than making stock at home this way.

One tip for best storing results is leave in place the fat cap that forms on top after the stock has chilled. It actually helps keep the stock fresher by forming a seal between it and the air. Just scrape the fat off and toss it out before using the stock.

Beef Stock

MAKES **about 3 quarts •** ***TIME*** **2 hours**

- 2 pounds beef or veal bones, cut into 2-inch pieces
- 1 pound oxtails
- 1 tablespoon tomato paste
- 3 tablespoons canola oil
- 1 teaspoon kosher salt
- 4 or 5 turns freshly ground black pepper
- 1 onion, skin on, root and stem removed, quartered
- 2 carrots, cut in thirds
- 4 celery stalks, cut in thirds
- 4 garlic cloves
- 2 bay leaves
- 4 thyme sprigs
- 6 parsley sprigs
- 1 teaspoon black peppercorns
- 2 or 3 whole cloves

1 Preheat the oven to 350°F.

2 Rub the bones and oxtails with the tomato paste. Spread the bones and oxtails evenly in a single layer in a roasting pan. Drizzle with 2 tablespoons of the canola oil and season with the salt and pepper. Roast, uncovered, for 45 minutes, until well browned.

3 Remove the bones from the roasting pan and set aside. Deglaze the roasting pan by setting it over two stove burners. Add 2 cups cold water and scrape up the browned bits from the bottom of the pan.

4 Set the pressure cooker over medium-high heat and heat the remaining 1 tablespoon canola oil until hot. Add the onion, carrots, and celery and sauté for 2 to 3 minutes, until softened but not at all browned. Add the bones, the deglazing liquid, garlic, bay leaves, thyme, parsley, peppercorns, cloves, and 3 quarts cold water and bring to a simmer. Skim off any foam and fat that floats to the surface of the stock.

5 Cover with the pressure cooker lid and securely lock it in place according to the manufacturer's directions. Increase the heat to high and bring the cooker to high pressure; you can tell it's there by the steam

escaping from the valve or a high-pitched whistling noise. Reduce the heat to medium and cook for 45 minutes, adjusting the heat as necessary to maintain a steady, consistent pressure.

6 Remove the pressure cooker from the heat and let the pressure come down for 10 minutes. If the cooker has a dedicated steam or pressure release valve, carefully discharge any remaining gentle pressure by releasing it. If the cooker has just the top pressure regulator, wait for the cover lock to release, then carefully remove the regulator cap. Let the pot stand for 3 to 4 minutes. Unlock and remove the lid.

7 Strain the stock through a cheesecloth-lined strainer set over a large pot or bowl. Discard the solids in the cheesecloth. Let cool, then refrigerate overnight or until the fat solidifies.

8 Store the stock in airtight containers in the refrigerator for 3 to 4 days or freeze for 4 to 5 months. Lift off and discard the fat before using the stock.

Chicken or Turkey Stock

MAKES **about 3 quarts** • ***TIME*** **1 hour**

1 tablespoon canola oil

4 pounds chicken bones (necks and backs) OR 1 leftover roasted turkey carcass, 1 turkey neck, and 1 smoked turkey leg

1 onion, skin on, root and stem removed, quartered

2 carrots, cut in thirds

4 celery stalks, cut in thirds

4 garlic cloves

2 bay leaves

4 thyme sprigs

6 flat-leaf parsley sprigs

1 teaspoon black peppercorns

2 or 3 whole cloves

1 Set the pressure cooker over medium-high heat and heat the canola oil until hot. Add the chicken or turkey parts and brown all over, 5 to 6 minutes.

2 Add the onion, carrots, and celery and sauté for 2 to 3 minutes, until softened but not at all browned. Add the garlic, bay leaves, thyme, parsley, peppercorns, cloves, and 3½ quarts cold water and bring to a simmer.

3 Cover with the pressure cooker lid and securely lock it in place according to the manufacturer's directions. Increase the heat to high and bring the cooker to high pressure; you can tell it's there by the steam escaping from the valve or a high-pitched whistling noise. Reduce the heat to medium and cook for 30 minutes, adjusting the heat as necessary to maintain a steady, consistent pressure.

4 Remove the pressure cooker from the heat and let the pressure come down for 10 minutes. If the cooker has a dedicated steam or pressure release valve, carefully discharge any remaining gentle pressure by releasing it. If the cooker has just the top pressure regulator, wait for the cover lock to release, then carefully remove the regulator cap. Let the pot stand for 3 to 4 minutes. Unlock and remove the lid.

5 Strain the stock through a cheesecloth-lined strainer set over a large pot or bowl. Discard the solids in the cheesecloth. Let cool, then refrigerate overnight or until the fat solidifies.

6 Store the stock in airtight containers in the refrigerator for 3 to 4 days or freeze for 4 to 5 months. Lift off and discard the fat before using the stock.

Seafood Stock

MAKES **about 2 quarts •** ***TIME*** **45 minutes**

2 pounds non-oily white fish bones and heads, such as cod, halibut, or tilapia

1 to 2 cups shrimp shells and/or tails

¼ cup bonito flakes

1 cup dry white wine

1 carrot, cut into 1-inch pieces

1 onion, cut into 1-inch pieces

2 celery stalks, cut into 1-inch pieces

½ teaspoon kosher salt

5 whole peppercorns

4 flat-leaf parsley sprigs

1 bay leaf

1 Clean the fish bones and heads under cold running water. Cut into 4-inch pieces and place in a pressure cooker.

2 Add the shrimp shells, bonito, wine, carrot, onion, celery, salt, peppercorns, parsley, bay leaf, and 2 quarts cold water to the pressure cooker and set over high heat. Bring to a simmer.

3 Cover with the pressure cooker lid and securely lock it in place according to the manufacturer's directions. Increase the heat to high and bring the cooker to high pressure; you can tell it's there by the steam escaping from the valve or a high-pitched whistling noise. Reduce the heat to medium and cook for 20 minutes, adjusting the heat as necessary to maintain a steady, consistent pressure.

4 Remove the pressure cooker from the heat and let the pressure come down for 10 minutes. If the cooker has a dedicated steam or pressure release valve, carefully discharge any remaining gentle pressure by releasing it. If the cooker has just the top pressure regulator, wait for the cover lock to release, then carefully remove the regulator cap. Let the pot stand for 3 to 4 minutes. Unlock and remove the lid.

5 Strain the stock through a cheesecloth-lined strainer set over a large pot or bowl. Discard the solids in the cheesecloth. Let cool, then refrigerate overnight.

6 Store the stock in airtight containers in the refrigerator for 3 to 4 days or freeze for 4 to 5 months. Remove and discard any fat before using the stock.

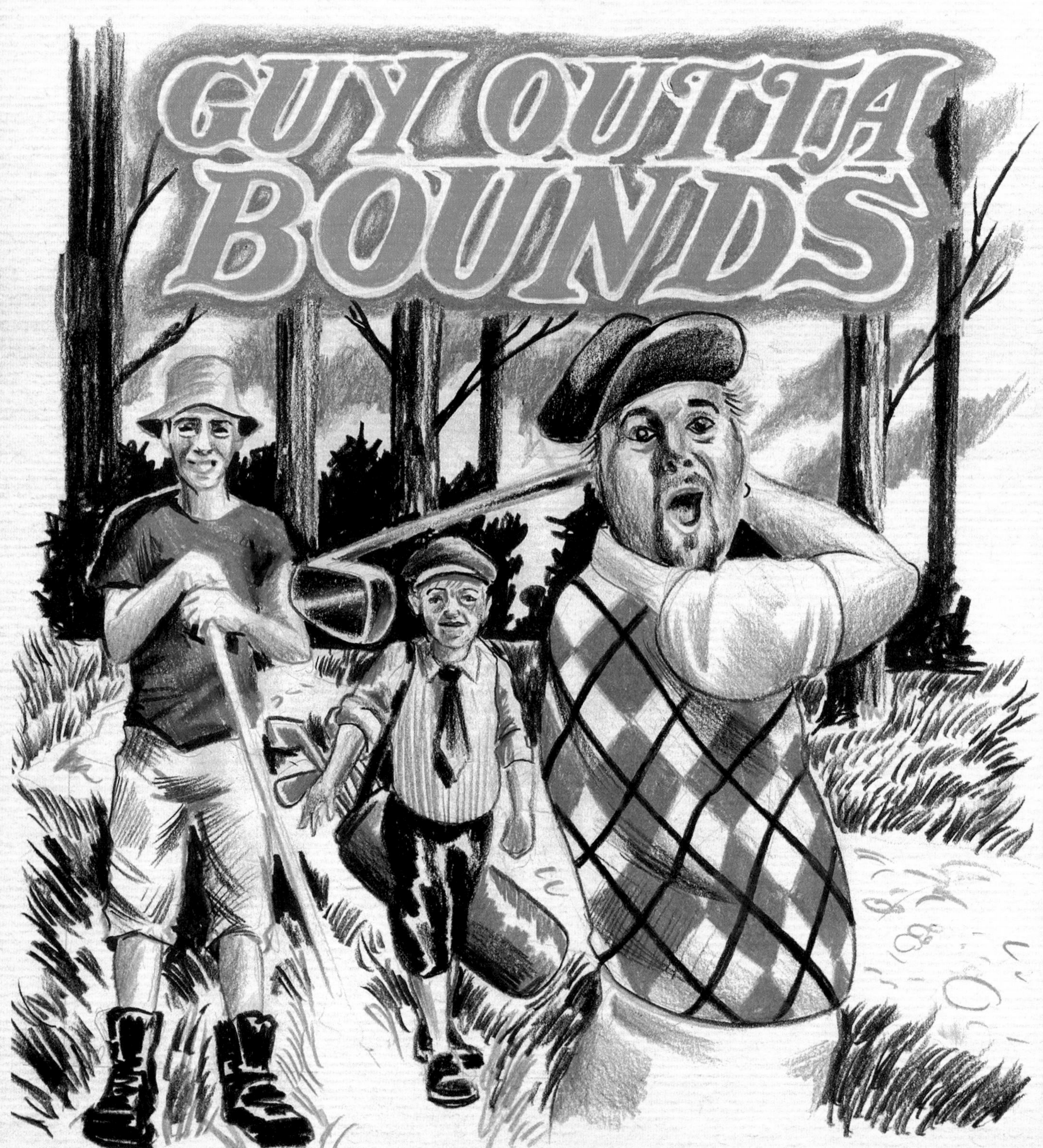
GUY OUTTA BOUNDS

Where Things Get Krazy

Here's the chapter that I'd turn into a full book if I could. This is the kind of stuff I love to cook when we're up at the ranch with the whole crowd and one of the crew shows up with two bushels of oysters and a bagged deer. That's when we fire up the grill, the smoker, and the oven—and if it's not nailed down, it's gettin' cooked. **If it were up to me, every single night would be an outta bounds night.** But not everybody is ready for roasted bone marrow. And—just being honest here—not every culinary adventure ends up in Flavortown, ya know what I mean? But you'll never win the game if you won't take the shot. So once in a while, when you've got a little extra time and you're ready to channel your inner culinary MacGyver, this is the chapter to come to. Just make sure you **don't MacGyver the whole meal.** Have some backups, maybe one or two easy family staples that everyone loves and enjoys. 'Cuz if it doesn't come out right, you may be having a dinner of nothing but sides—and that makes the whole crew grumpy.

Another family movie favorite: Caddyshack. Fooorrre!

OFF
THE
HOOK
The Reel Deal

Roasted Spatchcock Chickens Three Ways

I've said it before and I'll say it again. When you fire up a big heat source—whether it's the oven, grill, or smoker—you've gotta cook more than one thing! Take a look inside your oven and think about how much sense it makes to heat all that space for a single 4- or 5-pound roaster. I'll save you the suspense: It makes *no* sense! So the next time chicken is on the menu, don't buy just the one your family will eat on one night. Buy three and do 'em up three different ways. Then you'll have enough to keep the crew happy for days, especially when they see what's in store here. We've got a tropical-style huli huli machine—you've seen it on *Guy's Big Bite;* a red pepper–almond romesco; and a killer pesto.

Spatchcocking, where you take out the back bone and flatten the chicken, is a funny-sounding but really easy technique that shortens the cooking time and is the best way to ensure that the whole chicken cooks evenly; brining keeps it moist and juicy all the way to the bone.

MAKES **12 to 14 servings** • ***TIME*** **3½ hours, plus 4 hours for brining**

Chickens and brine

Three 4- to 5-pound whole chickens

1 gallon All-Purpose Brine (page 300)

Kosher salt and freshly ground black pepper, as needed

Huli huli rub and sauce

2 tablespoons garlic powder

2 tablespoons kosher salt

1 tablespoon paprika

1 tablespoon onion powder

1 teaspoon ground cumin

¼ teaspoon cayenne pepper

2 or 3 turns freshly ground black pepper

1 cup pineapple juice

½ cup ketchup

1 To spatchcock the chickens, place one breast side down on a clean, dry cutting board. Using kitchen shears, remove the backbone by cutting up from the tailbone to the neck on both sides. With the tip of a knife, remove and discard the wishbone. Flip the chicken over and use the palm of your hand to push the breast straight down flat on the cutting board, cracking the breastbone and flattening the chicken. Place it in a large dish and repeat with the other two chickens.

2 Pour the brine over the chickens, making sure they're completely immersed. Cover the dish with plastic wrap. Refrigerate for at least 4 hours or overnight.

3 To prepare the huli huli rub and sauce, in a small bowl, combine the garlic powder, salt, paprika, onion powder, cumin, cayenne, and black pepper. Mix well and set aside.

RECIPE CONTINUES →

We couldn't figure out
how to shoot three birds
so I just stacked the pans.
Looks cool, huh?

RECIPE CONTINUED FROM PAGE 233

1/2 cup low-sodium soy sauce

2 tablespoons seasoned rice vinegar

1/2 cup lightly packed light brown sugar

2 teaspoons ground ginger

Romesco sauce

1/2 cup golden raisins

1/2 cup extra-virgin olive oil

2 slices crusty bread, cut into 1/2-inch cubes (about 1 cup)

1/2 cup slivered almonds

5 garlic cloves, minced

1 cup drained Peppadew peppers

1/4 cup chopped flat-leaf parsley

2 tablespoons aged sherry vinegar

1 teaspoon kosher salt, plus more for seasoning

6 to 8 turns freshly ground black pepper, plus more for seasoning

Pesto

1/4 cup pine nuts, toasted (see page 22)

2 cups tightly packed basil leaves

4 garlic cloves, minced

1 teaspoon kosher salt

4 to 5 turns freshly ground black pepper

Pinch of red chili flakes

Juice and grated zest of 1 Meyer or regular lemon

3/4 ounce Parmesan cheese, grated (about 1/4 cup)

1/4 cup extra-virgin olive oil

4 In a medium saucepan over medium-low heat, bring the pineapple juice, ketchup, soy sauce, and vinegar to a simmer. Whisk in the brown sugar and ginger and simmer until the liquid begins to thicken, 7 to 8 minutes. Set the sauce aside to cool.

5 To prepare the romesco sauce, place the raisins in a small bowl and cover with boiling hot water. Let soak for 10 minutes. Drain and set aside.

6 In a large sauté pan over medium-high heat, heat 2 tablespoons of the olive oil. Add the bread and almonds and sauté until the nuts are fragrant and light brown, 3 to 4 minutes. Add the garlic and sauté for 1 minute, until fragrant. Set aside to cool for about 5 minutes.

7 Transfer the mixture to a food processor and add the plumped raisins, Peppadew peppers, parsley, vinegar, salt, and black pepper. Process the mixture until smooth. With the motor running, pour the remaining 6 tablespoons olive oil through the pour spout in a slow and steady stream. Process until the oil is fully incorporated into the sauce. Divide between two bowls and set aside. (Cover and refrigerate one bowl until serving.)

8 To prepare the pesto, in a dry skillet over medium heat, toast the pine nuts, stirring often, until golden brown, 4 to 5 minutes. Remove them from the pan and let cool.

9 In a food processor, pulse the basil, garlic, salt, black pepper, and chili flakes 3 or 4 times. Add the lemon juice and zest, Parmesan, and pine nuts. Pulse 3 or 4 times to coarsely chop the basil and pine nuts. With the motor running, pour the olive oil through the pour spout in a slow and steady stream. Process until completely combined. Divide between two bowls and set aside. (Cover and refrigerate one bowl until serving.)

10 Preheat the oven to 400°F.

RECIPE CONTINUES

RECIPE CONTINUED FROM PREVIOUS PAGE

11 Remove the chickens from the brine and pat dry with paper towels. Discard the brine. (Or, if roasting one or two chickens at a time, leave the remaining chicken[s] in the brine until ready to roast.) Coat one chicken evenly with the huli huli dry rub and set it aside on a baking sheet or pan, tucking the wingtips under the shoulders of the chicken so it lays flat.

12 On the other two chickens, use your fingers to separate the skin from the meat on the breasts, legs, and thighs. Using a spoon and your fingers, smear romesco sauce under the skin of one chicken and pesto under the skin of the other chicken. Place the chickens on baking sheets or pans, tucking the wingtips under the shoulders. Season lightly with salt and pepper.

13 To keep the chickens flat, place a second baking sheet with a weight such as a brick on top of each, or simply use a heavy cast-iron pan. Roast for 30 minutes.

14 Remove the pans from the oven and remove the baking sheet and weight or heavy pan from the top of the chickens. Reduce the oven temperature to 350°F. Baste each chicken liberally with its respective sauce.

15 Roast, uncovered, for 20 minutes, or until the skin is golden brown.

16 Cook for another 10 minutes, basting each chicken with its respective sauce two or three more times, until the internal temperature between the thigh and the leg reads 165°F on an instant-read thermometer.

17 Let rest for 15 minutes, then cut the chickens into pieces. Serve with the respective reserved sauces on the side.

Poutine French Fries

The best fries are fluffy on the inside and crisp and golden on the outside. But how often do we really get to eat the *best* fries? Not often enough, if you ask me. So when I make them myself, I make sure to do it right. That means soaking the sliced potatoes in vinegar and water to wash away the starch. Then you fry them not once but twice. The first time cooks the fries through so you get a nice fluffy interior. The second time, in hotter oil, gets you that crunchy, lightly colored exterior.

Sure, you could stop there and just dip them in some ketchup, but when you've come this far, why not go all the way . . . to Canada? Who knows who first figured out that tangy cheese curds and brown gravy are the perfect partners for french fries? The better question is . . . who am I to question genius?

MAKES 4 to 6 servings • TIME 1 hour, plus soaking time

8 russet potatoes

1/4 cup distilled white vinegar

Canola oil, for the baking sheet and for deep frying

Chunky beef gravy

2 tablespoons extra-virgin olive oil

2 pounds coarsely ground chuck

4 garlic cloves, minced

1 cup minced sweet onion

1/2 cup minced celery

1/2 cup minced carrot

1 teaspoon kosher salt

8 to 10 turns freshly ground black pepper

4 tablespoons (1/2 stick) unsalted butter

1/4 cup all-purpose flour

1 1/2 quarts Beef Stock (page 226 or use low-sodium store-bought)

Ask the butcher (or the grocery store meat department) to coarsely grind some chuck for you if you don't see anything labeled this way.

1 Scrub the potatoes. Cut them lengthwise into 1/4-inch-thick slices, then cut the slices lengthwise into 1/4-inch sticks. Transfer them to a large bowl and add cold water to just cover. Add the vinegar and mix well. Soak the potatoes for at least 30 minutes and up to 12 hours; for longer soaking, place the bowl in the fridge.

2 Preheat the oven to 200°F. Oil two rimmed baking sheets with the canola oil.

3 Drain the potatoes and pat them dry with a paper towel. Spread them evenly on the prepared baking sheets. Set the baking sheets in the oven and let the potatoes dehydrate for about 25 minutes. Set aside.

4 To prepare the gravy, heat the olive oil in a large saucepan over high heat until hot. Add the ground beef and sauté until well browned, 7 to 8 minutes. Add the garlic, onion, celery, and carrot and sauté until the onion is translucent, 4 to 5 minutes. Season with the salt and pepper.

RECIPE CONTINUES →

RECIPE CONTINUED FROM PREVIOUS PAGE

1 cup dry red wine

1/4 cup Worcestershire sauce

1 tablespoon kosher salt

3 or 4 turns freshly ground black pepper

1/4 pound white cheddar cheese curds or mozzarella, cut into 1/2-inch cubes (about 1 cup)

1 tablespoon minced chives, for garnish

5 Whisk in the butter and flour and mix well. Cook, whisking occasionally, until the flour is lightly browned and smells nutty and fragrant, 4 to 5 minutes. Deglaze the pan by adding the beef stock, wine, and Worcestershire sauce and scraping up the browned bits from the bottom of the pan. Whisk until well combined. Bring to a boil, then reduce the heat to a simmer and cook for 18 to 20 minutes, or until the gravy has thickened and the beef is tender. Set aside and keep warm.

6 To oil-blanch the french fries, pour 4 to 5 inches of canola oil into a heavy-bottomed pot such as a deep Dutch oven. Heat the oil over high heat to 300°F. Have ready two rimmed baking sheets lined with paper towels.

7 Working in small batches, cook the potatoes in the oil until just lightly golden, 4 to 5 minutes. Use a spider or large slotted spoon to lift the potatoes from the oil, carefully shake off the excess oil, and transfer to the lined baking sheets to drain. Let cool for about 10 minutes. Repeat with the remaining potatoes.

8 Increase the temperature of the oil to 375°F. Line two clean rimmed baking sheets with paper towels.

9 Working in small batches, fry the potatoes in the hot oil until golden brown and crispy, about 2 minutes. Use a spider or large slotted spoon to transfer them to the lined baking sheets to drain well. Repeat with the remaining potatoes. Transfer the fries to a large metal bowl and season with the salt and pepper.

10 To serve, place the hot crispy fries on a large platter. Sprinkle with the cheese, then ladle the chunky beef gravy over the top. Garnish with the chives and serve immediately.

You have to go to the gym just for looking at this.

Bacon Jalapeño Popcorn

I love the old-school sound of corn popping on the stovetop. I remember the very first time Ryder heard it—we were up at the cabin and he walked in to investigate what the heck was making all the noise. His eyes got as big as saucers when I showed him what was going on in the pot. There's nothing like seeing stuff you usually take for granted through the fresh eyes of kids. Most kids today only know pre-popped or microwave popcorn. For more flavor and the much-deserved anticipation, there is nothing like the stovetop method. For best results use a heavy-bottomed pot with a tight-fitting lid and a good handle.

MAKES **4 to 6 servings** • ***TIME*** **15 minutes**

½ pound applewood smoked bacon, cut into ¼-inch dice

3 jalapeños, seeded and cut into thin rings

3 tablespoons extra-virgin olive oil

1 cup popcorn kernels

¾ ounce Parmesan cheese, grated (about ¼ cup)

1 teaspoon kosher salt

This lets the steam escape so the popcorn doesn't get soggy.

1 Set a large, heavy-bottomed pot over medium heat. Add the bacon and cook until crispy and browned and the fat has rendered, about 8 minutes. Add the jalapeños to the pot and stir well. Cook for 2 minutes, or until the jalapeños are charred. Line a plate with a paper towel and use a slotted spoon to transfer the bacon and jalapeños to the plate. Set aside.

2 Add the olive oil to the pot and increase the heat to high. Add the popcorn kernels and toss well to coat them in the oil. Spread the kernels evenly on the bottom of the pot, then cover the pot with the lid. When the first kernels start to pop, very slightly uncover the pot. Shake the pot back and forth directly over the heat. Cook until the kernels stop popping, 2 to 3 minutes.

3 Remove the pot from the heat and pour the popcorn into a large bowl. Add the reserved bacon and jalapeños, the Parmesan, and the salt. Toss well to mix. Serve warm.

The kid loves popcorn.

Oysters Three Ways

A lot of people never consider eating oysters on the half shell unless they see them on a restaurant menu. It definitely doesn't have to be that way, because shucking an oyster isn't hard—just get yourself an oyster knife and follow the directions below. (Or type "shucking oysters" into your Internet search engine and you can spend the next two hours watching people demonstrate how to do it.) You'll get the hang of it once you've done a few, and before you know it you're going to be looking for excuses every other day to shuck a few dozen oysters. (As if you need an excuse.) When that happens, you're gonna need a plan for how to prepare all those oysters. Good thing I've got not one but *three* killer preparations for you right here.

***MAKES* 4 to 6 servings • *TIME* 1 hour**

Champagne mignonette

¼ cup Champagne vinegar

2 tablespoons minced shallot

2 tablespoons minced flat-leaf parsley

2 garlic cloves, minced

1 teaspoon sugar

4 or 5 turns freshly ground black pepper

Lemon caper butter

4 tablespoons (½ stick) unsalted butter

2 tablespoons drained capers

2 tablespoons minced flat-leaf parsley

Juice and grated zest of 1 Meyer or regular lemon

1 garlic clove, minced

5 or 6 turns freshly ground black pepper

Saltimbocca

2 ounces Provolone cheese, finely grated (about ½ cup)

¼ cup panko bread crumbs

1 To make the Champagne mignonette, combine all the ingredients in a medium bowl. Whisk until well combined, cover, and refrigerate until needed, up to 1 or 2 days.

2 To make the lemon caper butter, heat all the ingredients in a small saucepan over medium heat. As the butter melts, stir the mixture together until fragrant. Set aside to cool, then cover and refrigerate to firm up. The butter will keep for 2 to 3 days.

3 To make the saltimbocca mixture, pulse all the ingredients in a food processor until well combined. Refrigerate until needed.

4 Line two or three rimmed baking sheets with crumpled foil so the oysters will sit upright and not move around. Place the oysters in a large colander and run cold water over them while scrubbing with a firm-bristled brush. Discard any that are opened and do not close when you rap them on the counter. Working with one oyster at a time (and wearing gloves to protect your hands, if desired), insert the tip of an oyster knife into the hinge between the top and bottom shells. Holding the oyster steady with a kitchen towel, gently but firmly twist and turn the knife so you apply pressure to the hinge and "pop" it open. Carefully remove and discard

RECIPE CONTINUES 

Jamps ate all of these.

RECIPE CONTINUED FROM PAGE 242

8 thin slices prosciutto, finely chopped

10 sage leaves

2 or 3 turns freshly ground black pepper

3 tablespoons extra-virgin olive oil

Oysters and accompaniments

30 fresh medium oysters

½ sourdough baguette

¼ cup extra-virgin olive oil

Rock salt, for serving (optional)

2 lemons, cut in half, grilled or broiled

Special equipment

Oyster knife

Heavy gloves, if desired

the top shell. Gently scrape the oyster knife around and under the meat in the bottom half to detach it from the shell. Place the oyster on the foil-lined baking sheet and continue with the remaining oysters, putting 20 on one sheet (for baking) and 10 on another (for serving raw on the half shell). Place the sheets in the refrigerator.

Don't tip the bottom half or you'll lose all the briny oyster liquor!

5 Preheat the broiler to high and set a rack 4 to 5 inches from the heat source.

6 Cut the bread into ¼-inch-thick slices. Lightly drizzle the slices with the olive oil and place them on a rimmed baking sheet. Broil for 1 minute, or until golden. Turn the slices over and broil on the second side until golden, about 1 minute. Set aside.

7 Remove the baking sheet with 20 oysters on it from the refrigerator. Top 10 of the oysters with a teaspoon each of the saltimbocca mixture. Top the other 10 with a teaspoon each of the lemon caper butter mixture.

8 Broil for 2 to 3 minutes, until the oysters are bubbling and golden. Let cool slightly (the shells will be hot!).

9 Spread rock salt (if using) on a large serving platter. Arrange the broiled oysters on the salt. Place the remaining raw oysters on the salt. Stir the mignonette and spoon a little of it onto each of the raw oysters.

10 Serve with the crostini and grilled or broiled lemon halves.

Baked Stuffed King Crab Legs
with Shiitake Mushrooms and Corn

King crab legs have a great sweet flavor and firm texture, and they're almost always sold already cooked. This means that when we prepare them, our main job is to enhance their best qualities without overcooking them and turning them all rubbery. **Times like these, ya can't beat simplicity.** Nothin' more is needed than this corn and shiitake stuffing and a few minutes under the broiler.

MAKES **4 to 6 servings** • ***TIME*** **45 minutes**

- 1/2 cup panko bread crumbs
- 6 Ritz crackers, crushed
- 2 tablespoons unsalted butter
- 1/4 cup minced shallot
- 1 pound shiitake mushrooms, washed, stemmed, and finely diced
- 1 cup fresh or frozen corn kernels
- 2 tablespoons finely diced red bell pepper
- 2 garlic cloves, minced
- 1/4 cup dry sherry
- 1 teaspoon kosher salt
- 5 or 6 turns freshly ground black pepper
- 2 tablespoons minced chives
- Pinch of cayenne pepper
- 1/4 cup mayonnaise
- 3 pounds (4 or 5 whole legs) split Alaskan king crab legs, defrosted in the refrigerator
- 1/4 cup extra-virgin olive oil
- 2 lemons, cut into wedges

1 In a small bowl, combine the panko and crackers crumbs and set aside.

2 Melt the butter in a large sauté pan over medium-high heat. Add the shallot, mushrooms, corn, and bell pepper and sauté until the shallot is lightly browned and the mushrooms are tender, 6 to 7 minutes. Add the garlic and cook for 1 minute, until fragrant.

3 Deglaze the pan by adding the sherry and scraping up the browned bits from the bottom of the pan. Season with the salt and black pepper. Cook until the sherry has evaporated and the liquid in the pan has reduced completely, 4 to 5 minutes. Transfer to a medium bowl and let cool completely.

4 Add the chives, cayenne, and half of the crushed cracker and panko mixture to the mushroom mixture and stir to combine. Add the mayonnaise and mix well.

5 Pack the mixture on top of the flesh in each split crab leg, carefully but firmly pressing it so it sticks and holds its shape. Evenly space the legs on a rimmed baking sheet, stuffing side up. Sprinkle each with the remaining cracker and panko mixture. Drizzle liberally with the olive oil.

6 Preheat the broiler to high and set a rack 6 inches from the heat.

7 Broil for 3 to 4 minutes, until the stuffing is golden brown on top and warmed through. Serve with lemon wedges.

Java-Rubbed Bone-in Rib-Eye Steak
with Habanero Butter

When you're cookin' crazy-big, thick steaks like these monster rib-eyes, you've gotta keep two different things in mind: getting a killer sear on the outside and cooking the interior just right. The key is to start cooking the steaks at high heat so the outside gets that nice brown crust, then move 'em to a more moderate environment so the meat can be cooked just right without scorching the outside or overcooking the inside. That medium-heat situation can be achieved either by moving the steaks from the direct heat part of the grill to the indirect side or by putting them in a moderately hot oven.

Also keep in mind that the java rub is not the time to pull out your fancy ground coffee beans—what you really want is the punch that comes from instant coffee granules.

***MAKES* 4 servings • *TIME* 45 minutes**

Habanero butter

¼ pound (1 stick) unsalted butter, at room temperature

1 habanero, seeded and minced

Juice and grated zest of 1 lime

2 tablespoons minced shallot

2 tablespoons Roasted Garlic (page 298)

1 tablespoon minced flat-leaf parsley

1 teaspoon kosher salt

4 or 5 turns freshly ground black pepper

Java rub

¼ cup instant coffee granules

¼ cup black peppercorns, freshly cracked

1 To prepare the habanero butter, in a small bowl, mix all the ingredients with a wooden spoon until well blended. Refrigerate to firm up slightly. The butter can be prepared up to 2 to 3 days in advance; if made in advance, set at room temperature to soften slightly before serving.

2 To make the java rub, combine all the ingredients in a small bowl and stir to blend.

3 Make an indirect high-heat grill. If using charcoal, form the fire on one side of the grill; if using gas, heat one half of the grill to high. Remove the steaks from the refrigerator and let come to room temperature, about 20 minutes.

4 Pat the steaks dry with paper towels, then rub the java mix liberally all over them.

5 Wipe down the hot grill grates with canola-oil-blotted paper towels to clean them and create a nonstick surface.

2 tablespoons lightly packed dark brown sugar

2 tablespoons kosher salt

2 tablespoons granulated garlic

2 teaspoons paprika

1 teaspoon cayenne pepper

Steak

Two 48-ounce bone-in rib-eye steaks*

Canola oil, for grilling

*Yeah, these are crazy-big steaks and they're incredible, but if you can't get them easily, go ahead and get four smaller bone-in rib-eyes; they'll take a little less time to cook, but everything else will be the same—including the killer flavor.

6 Grill the steaks directly over the heat, without moving them, until well seared, 5 to 6 minutes. Flip the steaks over and repeat the process, then move the steaks to the cooler side of the grill. Cover the grill and cook until the steaks are pink on the inside and an instant-read thermometer reads 130°F to 135°F for medium-rare, 7 to 8 minutes longer. (For smaller steaks, grill on each side for 4 to 5 minutes, then cook for 5 to 6 minutes on the cooler side of the grill.)

7 Transfer the steaks to a tray and loosely tent with foil. Let the steaks rest for 5 minutes before serving.

8 To serve, top each java-rubbed steak with a few tablespoons of the habanero butter.

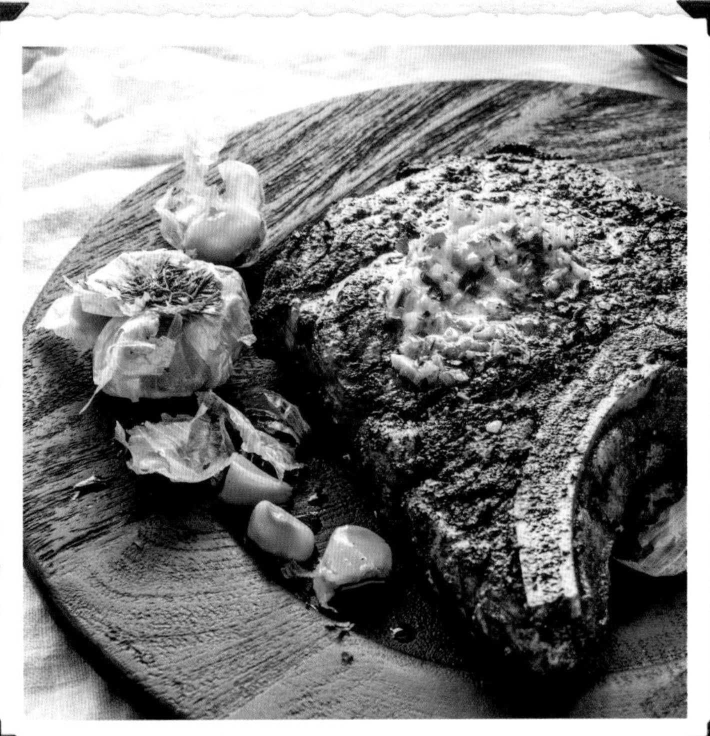

Jalapeño Lobster Mac 'n' Cheese
with Crunchy Crushed Corn Tortillas

Do you love sweet and tender lobster? Check. How about creamy, rich mac 'n' cheese? Check. With a crispy crunchy topping? Double and triple check. So here's your answer. But if you're gonna dive into this match made in heaven, make sure you get your money's worth. After you cook the lobster, put the shells back into the stock to simmer and deepen that righteous flavor in the cheese sauce.

MAKES 4 to 6 servings • TIME 2 hours

Lobster and stock

1 cup dry white wine

1 cup thinly sliced sweet onion

4 celery stalks

1 carrot

2 garlic cloves, smashed

2 thyme sprigs

2 bay leaves

2 tablespoons kosher salt

1 teaspoon black peppercorns

Two 2- to 2½-pound lobsters

1 pound cavatappi (corkscrew) pasta

Béchamel

3 cups half-and-half

6 tablespoons (¾ stick) unsalted butter

¼ cup minced shallot

1 jalapeño, seeded

1 teaspoon kosher salt

1 To prepare the lobster, in a large pot, combine 2 quarts water, the wine, onion, celery, carrot, garlic, thyme, bay leaves, 1 tablespoon of the salt, and the peppercorns. Bring to a boil over high heat. Add the lobsters and cover the pot. Reduce the heat to medium and simmer until the lobsters turn bright red, 8 to 10 minutes. Remove the pot from the heat and let the lobsters steep in the stock for 5 minutes. Remove the lobsters from the stock and set aside on a tray to cool. Set aside the pot with the stock.

2 Pull the claws and tail off a lobster. With a sharp knife, cut lengthwise through the tail. Remove the meat and set the shell and meat aside. Crack open the claws with the back of the knife or a lobster cracker. Remove the meat and set the shell and meat aside. Repeat with the other lobster. Chop the lobster meat into bite-size chunks and set it aside in a bowl.

3 Rinse the lobster shells and place them in the pot with the stock. If desired, rinse the green tomalley and the red or black roe (if present) out of the two body cavities and add them to the pot as well.

4 Bring the stock to a boil over high heat. Boil for 20 to 25 minutes, until the stock has reduced and concentrated in flavor. Strain the stock through a fine-mesh sieve. Discard the solids and set the lobster stock aside.

RECIPE CONTINUES

Lobster mac attack!

RECIPE CONTINUED FROM PAGE 248

¼ cup plus 2 tablespoons all-purpose flour

1 teaspoon Old Bay seasoning

2 or 3 gratings of nutmeg

Pinch of cayenne pepper

3 or 4 turns freshly ground black pepper

½ pound white cheddar cheese, grated (about 2 cups)

Topping

2 ounces white cheddar cheese, grated (about ½ cup)

1¾ ounces Parmesan cheese, grated (about ½ cup)

1 jalapeño, seeded and minced

1 red Fresno chile, seeded and minced

1 cup crushed corn tortilla chips

5 Meanwhile, in a large pot over high heat, bring 1 gallon water to a boil. When the water is boiling, season it with the remaining 1 tablespoon salt, then add the cavatappi and stir. Cook the pasta until al dente according to the package directions. Drain and set aside in a large bowl.

6 To prepare the béchamel, heat the half-and-half in a medium saucepan over medium heat until warm.

7 In a large saucepan over medium-high heat, heat the butter, shallot, jalapeño, and salt and sauté until the shallot is translucent and not at all brown, 4 to 5 minutes. Add the flour and mix well with the vegetables to make a roux. Pour in the half-and-half in a slow, steady stream and cook, whisking constantly, until the mixture is smooth and beginning to thicken. Add 2 cups of the reserved lobster stock and whisk until it comes to a simmer and is thickened. Add the Old Bay, nutmeg, cayenne, and black pepper. Simmer for 10 to 12 minutes, whisking often so it doesn't burn, until thick but pourable. Stir in the cheddar until melted.

8 Add one-third of the reserved lobster meat. Using an immersion blender, puree until smooth. Set aside.

9 Preheat the oven to 375°F.

10 Add the béchamel to the reserved pasta and mix until completely coated. Fold in the remaining lobster meat. Pour the lobster mac 'n' cheese into a large gratin dish (or divide it evenly among individual baking dishes).

11 To make the topping, in a small bowl, mix the cheddar and Parmesan. Sprinkle it on top of the mac 'n' cheese, followed by the minced chiles and crushed tortilla chips. Place the dish (or dishes) on a rimmed baking sheet to catch any spillover. Bake until the sauce is bubbling and the top is golden brown, 20 to 25 minutes (slightly less for smaller dishes).

12 Let stand for 5 to 10 minutes, then serve hot.

Cuban Fried Fish
with Sour Orange Mojo and Pigeon Pea Rice

I'm a fanatic about fresh fish, and this is one of my favorite ways to serve it. Not only because it tastes incredible, but because there's not much that is more fun to watch than when I drop a platter of Cuban fried whole fish on the table and let the crew dig in. You know for sure that dinner was a success when it looks like a cartoon tornado came through and stripped that fish clean.

There are a couple of cool ingredients here that you can find in Hispanic markets. Pigeon peas come in green and beige, and either is fine in this dish. Just like other beans, they come dried or canned (I use canned here). Sour orange juice tastes just like it sounds; if you can't find it, an easy sub is noted below.

MAKES **4 to 6 servings** • *TIME* **1 hour**

Sour orange mojo

1/4 cup extra-virgin olive oil

1/4 cup minced garlic

1 tablespoon kosher salt

1 cup sour (Seville) orange juice, or 2/3 cup fresh orange juice plus 1/3 cup fresh lime juice

1/2 cup pineapple juice

Juice of 2 limes

1/4 cup minced flat-leaf parsley

1/4 cup minced cilantro

3 tablespoons minced oregano

1 tablespoon ground cumin

1 teaspoon freshly ground black pepper

Pigeon pea rice

1 tablespoon extra-virgin olive oil

1/2 cup diced sweet onion

1 To prepare the sour orange mojo, in a small saucepan, combine the olive oil, garlic, and salt. Cook over medium heat until the garlic is fragrant, about 2 minutes. Remove from the heat and add the orange juice, pineapple juice, lime juice, parsley, cilantro, oregano, cumin, and pepper. Whisk well to combine. Cover and refrigerate for at least 30 minutes and up to 1 day.

2 Meanwhile, to prepare the rice, heat the olive oil in a medium saucepan over medium-high heat until hot. Add the onion, garlic, and salt and sauté until the onion is translucent and the garlic is fragrant, 3 to 4 minutes. Add the rice and tomato paste and stir well to coat the rice evenly. Cook for 1 minute to fry the tomato paste. Add the chicken stock, coconut milk, cumin, cayenne, and pigeon peas and stir well. Bring to a boil, then reduce the heat to a simmer. Partially cover the pan and simmer until the rice is tender and all the liquid has evaporated, 18 to 20 minutes. Fluff with a fork, cover, and set aside.

RECIPE CONTINUES →

The official fried fish of Flavortown.

RECIPE CONTINUED FROM PAGE 251

2 garlic cloves, minced

2 teaspoons kosher salt

2½ cups uncooked long-grain white rice

2 tablespoons tomato paste

3 cups Chicken Stock (page 228 or low-sodium store-bought)

One 14-ounce can coconut milk

1 teaspoon ground cumin

¼ teaspoon cayenne pepper

Two 15-ounce cans pigeon peas (gandulas), drained

Cuban fried fish

Canola oil, for deep frying

1½ cups all-purpose flour

½ cup cornstarch

1 tablespoon ground cumin

1 tablespoon paprika

2 teaspoons granulated garlic

1 teaspoon onion powder

2 teaspoons kosher salt

1 teaspoon freshly ground black pepper

1 large (about 2½-pound) whole red snapper, or 2 small (1¼-pound) snappers, scaled, gutted, and cleaned

3 In a Dutch oven or other heavy pot large enough to hold the fish, pour enough canola oil so that the fish can be covered by 1 inch. Heat the oil over high heat to 350°F. Set a wire rack over several layers of paper towels.

4 Meanwhile, in a large baking pan, combine the flour, cornstarch, cumin, paprika, granulated garlic, onion powder, salt, and pepper. Mix until well blended.

5 Cut deep, diagonal slices 1 inch apart into the sides of the snapper. Dredge the whole fish in the flour mixture, making sure to thoroughly dredge inside the just-cut slices. Shake off any excess flour.

6 Holding the fish by the tail, gently lower it headfirst into the hot oil and submerge as much of the fish as you can. If the tail is not completely submerged, use a large metal spoon to baste it with hot oil as the fish cooks. Cook until very crispy, 10 to 12 minutes.

7 Using tongs and a metal spatula, carefully remove the fish from the oil and let the excess oil drip off. Transfer to the wire rack to drain.

8 Spread the pigeon pea rice on a platter and place the fish upright on top of it (the rice will help it stand upright). Generously spoon the mojo over the fish. Serve.

Roasted Bone Marrow
with Grilled Sourdough and Bacon Marmalade

If the thought of eating bone marrow weirds you out, I'm not going to try to talk you into it. But if you're even a little curious about what all the buttery, meaty, succulent fuss is about, here's how you do it. (Okay, maybe I will try **just a little bit** to talk you into it.)

One important note—have your butcher cut the bones so it's really easy for you to get to the good stuff.

MAKES **4 servings** • *TIME* **1 hour 15 minutes**

Bacon marmalade

1 tablespoon extra-virgin olive oil

1/2 pound applewood smoked bacon, cut into 1/4-inch dice

1 large red onion, thinly sliced

1/4 cup lightly packed light brown sugar

2 tablespoons maple syrup

1 teaspoon red wine vinegar

1/4 teaspoon kosher salt

3 or 4 turns freshly ground black pepper

Sourdough toast

1/2 sourdough baguette, cut into 1/4-inch-thick slices

1/4 cup extra-virgin olive oil

Roasted bones

8 large beef marrow bones, split open lengthwise (about 5 pounds)

2 garlic cloves, minced or grated

2 tablespoons extra-virgin olive oil

4 thyme sprigs

1 To make the bacon marmalade, combine the olive oil and bacon in a medium skillet. Cook over medium heat for 7 to 8 minutes, or until the fat has rendered from the bacon and the bacon is golden brown. Add the onion and sauté until browned, 8 to 9 minutes. Add the brown sugar, maple syrup, vinegar, salt, pepper, and 2 tablespoons water. Mix well and bring to a boil. Reduce the heat to a simmer. Cook for 18 to 20 minutes, until the bacon and onion are very soft and the marmalade has thickened, adding water as necessary to keep the mixture from getting too dry. Remove from the heat and let cool. The marmalade can be stored in an airtight container in the refrigerator for up to 2 weeks.

2 Preheat the oven to 450°F and arrange a rack in the center of the oven.

3 To make the toast, brush the bread slices on both sides with olive oil and place on a rimmed baking sheet. Bake until golden brown, 3 to 4 minutes, turning once. Set aside.

4 To roast the bones, place the bones cut side up on two large rimmed baking sheets. In a small bowl, combine the garlic and olive oil. Using a pastry brush, lightly brush the mixture on the top of each marrow bone. Sprinkle the thyme over the top and season with flaky sea salt and pepper.

5 Roast until the marrow is soft and has begun to separate from the bone, 15 to 20 minutes, depending on the thickness of the bones.

2 teaspoons flaky sea salt

6 to 8 turns freshly ground black pepper

Juice and grated zest of 1 lemon, for serving

6 Arrange the bones on a platter and sprinkle on top a squeeze of lemon juice and a little grated lemon zest.

7 Serve with the grilled sourdough toasts and the bacon marmalade. To eat, scoop the marrow out of the bones, spread it on the grilled sourdough toasts, and top with a spoonful of bacon marmalade.

Turkey Pastrami

This is a recipe from way back, when my buddies and I formed our BBQ team, Motley Que, and began playing around with brining, curing, and cooking all sorts of meats. I love pastrami, man, and I got to thinking about whether it was possible to get that intense flavor into something a little healthier. It turns out turkey is the perfect canvas for it. It's got the right texture and stands up beautifully to the brining and curing that make great pastrami. But you don't only get great-tasting, healthier pastrami out of this recipe; you also get to turn your regular oven into a kickin' smoker! (Ya might want to turn off your smoke detector for a little while—just make sure to turn it back on when you're done!)

This makes killer sandwiches, sliced thin, and served on pumpernickel or rye.

MAKES **about 4 pounds** • *TIME* **2 hours, plus 3 to 4 days for brining and curing**

Brine

1/4 cup lightly packed dark brown sugar
1/4 cup kosher salt
1/4 cup crushed juniper berries
1/4 cup freshly cracked black peppercorns
8 garlic cloves, smashed
Pinch of red chili flakes
2 cups ice cubes

One 5-pound boneless, skinless turkey breast

Spice rub

1/2 cup juniper berries
1/4 cup black peppercorns
1/4 cup lightly packed dark brown sugar
1 teaspoon red chili flakes

Special equipment

1 cup hickory chips

1 To prepare the brine, in a large saucepan combine 2 cups water and all the ingredients except the ice cubes and mix well. Heat over high heat, stirring, until the sugar and salt have dissolved. Remove from the heat and add the ice cubes to cool. Set aside to cool completely.

2 Place the turkey breast and the brine in a 2-gallon resealable plastic bag. Seal the bag and place it in another resealable bag. Place the bags in a shallow pan and refrigerate for 2 to 3 days.

In case there are any small holes.

3 To prepare the spice rub, pulse the juniper berries and peppercorns in a spice grinder until well ground. Transfer to a small bowl and add the brown sugar and chili flakes.

4 Remove the turkey breast from the brine and dry well with paper towels. Rub the spice rub evenly all over the turkey. Wrap tightly in plastic wrap and refrigerate for about 24 hours.

5 When ready to cook, place the hickory chips in a bowl and cover with water, making sure the chips are completely submerged. Soak for 15 minutes. While the chips are soaking, place an oven rack 4 inches below the broiler and preheat the broiler to high.

6 Fold a 2-foot-long sheet of heavy-duty aluminum foil crosswise in half and crimp the edges up slightly to create a rim. Place the foil on a rimmed baking sheet. Drain the hickory chips and spread them on top of the foil. Broil for 5 to 7 minutes, until smoking, stirring the chips occasionally to promote more smoking. Remove the baking sheet from the oven. Push the chips to one side of the foil. Fold the other half of the foil up and over the top of the chips and crimp the edges to close and create a sealed pouch. Poke several holes in the top of the package with a knife to release smoke. Place on the bottom rack of the oven. Heat the oven to 250°F.

7 Unwrap the turkey breast and put it on a rack set on a rimmed baking sheet. Place the baking sheet on an oven rack above the "smoker" and roast for 1 hour.

8 Increase the oven temperature to 325°F, then carefully turn the breast over and roast until the internal temperature reaches 160°F on an instant-read thermometer, 30 to 35 minutes.

9 Cover loosely and let cool, then slice and serve. To store, tightly wrap the unsliced pastrami in plastic wrap and store in the refrigerator for 3 to 5 days.

BREAKFAST & BRUNCH

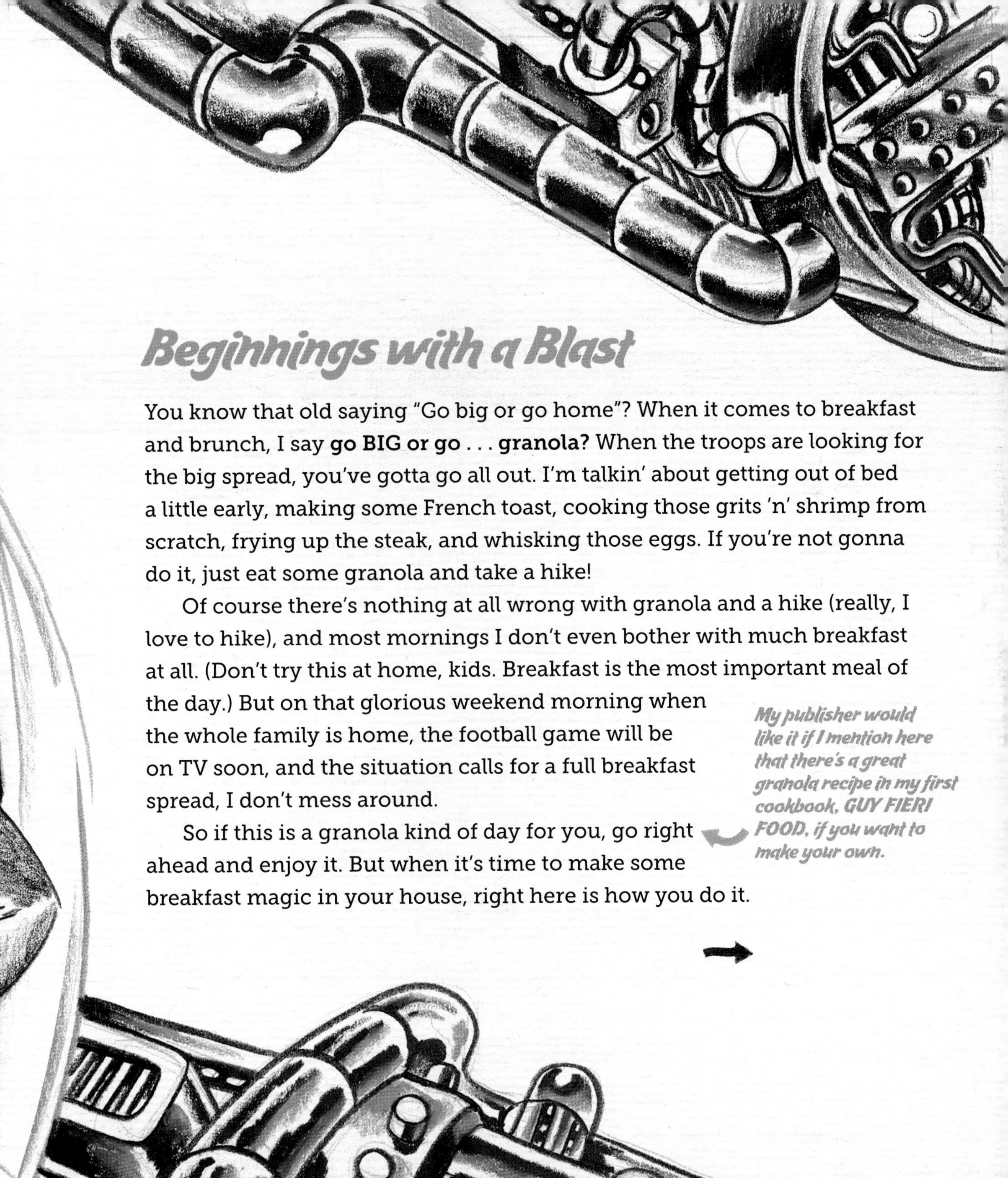

Beginnings with a Blast

You know that old saying "Go big or go home"? When it comes to breakfast and brunch, I say **go BIG or go . . . granola?** When the troops are looking for the big spread, you've gotta go all out. I'm talkin' about getting out of bed a little early, making some French toast, cooking those grits 'n' shrimp from scratch, frying up the steak, and whisking those eggs. If you're not gonna do it, just eat some granola and take a hike!

Of course there's nothing at all wrong with granola and a hike (really, I love to hike), and most mornings I don't even bother with much breakfast at all. (Don't try this at home, kids. Breakfast is the most important meal of the day.) But on that glorious weekend morning when the whole family is home, the football game will be on TV soon, and the situation calls for a full breakfast spread, I don't mess around.

So if this is a granola kind of day for you, go right ahead and enjoy it. But when it's time to make some breakfast magic in your house, right here is how you do it.

My publisher would like it if I mention here that there's a great granola recipe in my first cookbook, GUY FIERI FOOD, if you want to make your own.

→

Vodka Lox
with Herbed Cream Cheese and Everything Bagels

There's something special about salmon and vodka. If you've never tried this ridiculously good combination, and if by chance you've never cured your own salmon, you've definitely come to the right place. First you're gonna coat a nice side of salmon with vodka (a swig for you, a swig for the fish, repeat as necessary) and then cure it in a sugar-and-salt mixture. It's not at all difficult, it just takes the time it takes—two 12-hour cures—so don't try to rush it. **And when the salmon is cured you'll be ready for the most real-deal bagel with lox this side of New York City.**

MAKES **4 to 6 servings •** ***TIME*** **1 hour, plus 24 hours for curing the salmon and resting the herbed cream cheese**

Vodka lox

¼ cup vodka

3 garlic cloves, minced

½ teaspoon freshly ground black pepper

1 center-cut skin-on side of fresh salmon (about 2½ pounds), scaled, pin bones removed, belly trimmed

3 cups sugar

3 cups kosher salt

Zest of 2 lemons

1 bunch dill fronds (about 2 cups lightly packed)

Herbed cream cheese

Zest of 1 lemon

2 tablespoons minced chives

2 tablespoons minced dill

2 tablespoons minced flat-leaf parsley

¾ pound (1½ cups) cream cheese, at room temperature

1 To prepare the vodka lox, in a small bowl, combine the vodka, garlic, and pepper. Rub the vodka mixture all over both sides of the salmon.

2 In a large bowl, mix together the sugar, salt, lemon zest, and dill and set aside.

3 Line a rimmed baking sheet with a large piece of plastic wrap. Sprinkle a third of the sugar-salt cure mixture on the plastic. Place the salmon fillet skin side down in the center of the cure mixture. Cover the fillet with half of the remaining cure mixture, mounding it on top and around the fillet so it is well covered (set aside the remaining cure). Wrap the plastic wrap around the salmon. Use more plastic wrap to wrap the fish tightly and completely to keep the cure pressed up very snugly against the fish.

4 Place another baking sheet on top of the fillet and put a weight, such as a few bricks or cans of beans or bottles of vodka, on top to apply pressure. Place in the refrigerator to cure for 12 hours.

This recipe requires precision, so stick as close to 12 hours as possible.

RECIPE CONTINUES 

Wow, what a picture!

RECIPE CONTINUED FROM PAGE 261

½ cup finely chopped fire-roasted red bell pepper (see page 32)

2 tablespoons drained capers, minced

½ cup minced red onion

1 teaspoon kosher salt

5 or 6 turns freshly ground black pepper

For serving

6 everything bagels, sliced in half and toasted

¼ cup Pickled Red Onions (page 294)

Drained nonpareil capers (optional)

Kosher salt (optional)

5 Drain off any juices that have collected and lightly repack the fillet as in step 3 with the remaining sugar-salt cure mixture (the salmon will have shrunk slightly at this stage, so there will be enough cure). Again, put the baking sheet and weights on top. Place in the refrigerator to cure for another 12 hours.

6 To make the herbed cream cheese, in a small bowl, combine the lemon zest, chives, dill, and parsley. Stir well and set aside. In a medium bowl, combine the cream cheese, bell pepper, capers, onion, salt, and pepper and stir with a rubber spatula to blend well. Add the zest and herbs and stir gently until combined. Cover the bowl with plastic wrap and refrigerate overnight to let the flavors meld together.

7 Remove the salmon fillet from the plastic wrap and cure mixture. Rinse under cold running water to remove any excess sugar and salt. Pat the fillet dry with paper towels. Wrap it tightly in plastic and keep refrigerated until ready to serve. (As long as it remains completely wrapped, the lox will last for at least 1 week. Once it's exposed to air it'll last no longer than 1 week—that is, if you don't eat it all up before then. Always use the "smell" test before you eat it.)

8 To cut the salmon, place the fillet skin side down on a cutting board. Holding a knife at a sharp angle to the cutting board, thinly slice large, flat pieces, cutting the salmon away from the skin as you slice and leaving the skin behind.

9 To serve, smear both cut sides of the toasted bagels with herbed cream cheese. On the bottom halves, layer some pickled red onions and stack high with the lox. Add a few capers and a sprinkle of salt, if desired. Top with the bagel tops and serve.

Spring Vegetable Frittata

We have a huge garden at home where we grow . . . well, you name it and we probably grow it. Sometimes it all grows a little faster than we can eat it, and when that happens we bring in our highly technical overripe vegetable management system: chickens! Man, sometimes I think those chickens eat better than we do. But I'll tell ya, the payoff is huge because the eggs they lay have yolks that are **as orange as the sun.** I'll never forget the first day Ryder saw a supermarket egg—he didn't understand that it was the same food as what our hens lay! It just goes to show you how different food is the closer to the source you are. (And that's my shameless plug for your local farmers' market. I hope you didn't blink and miss it.)

MAKES **4 servings** • ***TIME*** **1 hour**

10 large eggs

3/4 cup heavy cream

1 3/4 ounces Parmesan cheese, finely grated (about 1/2 cup)

2 teaspoons kosher salt, plus more for the spinach

Freshly ground black pepper

7 tablespoons extra-virgin olive oil

1/2 cup minced sweet onion

1/2 red bell pepper, seeded and minced

1/2 jalapeño, seeded and minced

8 asparagus, trimmed and finely sliced

1 medium zucchini, sliced into thin half-moons

1 garlic clove, minced

4 cups lightly packed baby spinach

1 tablespoon fresh lemon juice

1 Preheat the oven to 350°F.

2 In a large bowl whisk the eggs until light and frothy, about 1 minute. Add the cream and 1/4 cup of the Parmesan and whisk until well blended. Add 1 teaspoon of the salt and a few turns of pepper. Set aside.

3 In a medium cast-iron skillet, heat 2 tablespoons of the olive oil over medium heat. When the oil is hot, add the onion, bell pepper, jalapeño, asparagus, zucchini, garlic, the remaining salt, and a few turns of pepper. Sauté until the onion is just translucent, 3 to 4 minutes.

4 Raise the heat to high, add 2 tablespoons of the oil to the pan, and stir. Pour the egg mixture into the pan. Using a rubber spatula, gently incorporate the vegetables, stirring the eggs until slightly congealed, 4 to 5 minutes.

5 Transfer the pan to the oven and cook until golden brown on top and slightly puffy in the center, 14 to 16 minutes. Let cool slightly in the pan.

6 In a medium bowl, drizzle the baby spinach with the remaining 3 tablespoons olive oil and the lemon juice. Season with a little salt and pepper and toss gently to coat.

7 To serve, cut the frittata into large pieces and arrange on plates with the spinach on the side. Garnish with the remaining Parmesan and serve.

Louisiana Shrimp with Stone-Ground Grits

I'm not as big a fan of cheesy grits as some people are. All that cheddar or Jack overwhelms the flavor of the real star of the show, which should be the stone-ground grits. What's that? You didn't think grits had flavor? That might be because tasteless *instant* grits are so common. When you think of instant grits, I want you to think of instant pizza. Having trouble? That's because there's no such thing, man. Do yourself a favor and pick up a bag of the real thing, true stone-ground cornmeal. Your grits'll never be the same.

Oh, I know I said no cheese, but a little hit of Parm is never a bad thing, and its deep umami taste balances the stone-ground corn instead of overshadowing it. **You're so gonna love this.**

MAKES **4 to 6 servings •** ***TIME*** **1 hour**

Stone-ground grits

4 cups half-and-half

1 teaspoon kosher salt

2 cups stone-ground cornmeal

3¼ ounces Parmesan cheese, grated (about 1 cup)

2 tablespoons unsalted butter

Shrimp

4 tablespoons extra-virgin olive oil

1 cup minced sweet onion

1 red bell pepper, seeded and minced

1 jalapeño, seeded and minced

2 teaspoons kosher salt

4 garlic cloves, minced

2 tablespoons tomato paste

½ cup Chicken Stock (page 228 or use low-sodium store-bought)

2 tablespoons distilled white vinegar

1 To make the grits, in a heavy-bottomed saucepan over medium-high heat, bring 4 cups water, the half-and-half, and the salt to a boil. Add the cornmeal in a gentle stream, whisking vigorously as you pour it in. Reduce the heat to medium-low and simmer, stirring frequently, for 2 to 3 minutes. Whisk in the Parmesan and cook until thick and creamy, 35 to 40 minutes, stirring every few minutes. Stir in the butter, remove from the heat, cover to keep warm, and set aside.

Make sure to scrape the bottom of the pan each time you stir to prevent sticking.

2 Meanwhile, to prepare the shrimp, heat 2 tablespoons of the olive oil in a large sauté pan over medium heat until hot. Add the onion, bell pepper, jalapeño, and 1 teaspoon of the salt. Sauté until the onion is translucent and lightly browned, 5 to 6 minutes. Add half the garlic and cook for 1 minute, until fragrant.

3 Add the tomato paste and sauté for 2 minutes to coat the vegetables. Deglaze the pan by adding the chicken stock, vinegar, Worcestershire sauce, and hot sauce and scraping up the browned bits from the bottom

2 tablespoons Worcestershire sauce

1 tablespoon Louisiana hot sauce

1½ pounds 31/35 (large) shrimp, peeled, deveined, and butterflied

¼ teaspoon cayenne pepper

5 or 6 turns freshly ground black pepper

2 tablespoons chopped flat-leaf parsley

4 tablespoons (½ stick) unsalted butter, cubed

½ cup finely sliced green onions (white and light green parts), for garnish

of the pan. Bring to a boil, then reduce the heat and simmer, stirring often, until the sauce has reduced by one-third, 9 to 10 minutes.

4 Pour two-thirds of the sauce into a large bowl and the remainder into a blender. Puree until smooth, about 1 minute. Transfer to the bowl with the unpureed sauce and mix together. Set aside.

This thickens the sauce.

5 Season the shrimp with the remaining 1 teaspoon salt, the cayenne, and the black pepper. Pour the remaining 2 tablespoons olive oil into the now-empty sauté pan and heat it over medium-high heat until hot. Add the shrimp and sauté both sides, until it starts to curl and change color, 3 to 4 minutes. Add the remaining garlic and cook for 1 minute, until fragrant. Add the parsley and the reserved vegetable sauce and bring to a simmer, then reduce the heat and cook until the shrimp are completely pink and the sauce has slightly thickened, about 2 minutes. Add the butter and swirl the pan to melt it into the sauce. Remove from the heat.

6 To serve, pour the grits onto a large serving platter. Spoon the sauce and shrimp over the top. Garnish with green onions and serve.

Big Breakfast Burrito

This is the perfect breakfast to make for everybody when they're headed out for a hunting trip, sporting event, or anything else that requires the crew to get up before the sun does. To take these big burritos to go, wrap 'em up tight in foil and they'll stay nice and warm.

MAKES **4 servings** • ***TIME*** **45 minutes**

8 large eggs

1 tablespoon kosher salt

8 to 10 turns freshly ground black pepper

4 tablespoons canola oil

1 cup diced sweet onion

½ pound diced unpeeled potatoes

4 garlic cloves, minced

Four 12-inch flour tortillas

½ pound pepper Jack cheese, grated (about 2 cups)

2 cups finely sliced lettuce

1 pound skirt steak, grilled (see Ancho Skirt Steak Hash with Red Pepper Hollandaise, page 271, or Java-Rubbed Bone-in Rib-Eye Steak with Habanero Butter, 246)

½ cup Salsa Rojo (page 291)

1 cup Roasted Tomatillo Salsa (page 289)

1 cup Pico de Gallo (page 290)

Hot sauce, for serving

1 lime, cut into wedges, for serving

1 In a large bowl, whisk the eggs and season with half the salt and pepper. Heat 1 tablespoon of the canola oil in a medium nonstick sauté pan over medium heat. Add the eggs and scramble, stirring with a rubber spatula, until firm, about 2 minutes. Transfer to a plate and set aside.

2 Heat 1 tablespoon of the canola oil in a large sauté pan over medium-high heat until hot. Add the onion and remaining salt and sauté until translucent, 4 to 5 minutes. Reduce the heat to medium and add the potatoes. Cook until the potatoes are tender and lightly browned, about 10 minutes. Add the garlic and cook for 1 minute, until fragrant. Remove from the heat and set aside.

3 Preheat a griddle to medium-high. Pour the remaining 2 tablespoons canola oil on the hot griddle and spread it over the whole surface.

4 While the griddle is heating, assemble the breakfast burritos. Place the flour tortillas on a flat surface and sprinkle each one liberally with cheese, keeping a 1-inch edge clean all around the perimeter of the tortilla. Divide each of the following equally among the tortillas, spreading each one evenly across the burrito, keeping the 1-inch edge clear: lettuce, sliced steak, the potato-and-onion mixture, and the scrambled eggs. Spoon some salsa rojo on top of each.

5 If necessary, use the back of a spoon to spread the fillings out to 1 inch from the edge of the tortillas. Working with one at a time, fold two opposite sides of the tortilla up around the fillings. While holding those in place with your fingers, use your thumbs to flip the bottom part of the tortilla up and close it over the filling, then continue to roll forward to tightly enclose the filling. Repeat this process with the remaining burritos.

6 Place the burritos fold side down on the griddle and cook for 2 to 3 minutes to melt the cheese and brown the burrito while sealing up the wrap. Flip and cook on the other side for 2 to 3 minutes. Remove the burritos from the griddle and wrap each burrito tightly in foil to keep warm.

7 Serve with the roasted tomatillo salsa, pico de gallo, hot sauce, and lime wedges.

Nice burrito in a foil tuxedo!

Ancho Skirt Steak Hash
with Red Pepper Hollandaise

Hash originated as a way to use up leftovers. **It was all about preserving, repurposing, and economizing.** Back in the day people couldn't store whatever might be left from last night's dinner for very long, and no one would have dreamed of throwing good food away anyway. They'd chop up whatever meat, vegetable, and starch was left from the day before, fry it all up in a skillet, maybe drop an egg on top, and breakfast was served. This is probably part of the reason that the key to the best hash—one that's crispy and browned—is never to begin with raw potatoes. They tend to steam more than brown, so even though they're cooked, there's no texture. When the potatoes are already cooked before they hit that pan, they'll get browned and full of flavor. That's why almost every time I'm baking or steaming potatoes for any reason, I throw a few extra in . . . for breakfast.

By the same token, this recipe for griddled ancho steak is righteous (and makes killer burritos—see page 268), but if you've already got leftover steak or other protein from last night, use it instead.

MAKES **4 servings** • *TIME* **1 hour**

Dry rub

¼ cup All-Purpose Dry Rub (page 301)

1 teaspoon instant espresso powder

Steak

One 1½-pound skirt steak, trimmed and cut into 2 chunks

Canola oil, for the griddle

½ pound asparagus, root ends trimmed, sliced on the bias ¼ inch thick

¼ cup extra-virgin olive oil, plus more for the asparagus

1½ teaspoons kosher salt, plus more for the asparagus

Freshly ground black pepper

1 To prepare the rub, combine all the ingredients in a small bowl and stir until well mixed. Remove and set aside 1 tablespoon of the mixture. Rub the remainder all over the steaks.

2 Preheat a large cast-iron griddle over high heat. Soak a paper towel with canola oil and thoroughly rub it over the surface of the griddle to clean it and create a nonstick surface. Cook the steaks on one side until well seared, about 8 minutes. Flip the steaks and cook for 4 more minutes. Remove the steaks from the griddle and set aside to rest for 10 minutes.

3 While the steaks are cooking, toss the asparagus with a drizzle of olive oil and a few pinches of salt and black pepper.

4 Pour the olive oil into a skillet and heat over medium-high heat. Add the halved potatoes, the reserved 1 tablespoon of rub, ¾ teaspoon of the salt,

RECIPE CONTINUES →

RECIPE CONTINUED FROM PREVIOUS PAGE

½ pound baby bliss potatoes, boiled until tender, then halved (about 2 cups)

1 small yellow onion, cut into ¼-inch slices

1 medium red bell pepper, seeded and cut into ¼-inch slices

½ medium green bell pepper, seeded and cut into ¼-inch slices

2 garlic cloves, minced

Roasted Red Pepper Hollandaise (recipe follows), for serving

¼ cup finely sliced green onions (white and light green parts), for garnish

¼ teaspoon smoked paprika, for garnish

and a few turns of black pepper. Cook until golden brown all over, about 10 minutes.

5 Add the asparagus, onion, bell peppers, and garlic. Cook for 5 to 7 minutes, until the vegetables are wilted and cooked through. Season with the remaining ¾ teaspoon salt and a few more turns of black pepper and stir well.

6 Slice the steak against the grain into ½-inch strips. Arrange the steak on top of the hash in the pan. Drizzle liberally with hollandaise and garnish with chopped green onions and a sprinkle of smoked paprika. Serve family style in the pan.

Roasted Red Pepper Hollandaise

MAKES **about 2 cups**

3 large egg yolks

1 tablespoon fresh lemon juice, plus more as needed

½ teaspoon smoked paprika

½ teaspoon salt, plus more as needed

Pinch of cayenne pepper, plus more as needed

10 tablespoons (1 stick plus 2 tablespoons) unsalted butter, melted

2 red bell peppers, fire-roasted (see page 32) and sliced

1 Place the egg yolks, lemon juice, paprika, salt, and cayenne in a blender. Blend at medium speed until lightened in color, about 25 seconds. Reduce the speed and, with the blender running, slowly drizzle in the melted butter. Add the roasted bell peppers and blend until the mixture is smooth and consistent.

2 Taste for seasoning and add more salt, cayenne, or lemon juice if desired. Transfer to a small saucepan and keep warm over very low heat, stirring frequently, until ready to use.

3 Store any unused sauce in an airtight container in the refrigerator for 1 day (hollandaise is always great on eggs). Gently reheat in a saucepan over very low heat, whisking constantly until warm.

Stacked French Toast
with Berries and Lemon-Vanilla Cream Cheese

When it comes to French toast, the key is always to begin with thick batter and thick slices of bread. When these elements are too thin, the liquid gets absorbed so quickly that the result is just hot, soggy bread with no bite. **Thick bread like Texas toast and a nice, dense batter gets you the spongy, cakey texture I'm talkin' about.**

MAKES **4 to 6 servings •** ***TIME*** **1½ hours**

Macerated berries

1 pint strawberries, hulled and quartered

1 pint raspberries

1 pint blackberries

¼ cup sugar

Lemon-vanilla cream cheese

¾ pound whipped cream cheese, at room temperature

¼ cup powdered sugar

1 teaspoon pure vanilla extract

Grated zest of 1 lemon

French toast

2 cups half-and-half

6 large eggs

2 tablespoons sugar

2 teaspoons pure vanilla extract

1 teaspoon ground cinnamon

4 or 5 gratings of nutmeg

12 slices Texas toast

4 tablespoons (½ stick) unsalted butter, for cooking

1 To prepare the berries, combine all the ingredients in a medium bowl and stir well. Cover and refrigerate for at least 30 minutes and up to overnight.

2 To prepare the cream cheese, combine all the ingredients in a medium bowl and stir well until completely mixed together. Set aside at room temperature. For longer storage, transfer to an airtight container and refrigerate for up to 5 to 7 days. Set out at room temperature for 20 minutes before serving.

3 To prepare the French toast, place the half-and-half, eggs, sugar, vanilla, cinnamon, and nutmeg in a flat, rimmed dish large enough to hold the bread in a single layer (such as a baking sheet). Whisk to combine, until the sugar has dissolved. Place the bread in the batter, turning to coat thoroughly. Arrange the toast slices evenly in the dish, cover loosely with plastic wrap, and set aside in the refrigerator until the bread completely soaks up the batter, about 15 minutes.

I hate doing dishes, so I do it right in the flat dish. If that's not your gig and you don't mind washing an extra dish, whisk it in a large bowl and pour it into the flat dish.

4 Heat a large, flat griddle over medium heat until hot. Place a tablespoon of the butter on the griddle and spread it evenly. Cook 3 slices of bread for 4 to 5 minutes on each side, until golden

RECIPE CONTINUES →

RECIPE CONTINUED FROM PREVIOUS PAGE

1 cup maple syrup, for serving

2 tablespoons powdered sugar, for serving

brown and crispy around the edges. Transfer to a plate and cover with a kitchen towel to keep warm. Repeat with the remaining butter and bread.

5 For each serving, spread some cream cheese on a slice of French toast. Top with a layer of berries and a drizzle of maple syrup. Repeat one or two times for each stack. Dust with powdered sugar and a drizzle of maple syrup. Serve.

Big Warriors fan! Go Dubs!

This is so wrong . . . and yet Ryder thought it was so right.

A one-way ticket back to
childhood Flavortown.

It's pronounced Ay-bel-skee-ver.

Aebleskivers (Cast-Iron Danish Pancakes)

An aebleskiver is a Danish pancake that's kind of a cross between a donut and Yorkshire pudding. It looks a little like a racquetball and tastes (to me, anyway) like all the good, warm, and sweet things from childhood. This is probably because when I was a kid they were a Ferndale tradition thanks to the aebleskiver breakfast hosted by the area Danish Lodges every year. The ladies of the Lodges would begin early in the morning making their batter and heating up their special cast-iron pans, which looked as if they'd make little rounded cupcakes. By the time they were ready to open the doors, there was a line down the street, but there was no rushing those nice ladies or the aebleskivers themselves.

Poured into the piping-hot oiled pans, the batter would sizzle and pop as it cooked and the amazing aroma would carry all the way down the street to my mom and dad's Western clothing store. They'd send me up to wait in line and secure a bag to bring back to the shop. I'd watch as each aebleskiver was turned little by little with two long toothpicks so that each turn cooked a little more of the batter, until each one was a perfect sphere. I'd get my bagful and run back to the store; I can remember like it was yesterday how the smell of those still-warm aebleskivers would fill the whole store when I opened the bag. Now I don't have to just remember it, though, because whenever I want to relive it, I've got this recipe. And now you do, too!

MAKES **about 20 aebleskivers** • ***TIME*** **45 minutes**

2 large eggs

2 cups buttermilk

4 tablespoons (1/2 stick) unsalted butter, melted

2 cups all-purpose flour

2 teaspoons baking powder

1 tablespoon sugar

1/2 teaspoon baking soda

1/2 teaspoon kosher salt

1/4 teaspoon ground cinnamon

1 Preheat the oven to 350°F. Place the aebleskiver pan in the oven for at least 15 minutes. (If your pan is electric, you can skip the oven and turn the pan on according to the manufacturer's instructions to preheat it.)

2 Have ready a small bowl and a clean, dry large bowl. Separate the eggs, dropping the whites into the large bowl and the yolks into the small one. Add the buttermilk and melted butter to the egg yolks. Whisk to combine and set aside. With a clean whisk or electric mixer, whisk the egg whites until they hold stiff peaks. Set aside.

RECIPE CONTINUES →

← *RECIPE CONTINUED FROM PREVIOUS PAGE*

1 cup vegetable oil, or as needed, for cooking

2 to 3 tablespoons powdered sugar, for serving

1 cup lingonberry preserves, for serving

Special equipment

Aebleskiver pan (you can find these pans in cooking equipment stores or online)

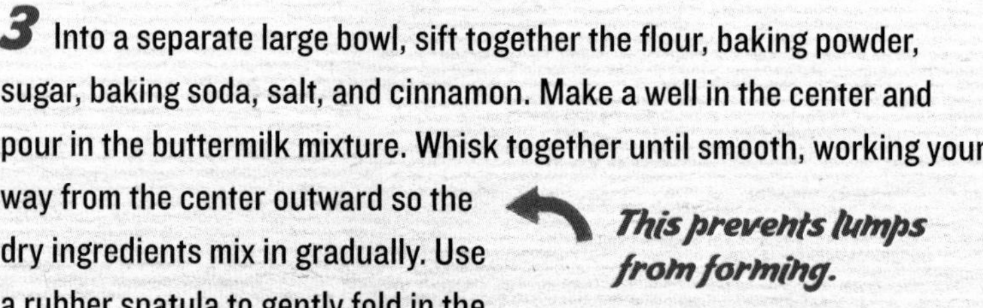

3 Into a separate large bowl, sift together the flour, baking powder, sugar, baking soda, salt, and cinnamon. Make a well in the center and pour in the buttermilk mixture. Whisk together until smooth, working your way from the center outward so the dry ingredients mix in gradually. Use a rubber spatula to gently fold in the egg whites; don't overmix so that the batter stays nice and light—it's fine if there are some streaks of egg white.

This prevents lumps from forming.

4 Line a large bowl with a clean kitchen towel. Place the hot aebleskiver pan over medium heat.

5 Pour 2 teaspoons of the vegetable oil into each cup in the pan and heat until hot. Put 2 tablespoons of batter into each cup (each cup should be filled about two-thirds with batter). Cook until bubbling and firm around the edges, about 2 minutes. Using two toothpicks, quickly and carefully turn each pancake over so the cooked dome is on top and the uncooked batter that was on top drips out to form the bottom half of the sphere. Cook on the second side until golden brown and crispy, about 3 minutes. Carefully remove the pancakes from the pan and place them in the bowl. Loosely cover with the towel to keep warm. Repeat with the remaining batter, adding 2 teaspoons vegetable oil to each cup before each batch to prevent sticking.

6 Serve warm, dusted with powdered sugar and with lingonberry preserves on the side.

Two-Way Waffles

My mom was the original Waffle Queen. When I was a kid, the mornings she'd plug in her old waffle iron and start mixing up the batter, I couldn't sit still watching her and waiting for the first crispy-on-the-outside, tender-in-the-middle waffle to come off that iron. Oh, that iron. It was a real piece of work. It gave off sparks and didn't work sometimes . . . I think it came over on the *Mayflower*! Can you imagine my devastation when every now and then it would go off completely? My little heart would sink!

Now my family loves waffles, but they didn't love them as much as I did until we featured Funk 'n' Waffles in Syracuse, New York, on *Diners, Drive-ins and Dives* a few years back. Those guys make the most righteous waffles I've ever tasted, and their approach—perfect buttermilk waffles served with any of a couple dozen or more sweet or savory accompaniments—is my inspiration for these waffles. Whip up both fillings—sweet cinnamon apples and ham and melting Brie—and a full batch of waffles so people can choose whether they want sweet or savory. Just make sure your waffle iron is on point before you begin.

MAKES **4 to 6 servings** • ***TIME*** **1 hour**

Cinnamon apple filling

4 Granny Smith apples, peeled, cored, and thinly sliced

4 tablespoons (½ stick) unsalted butter

½ cup granulated sugar

1 teaspoon ground cinnamon

Pinch of ground cloves

2 tablespoons powdered sugar, for serving

Ham and Brie filling

6 ounces shaved maple ham, coarsely chopped

1½ tablespoons unsalted butter

¼ pound Brie cheese, cut into ¼-inch cubes, at room temperature

Dijonnaise Sauce (page 281), for serving

1 To prepare the cinnamon apple filling, in a large sauté pan over medium-high heat, cook the apples in the butter until the apples are softened, 2 to 3 minutes. Add the granulated sugar, cinnamon, and cloves and sauté until the apples are caramelized with sugar, 4 to 5 minutes. Remove from the heat and set aside to cool completely.

2 To prepare the ham and Brie filling, in a medium sauté pan over medium-high heat, cook the ham in the butter until the butter is bubbling and nutty and the ham is browned, 2 to 3 minutes. Remove from the heat and set aside to cool completely. Stir in the Brie cubes.

3 To prepare the waffle batter, have ready a small bowl and a clean, dry medium bowl. Separate the eggs, dropping the whites into the medium bowl and the yolks into the small one. Whisk the yolks until pale and set aside. With a clean whisk or a hand mixer, whisk the whites until they hold firm peaks. Set aside.

RECIPE CONTINUES →

← RECIPE CONTINUED FROM PREVIOUS PAGE

French waffles

2 large eggs

1½ cups fine cornmeal

1¼ cups all-purpose flour

1 tablespoon baking powder

1 teaspoon sugar

1 teaspoon kosher salt

1¾ cups buttermilk

4 tablespoons (½ stick) butter, melted

4 In a large bowl, whisk together the cornmeal, flour, baking powder, sugar, and salt. Make a well in the center and add the buttermilk, melted butter, and beaten egg yolks. Whisk until smooth, working your way from the center outward so the dry ingredients are gradually incorporated. Use a rubber spatula to gently fold in the egg whites; don't overmix so that the batter stays nice and light—it's fine if there are some streaks of egg white.

This prevents lumps from forming.

5 Preheat a waffle maker and preheat the oven to 325°F. Place a wire rack over a baking sheet.

6 Transfer half of the waffle batter to another bowl. To one bowl of batter add the ham and Brie filling and mix well. To the other bowl of batter add 1 cup of the cinnamon apple filling and mix well (reserve the remaining apple filling for garnish).

7 To cook the waffles, working in batches and cooking all of one type before the other, ladle the batter onto the waffle iron (follow the manufacturers' instructions). Cook until the waffles are crispy and golden brown, 3 to 4 minutes. Place the waffles on the wire rack and keep them warm in the oven as you finish cooking the rest of the batter.

8 To serve the cinnamon apple waffles, place the waffles on large round plates. Spoon some of the reserved apple filling on top and dust with powdered sugar.

9 To serve the ham and Brie waffles, place the waffles on large round plates. Drizzle some Dijonnaise sauce on top.

Dijonnaise Sauce

MAKES **1½ cups**

- 1 cup mayonnaise
- ¼ cup heavy cream
- Juice and grated zest of 1 lemon
- 2 tablespoons minced chives
- 2 tablespoons drained capers, minced
- 2 tablespoons Dijon mustard
- 3 or 4 dashes of Worcestershire sauce
- Pinch of cayenne pepper
- 3 or 4 turns freshly ground black pepper

1. Combine all the ingredients in a small bowl and whisk until smooth.
2. Use at once or cover and refrigerate until needed.

Sweet and savory waffles in a single recipe? What a world we live in!

SAUCES & SALSAS

The First and Last Stop on the Flavor Train

Even though we're getting close to the end of the book, the fact is that the recipes in this chapter are the foundation of many of the recipes in the rest of the book. Ya know, the catchphrase "building flavor" is tossed around a lot these days, but it's important to understand something fundamental about it. Complex flavor isn't something you magically apply at the end of cooking. When you taste a barbecued pork rib or roasted chicken and you have that moment of revelation—"Wait a second—**why does that taste so fantastic?!**"—it's likely because whoever cooked it began with quality ingredients and then took a little extra time to brine it and cover it in a spice rub. And when the sauce, dressing, or salsa served with it is also totally on point, then all the components work together to make something that's smokin'.

These sorts of flavor builders are kinda like the backup singers in a band. You may

→

not consciously notice them, but without them something would definitely be missing. If you listen carefully, you can tell that they're setting up the lead singer to sound great. In the same way, a good brine, rub, and sauce are the unsung heroes on the plate: You may not be able to pick out each one individually, but they're the difference between a regular dish and a dish that comes straight from Flavortown.

Salsa Molcajete

This "house salsa" at El Burro Borracho is restrained in terms of heat but there's nothing restrained about its bright flavor and awesome texture. You don't need an authentic *molcajete* and *tejolote*—a stone mortar and pestle—to make this real-deal salsa, but if you have one, you'll be just a little more legit.

MAKES **about 4 cups** • ***TIME*** **30 minutes**

6 Roma tomatoes, cored and halved

1/4 sweet onion, diced

1 serrano chile, halved and seeded

6 garlic cloves, coarsely chopped

2 tablespoons extra-virgin olive oil

2 teaspoons kosher salt

2 tablespoons chopped cilantro

1 teaspoon ground cumin

Juice of 1 lime

1 Place an oven rack 6 inches from the broiler and preheat the broiler to high.

2 Spread the tomatoes, onion, serrano, and garlic on a rimmed baking sheet. Drizzle with the olive oil and season with a pinch of the salt. Broil until the edges of the vegetables are charred and black, 8 to 10 minutes. Let cool slightly.

3 Place a quarter of the mixture in a food processor and pulse until pureed. Pound the remaining ingredients in a molcajete until they're well mixed together but still have some texture and chunkiness. (Alternatively, coarsely chop the remaining ingredients into 1/4-inch pieces.)

4 In a medium bowl, combine the crushed or chopped vegetables with the pureed vegetables. Add the cilantro, cumin, lime juice, and the remaining salt. Mix well and serve. Store in an airtight container in the refrigerator for up to 3 days.

Guy's Guac Bar

The idea for a full guacamole "bar" with all sorts of different toppings and stir-ins first came to me when we were creating the menu for El Burro Borracho, where we didn't want to offer just ordinary guac, and it's turned into one of the most popular things we serve. But you don't have to make a trip to Nevada for this sort of awesomeness (although if you're there, stop in to see us in Laughlin or Vegas!). All you've gotta do is mix up some avocado and lime and set up some sliced and diced additions so that each member of the crew can mix up their own signature concoctions.

MAKES **6 to 8 servings** • ***TIME*** **30 minutes**

2 tablespoons canola oil

½ pound uncooked (Mexican) chorizo

Kosher salt

¼ cup frozen shelled edamame

¼ cup pepitas

Freshly ground black pepper

1 fresh corn cob, husked and silks removed

4 ripe Hass avocados, pitted and peeled

Juice of 1 lime

2 tablespoons chopped cilantro

1 teaspoon flaky sea salt

4 small radishes, cut into fine matchsticks

1 ounce Cotija cheese, crumbled (about ¼ cup)

½ cup Pico de Gallo (page 290)

¼ cup diced fire-roasted poblanos (see page 32)

Tortilla chips, for serving

1 In a large sauté pan, heat the canola oil over medium heat until hot. Add the chorizo and cook until fragrant and lightly browned, 5 to 7 minutes, using a wooden spoon to break up the chorizo as it cooks. Transfer to a small serving bowl and cover loosely with foil to keep warm.

2 Bring a small saucepan of water to a boil. Add several pinches of kosher salt and the edamame. Boil for 2 to 3 minutes, until bright green and tender. Drain and set aside to cool, then transfer to a small serving bowl.

3 Toast the pepitas in a dry skillet over high heat for 3 to 4 minutes, until browned, shaking the pan as they cook so they brown evenly. Season with salt and black pepper and transfer to a small serving bowl.

4 Heat a grill to high, or set an oven rack 6 inches from the heat source and heat a broiler to high. Grill or broil the corn for 4 minutes on each side, until charred all over. Let cool slightly, then stand the corn upright in a large bowl (to catch the kernels) and, using a sharp knife, cut down to remove the kernels from the cob. Set the kernels aside in a small serving bowl.

5 In a large bowl (or molcajete; see page 285), crush the avocados with a fork (or tejolote) until well broken up. Add the lime juice, cilantro, flaky sea salt, and black pepper to taste. Mix to combine.

6 Place the radishes, Cotija, pico de gallo, and poblanos in small serving bowls. Serve the avocado with all the condiments around it and a big bowl of chips.

Roasted Tomatillo Salsa (opposite), Spicy Mango Habanero Salsa (page 290), Salsa Molcajete (page 285).

Roasted Tomatillo Salsa

(Salsa Verde)

This mild salsa is great for kids or anyone who prefers a little less of a spice kick. And if you haven't tried tomatillos—canned or fresh—well, you're in for a surprise.

MAKES **3 cups** • *TIME* **35 minutes**

- 8 fresh tomatillos, husks removed, well rinsed
- 2 tablespoons extra-virgin olive oil
- 1/4 sweet onion, diced
- 2 garlic cloves, minced
- 3 tablespoons chopped cilantro
- 1 tablespoon distilled white vinegar
- 2 tablespoons hot sauce, or to taste
- 1/2 teaspoon ground cumin
- 1 teaspoon kosher salt
- 4 or 5 turns freshly ground black pepper

1. Set an oven rack 6 inches from the heat source and preheat the broiler to high. Rub the tomatillos with the olive oil and place them on a rimmed baking sheet. Broil until browned all over, turning occasionally, 7 to 8 minutes.

2. In a blender, blend the tomatillos, onion, garlic, cilantro, vinegar, hot sauce, cumin, salt, and pepper until the mixture is well broken down but still has some texture.

3. Serve at room temperature. Store in an airtight container in the refrigerator for up to 3 days.

Spicy Mango Habanero Salsa

Combining fiery habaneros with sweet, juicy mango tames their bite and results in a balanced salsa with great kick and not too much heat.

MAKES **4 cups** • ***TIME*** **15 minutes, plus 1 hour for chilling**

- 3 ripe but firm mangos, peeled, seeded, and cut into ¼-inch dice
- ¼ cup fire-roasted red bell pepper (see page 32), cut into ¼-inch dice
- ½ red onion, cut into ¼-inch dice
- 1 habanero chile, seeded and minced
- Juice of 1 lime
- 2 tablespoons chopped cilantro
- 2 teaspoons kosher salt

1 In a medium bowl, combine all the ingredients and mix well. Cover and refrigerate for about 1 hour to allow the flavors to meld together.

2 Serve at room temperature. Store in an airtight container in the refrigerator for up to 2 days.

Tip: Wear gloves when you chop the habanero to avoid getting your hands covered in capsaicin, the compound that makes all that heat—I like those black rubber gloves you see in tattoo parlors for this. Also, chop them on a cutting board that you can put in the dishwasher as soon as you're done.

Pico de Gallo

The celery juice adds a bright, grassy flavor, and it's a natural preservative, so it helps extend the shelf life of this classic Mexican fresh red salsa.

MAKES **about 3 cups** • ***TIME*** **15 minutes, plus 1 hour for chilling**

- 4 Roma tomatoes, cored and finely diced
- 2 tablespoons chopped cilantro
- ½ red onion, minced
- 1 garlic clove, minced
- 1 jalapeño, seeded and minced
- Juice of 1 lime
- 1 teaspoon fresh celery juice (optional)
- ½ teaspoon kosher salt
- Freshly ground black pepper

1 In a medium bowl, combine all the ingredients and mix well. Cover and refrigerate for about 1 hour to allow the flavors to meld together.

2 Drain any excess liquid before serving. Store in an airtight container in the refrigerator for up to 3 days.

Salsa Rojo

This smoky red salsa brings the heat to dishes like burritos, chilaquiles, and tacos.

MAKES **about 2 cups** • ***TIME*** **45 minutes**

- 2 dried ancho chiles
- 2 dried guajillo chiles
- 2 dried pasilla chiles
- 4 Roma tomatoes, quartered
- 1 medium sweet onion, sliced
- 1 jalapeño, halved and seeded
- 3 garlic cloves
- 1/4 bunch cilantro, rinsed
- 1 tablespoon Mexican dried oregano
- 1 teaspoon apple cider vinegar
- 1 tablespoon kosher salt

1 Remove the stems and seeds from the dried chiles, and tear them into large pieces.

2 In a large skillet over medium-high heat, toast the chiles until they start to change color, about 2 minutes. Transfer them to a small saucepan and add about 2 cups hot water, or just enough to cover them. Place the pan over medium-low heat and simmer until the chiles are soft and tender, 13 to 15 minutes. Remove from the heat and set aside to cool.

3 Meanwhile, place an oven rack 6 inches from the broiler and preheat the broiler to high.

4 Place the tomatoes, onion, jalapeño, and garlic on a rimmed baking sheet. Broil until the vegetables are well charred on the top, about 10 minutes.

5 Transfer the chiles with their cooking liquid to a blender and puree until smooth, about 2 minutes. Pour into a medium saucepan and set aside.

6 Puree the roasted vegetables, cilantro, and oregano in the blender until smooth. Add to the chiles in the saucepan along with the vinegar and salt.

7 Bring the mixture to a simmer over medium heat and cook gently for 8 to 10 minutes to blend the flavors. Remove from the heat. If the mixture is too thick, thin with a little hot water.

8 Store in an airtight container in the refrigerator for up to 3 days.

Guy Fieri's
PLAYA DEL CARMEN
KITCHEN + BAR

Ranch Dressing

This old-school dressing is my go-to for salads and sandwiches and as a dipping sauce. For a seriously geared-up version, add some sriracha, as on pages 7 and 87.

MAKES **about 3 cups •** ***TIME*** **15 minutes**

1 cup mayonnaise

½ cup buttermilk

½ cup sour cream

3 tablespoons chopped dill

1 teaspoon garlic powder

1 teaspoon onion powder

½ teaspoon paprika

2 teaspoons sugar

Pinch of cayenne pepper

½ teaspoon kosher salt

4 or 5 turns freshly ground black pepper

1 Combine all the ingredients in a medium bowl. Whisk until well combined and creamy in texture.

2 Cover and refrigerate until ready to serve, or for up to 3 to 5 days.

Quick Pickled Vegetables

If this is the first time you've quick-pickled vegetables, you'll wonder why the universe has been keeping this secret hidden from you. With just a few minutes of simmering and enough time to let 'em cool, you can turn all kinds of vegetables tucked in your crisper drawer into tangy, sweet, spicy, crunchy pickles, *and* you get a kickin' brine that's good enough to use as a dressing for grain or chopped vegetable salads. You can use these pickles in place of any giardiniera veggies I call for in this book. If you can't find Fresno chiles where you are, use jalapeño or serrano in their place.

MAKES **about 6 cups** • ***TIME*** **30 minutes, plus cooling time**

1½ cups apple cider vinegar
½ cup superfine sugar
2 teaspoons kosher salt
2 teaspoons ground turmeric
1½ teaspoons celery seed
1½ teaspoons mustard seed
1½ teaspoons dry mustard
2 bay leaves
½ small green cabbage, cut into ½-inch pieces
¼ cauliflower head, cut into bite-size florets
1 carrot, sliced on the bias ½-inch thick
¼ medium daikon radish, peeled and cut into ½-inch dice
½ sweet onion, diced
1 red bell pepper, seeded and julienned
2 Fresno, jalapeño, or serrano chiles, seeded and minced

1 In a large, heavy-bottomed saucepan, combine the vinegar, 1½ cups water, the sugar, salt, turmeric, celery seed, mustard seed, dry mustard, and bay leaves. Bring to a boil over medium-high heat. Reduce the heat and simmer for 5 minutes.

2 Add the cabbage, cauliflower, carrot, daikon, onion, bell pepper, and chiles and return to a boil. Reduce the heat and simmer until the carrots and cauliflower are tender, 7 to 8 minutes. Set the pan aside to cool.

3 Transfer the cooled vegetables with the brine to a covered container and refrigerate until cold. Use at once or store for up to 2 weeks.

Pickled Red Onions

It only takes a few minutes to pull together a pickling brine and slice a couple red onions. Then all you've gotta do is mix it together and cool your heels overnight so they can be transformed into **the ultimate sandwich topping,** as demonstrated by the Pork Chop Torta (page 14). Pickled red onions are also awesome on tacos. Now *that's* sweet.

MAKES **about 1½ cups** • ***TIME*** **15 minutes, plus overnight pickling time**

1 small red beet, peeled and quartered

1 cup red wine vinegar

½ cup sugar

2 tablespoons kosher salt

3 or 4 black peppercorns

1 bay leaf

2 medium red onions, peeled and sliced into thin lengthwise strips

1 In a medium saucepan, combine the beet, vinegar, sugar, salt, peppercorns, bay leaf, and ½ cup water. Bring to a boil over medium-high heat, stirring to dissolve the sugar and salt, 7 to 8 minutes.

2 Place the onions in a large bowl and pour the hot liquid over them. Let cool, then transfer to an airtight container and refrigerate overnight.

3 Remove and discard the beet and bay leaf before serving. Store in the refrigerator for up to 2 weeks.

Pizza Sauce

To make insane—and insanely good—pizzas like the ones on pages 191 and 192, you've gotta have a sick sauce like this one.

MAKES **about 4 cups** • ***TIME*** **45 minutes**

1 tablespoon extra-virgin olive oil
½ medium yellow onion, diced
1 garlic clove, minced
¼ teaspoon red chili flakes
2 tablespoons tomato paste
One 28-ounce can crushed tomatoes
1 teaspoon dried marjoram
1 teaspoon dried oregano
1 tablespoon torn basil leaves
1 teaspoon kosher salt
6 or 7 turns freshly ground black pepper

1 In a large saucepan, heat the olive oil over medium-high heat until hot. Add the onion and sauté until translucent, 3 to 4 minutes. Add the garlic and chili flakes and cook for 1 minute, until fragrant. Add the tomato paste and cook, stirring, for 2 to 3 minutes. Stir in the crushed tomatoes. Reduce the heat to a simmer and cook for 20 minutes, stirring occasionally, until thickened.

2 Stir in the marjoram and oregano and simmer for 15 minutes. Stir in the basil, salt, and black pepper.

3 Let the sauce cool completely before using on pizzas. Store in an airtight container in the refrigerator for up to 5 days.

Cheese Sauce

Stir this crazy-good and crazy-easy-to-make cheese sauce into cooked pasta for a quick mac 'n' cheese or spoon it over any cooked vegetable.

***MAKES* 2 cups • *TIME* 25 minutes**

1½ tablespoons unsalted butter
1½ tablespoons all-purpose flour
2 cups whole milk
½ pound sharp white cheddar cheese, grated (about 2 cups)
¼ teaspoon kosher salt
1 or 2 turns freshly ground black pepper
1 or 2 gratings of nutmeg
Pinch of cayenne pepper

1 In a medium saucepan over medium heat, melt the butter, then whisk in the flour to make a roux. Cook, whisking constantly, until it turns pale yellow in color, about 5 minutes.

2 Slowly add the milk and cook, whisking constantly, until you have a smooth, medium-thick sauce, about 10 minutes.

3 Add the cheddar and whisk until melted. Whisk in the salt, black pepper, nutmeg, and cayenne. Set aside to cool to room temperature.

Donkey Sauce (Almost world famous)

Use this ev-er-y day, in ev-er-y way. . . .

***MAKES* 1½ cups • *TIME* 10 minutes**

1 cup mayonnaise
¼ cup Roasted Garlic puree (page 298)
1 teaspoon yellow mustard
4 dashes of Worcestershire sauce
¼ teaspoon kosher salt
4 turns freshly ground black pepper

1 In a medium bowl, combine all the ingredients and stir until smooth.

2 Transfer to a container with a tight-fitting lid and store in the refrigerator for up to 6 days.

Basil Oil

This bright green oil doesn't just add a splashy shot of color when swirled on top of dishes like Charred Tomato and Red Bell Pepper Soup (page 146); it also adds intense flavor. Some people strain basil oil after it's blended, but I don't think it's necessary.

MAKES **about 2 cups •** ***TIME*** **30 minutes, plus 15 minutes for chiling**

Kosher salt

2½ cups basil leaves

½ cup flat-leaf parsley

1 cup extra-virgin olive oil

1 teaspoon fresh lemon juice

1 teaspoon kosher salt

4 or 5 turns freshly ground black pepper

1 Bring a large saucepan of water to a boil over medium-high heat. Prepare a large bowl of ice water.

2 Add several pinches of salt to the boiling water, then add the basil and parsley. Boil for about 10 seconds, until wilted. Remove with a strainer and immediately plunge the herbs into the bowl of ice water. Let cool completely, about 20 seconds. Drain the herbs, then lay them on paper towels to dry and remove excess water.

3 Transfer the blanched basil and parsley to a blender. Add the olive oil, lemon juice, salt, and pepper. Blend until completely pureed.

4 Pour into a bowl, cover, and refrigerate for 15 minutes before using.

This lets the froth and foam caused by the blender to settle and leaves a glossy, smooth oil.

5 Store in an airtight container in the refrigerator for 3 to 5 days; longer than that and it'll start to lose its vibrant green color.

Roasted Garlic Butter

This amazing flavored butter is great used lots of ways, but especially spread on sandwich rolls before you toast or grill 'em off. Make sure the butter is completely soft before you mix it up!

MAKES **about 1 cup** • ***TIME*** **1 hour**

½ pound (2 sticks) unsalted butter, at room temperature

2 tablespoons Roasted Garlic (recipe follows)

½ teaspoon kosher salt

3 or 4 turns freshly ground black pepper

1 Mix all the ingredients in a bowl until evenly incorporated.

2 Cover and refrigerate until ready to use. Bring to room temperature before using.

3 Store in the refrigerator for 3 to 5 days.

Roasted Garlic

MAKES **about ¼ cup**

2 garlic heads

2 teaspoons extra-virgin olive oil

½ teaspoon kosher salt

4 or 5 turns freshly ground black pepper

1 Preheat the oven to 350°F.

2 Cut enough off the top of the garlic heads to just expose the garlic cloves. Place them on a sheet of aluminum foil and drizzle with the olive oil. Season with the salt and pepper. Wrap up the foil into a tight pouch. Place on a rimmed baking sheet if desired.

3 Roast until tender and medium brown in color, 35 to 40 minutes. Let cool.

4 Squeeze the pulp from the skins and puree in a food processor.

5 Store in an airtight container in the refrigerator for up to 3 days.

All-Purpose Brine

Here's what you need to lock flavor and moisture into roasted or grilled meats. This is the ultimate brine for pork, lamb, chicken like the Roasted Spatchcock Chickens Three Ways (page 233), and turkey such as the Bacon-Roasted Turkey with Scalloped Potatoes and Caramelized Balsamic Brussels Sprouts (page 101).

MAKES **1 gallon** • ***TIME*** **15 minutes**

- ¼ cup apple cider vinegar
- 1 small yellow onion, sliced into thin wedges
- 4 garlic cloves, smashed
- 6 thyme sprigs
- 6 parsley stems
- ½ teaspoon red chili flakes
- 2 bay leaves
- ¼ cup kosher salt
- 1 teaspoon black peppercorns
- 2 strips lemon peel
- 4 cups ice cubes

1 In a large stockpot, combine 2 quarts cold water, the vinegar, onion, garlic, thyme, parsley, chili flakes, bay leaves, salt, peppercorns, and lemon peel. Heat over medium-high heat, stirring occasionally, until the salt has dissolved, 7 to 8 minutes.

2 Remove from the heat and add 1 quart cold water and the ice. Stir until the ice melts.

3 Store the brine in an airtight container in the refrigerator until needed, up to 1 to 2 days.

All-Purpose Dry Rub

For pork, turkey, chicken, steaks, or lamb, this rub is da bomb as is, or you can use it as a platform to take it in any direction you want. Add instant coffee (as in the Ancho Skirt Steak Hash with Red Pepper Hollandaise on page 271), or a bunch of dried rosemary, or ground chiles for more heat, or dark brown sugar and dried ginger. The possibilities are limited only by your pantry and spice cabinet, and the results will be right on no matter what.

MAKES **1 cup** • ***TIME*** **5 minutes**

3 tablespoons chili powder
3 tablespoons granulated garlic
2 tablespoons paprika
1 tablespoon smoked paprika
1 tablespoon light brown sugar
2 teaspoons dry mustard
2 teaspoons rubbed sage
2 teaspoons dried thyme
1 teaspoon dried oregano
3 tablespoons kosher salt
2 teaspoons freshly ground black pepper

1 In a medium bowl, combine all the ingredients and mix well until evenly incorporated.

2 Store in an airtight container until ready to use.

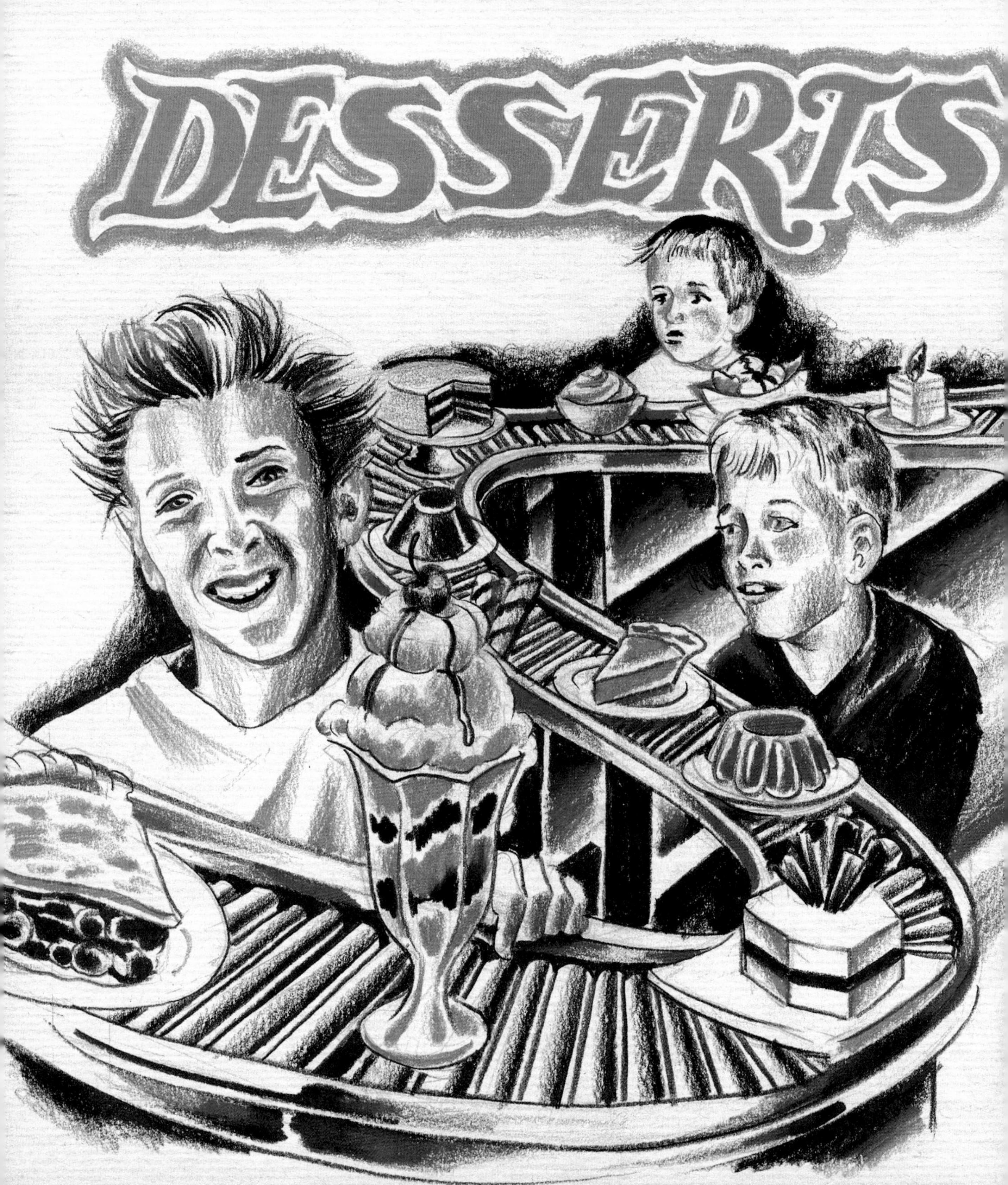
DESSERTS

If They Want It, Make It Worth It

Everybody who knows me well knows that dessert isn't my absolute favorite course. But when you're raising two growing boys, let me tell you, mastering some big-time, go-to desserts can really help get you closer to that Dad of the Year award. I've learned that as much as I love an amazing meal that consists only of a main course and a bunch of sides and salads, there are a few people in my house who are far more likely to clean their plates if they know a kickin' chocolate cake or some ice cream and homemade waffle cones are waiting for them on the other side.

So over the years I've come up with a handful of righteous desserts that even *I* think are awesome.

I've also begun to understand (other) people's love for dessert a little better. I think people craving a sweet

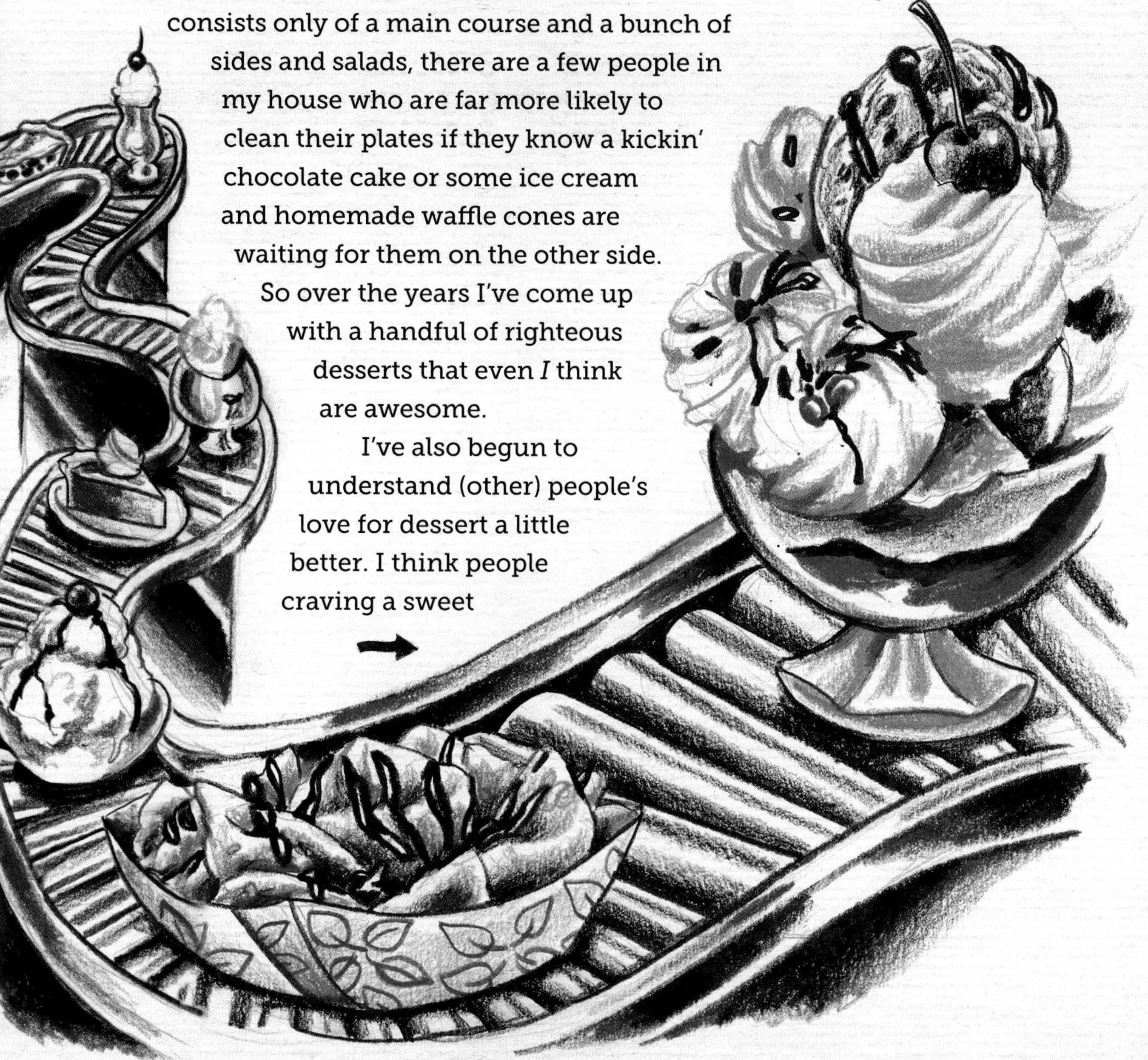

ending to a great meal is kind of like the audience at the end of a righteous concert. Even when everything has come together perfectly and the band has nailed every note, people will still stay rooted to their seats after the last song and they won't leave until the band comes out and plays an encore. In kinda the same way, even when you've cooked a symphony of a dinner, everyone still wants dessert.

So here's my encore—in the form of a few positively killer desserts. 'Cause if you're gonna do it, you've gotta do it right.

Deep-Fried Ice Cream "Boulders"

This all started with my humble beginnings as a dishwasher in a Mexican restaurant. Fried ice cream was always a favorite. . . . Here is my family's recipe.

***MAKES* 4 servings • *TIME* 1 hour, plus up to 48 hours for freezing**

"Boulders"

2 quarts good-quality vanilla ice cream

4 cups cornflakes

½ cup sugar

1 tablespoon ground cinnamon

Pinch of cayenne pepper

4 large eggs

Canola oil, for frying

For serving

2 cups Strawberry Compote (page 308)

1 cup Chocolate Sauce (page 307)

2 cups sweetened whipped cream

2 tablespoons finely grated bar chocolate

1 cup toasted unsweetened coconut flakes

6 to 8 maraschino cherries

¼ cup powdered sugar

1 Scoop the ice cream into 4 large "boulders" (about 5 inches in diameter) and place them on a rimmed baking sheet lined with parchment paper. Freeze overnight until rock hard. (To make perfect round balls without a large scoop, use a large soup ladle to form 8 half-spheres and freeze until almost solid. To make each large ball, press the flat sides of two half-spheres together. Freeze overnight.)

2 Place the cornflakes in a food processer and pulse 7 or 8 times, until you have a mixture of finely crushed flakes with some big pieces remaining. Transfer the cornflakes to a medium bowl and add the sugar, cinnamon, and cayenne. Mix well and set aside.

The smaller pieces will coat and fill the gaps in the coating while the large pieces will give the crunchy texture.

3 Remove the ice cream boulders from the freezer and roll each one in the cornflake mixture, coating the ball evenly and thoroughly. Shake off any excess, then return to the baking sheet and freeze for 1 hour, until firm, reserving the cornflake mixture.

4 In a separate bowl, beat the eggs. Remove the boulders from the freezer and, working with one at a time, dip a boulder into the eggs and then into the cornflakes, lightly pressing the crumb mixture into the ball so it sticks and is evenly and thoroughly coated. Return to the baking sheet and repeat with the remaining boulders. Discard any extra egg or

RECIPE CONTINUES →

RECIPE CONTINUED FROM PAGE 305

The ice cream needs to be completely solid so it doesn't melt when you fry it.

cornflake mixture. Freeze for 2 hours or overnight, depending on how soft the ice cream got during coating.

5 To fry the ice cream, pour canola oil in a large, heavy pot to a depth of 5 inches and heat it over high heat to 400°F on a thermometer.

6 Remove one ice cream ball at a time from the freezer. Place it on a slotted spoon and quickly submerge it in the preheated oil. Fry for 30 to 40 seconds. Immediately place it in a shallow bowl and garnish with strawberry compote, chocolate sauce, whipped cream, grated chocolate, toasted coconut, and 1 or 2 maraschino cherries. Finish with a light dusting of powdered sugar. Serve immediately.

7 Make sure that the oil returns to 400°F before frying the next boulder. Repeat with the remaining boulders and garnishes, serving each one as soon as it is fried and garnished.

Chocolate Sauce

MAKES **about 2 cups**

1 cup heavy cream
1 tablespoon unsalted butter
½ pound semisweet chocolate, coarsely chopped

1 In a medium saucepan over medium heat, heat the cream and butter just until warm. Add the chocolate and continue to heat gently (without simmering), stirring, until the chocolate has melted completely and the mixture is smooth.

2 Unless you're using the sauce right away, remove it from the heat and cool to room temperature. Store in an airtight container in the refrigerator for up to 5 days. To reheat, place the container in a bowl of warm water and stir the sauce occasionally until warmed through.

RECIPE CONTINUES

RECIPE CONTINUED FROM PREVIOUS PAGE

Strawberry Compote

MAKES about 1½ cups

1 pint strawberries, hulled and quartered
3 tablespoons powdered sugar
1 tablespoon fresh lemon juice
½ teaspoon pure vanilla extract

1 In a medium nonreactive saucepan, combine all the ingredients with ¼ cup water. Mix well, then bring to a light simmer over medium heat. Cook for 15 minutes, stirring occasionally, until the sauce has thickened and the berries start to break down.

2 Remove from the heat and puree in a blender until smooth. Let cool to room temperature. Serve.

3 Store in an airtight container in the refrigerator for 3 to 5 days.

Cheesecake Challenge

There's a reason this flies out of the kitchen in every restaurant where we serve it. **Challenge is good, right?** When it comes in the form of a marbled cheesecake studded with chips and pretzels and drizzled with chocolate sauce, the answer is a big-time *yes*.

For a totally outta-sight presentation, serve it a full half-cake at a time, the way we do it at the restaurants (pictured on page 311). Then pass out spoons and let everyone dig in. If you prefer a more down-to-earth presentation, put the whole cheesecake on a cake plate and garnish it with the pretzels, chips, and chocolate sauce.

Nah, I'm not gonna make you guess: We serve up this particular challenge at Guy's Vegas Kitchen and Bar (where it was born), Guy Fieri's Chophouse in Atlantic City, Guy's Baltimore Kitchen and Bar, Guy's Mt. Pocono Kitchen, and Guy Fieri's American Kitchen and Bar: Cancun.

MAKES **4 to 6 servings •** ***TIME*** **1½ hours, plus 4 hours for cooling**

Graham cracker crust

1½ cups graham cracker pieces (about ½ inch each)

½ cup sugar

6 tablespoons (¾ stick) unsalted butter, melted

½ teaspoon ground cinnamon

Cheesecake

2 pounds cream cheese (four 8-ounce packages), at room temperature

¾ cup sugar

1½ teaspoons all-purpose flour

1 teaspoon pure vanilla extract

4 large eggs

¾ cup sour cream

1 cup Chocolate Sauce (page 307)

1 cup small hard sourdough salted pretzels, for garnish

1 cup salted ruffled potato chips, for garnish

1 To prepare the graham cracker crust, place all the ingredients in a food processor. Pulse until well combined. Transfer the crumb mixture to a 10-inch nonstick springform pan. Using your fingers, press the crumbs evenly into the base of the pan and ¼ inch up the sides. Use a flat-bottomed glass to press the crumb mixture firmly and pack it tightly. Set aside.

2 Preheat the oven to 325°F.

3 To prepare the cheesecake, in the bowl of a stand mixer fitted with the paddle attachment, combine the cream cheese, sugar, flour, and vanilla. Cream the mixture on medium speed until it is smooth and lump free, stopping occasionally to scrape down the sides, 5 to 6 minutes.

4 Reduce the speed to low and add the eggs one at a time, completely incorporating each one before adding the next. Add the sour cream and mix until just incorporated and smooth, 1 to 2 minutes.

5 Pour the batter over the crumb base and gently tap the pan on a flat surface to remove any air bubbles and smooth out the top. Using a spoon

RECIPE CONTINUES →

RECIPE CONTINUED FROM PREVIOUS PAGE

or fine-tipped pastry bag, evenly drizzle 3 tablespoons of the chocolate sauce in a thin stream over the whole surface of the cheesecake batter. Drag the tip of a long skewer through the chocolate sauce to swirl it into the cheesecake batter in a marble-patterned design.

6 Wrap the bottom of the pan in a large sheet of heavy aluminum foil (to form a water seal) and place the pan in a large, deep baking dish, such as a lasagna pan. Pour 1 inch of water into the baking dish, taking care not to get any within the foil or in the springform pan.

7 Bake until the cheesecake is just firm and the outside has just turned a very light brown, 40 to 45 minutes. Remove the pan from the water bath and set aside to cool for 30 minutes. Refrigerate the cheesecake for about 3½ hours to set up.

8 When ready to serve, carefully release the spring and remove the pan ring. Dip a sharp knife in hot water and cut the cheesecake in half.

9 Cut a sliver off the outer edge of one half, just off center. Stand the cheesecake half upright on a serving plate on the flat side you just cut off. Repeat with the other half, and place it on the same or a different serving plate. Garnish by sticking pretzels and potato chips into the cheesecake slice and drizzle it liberally with the remaining chocolate sauce.

Straight outta Vegas, baby.

Chocolate Whiskey 7-Layer Cake

Sure, a cake with two or three layers is nice, but **a totally kickin' cake will reach seven layers high.** The best part about this cake—for the kids passing through the kitchen—is that one domed layer doesn't get used in the final stack. Just set it out on the counter and it'll be gone before you're done stacking and frosting this baby.

In case you're curious, most of the alcohol in the cake cooks off. The whiskey in the anglaise sauce is not cooked, but it can be replaced with 1 teaspoon pure vanilla extract if desired.

MAKES **10 to 12 servings** • ***TIME*** **2 hours**

Chocolate fudge frosting

½ pound (2 sticks) unsalted butter, cubed

10 ounces dark chocolate, chopped

¼ cup dark cocoa powder

8 cups powdered sugar

1 cup half-and-half

1 tablespoon pure vanilla extract

Pinch of sea salt

Chocolate cakes

Vegetable cooking spray, for the pans

2 cups sugar

2 cups all-purpose flour

1½ cups dark cocoa powder

1 tablespoon baking powder

2 teaspoons baking soda

½ teaspoon kosher salt

1⅓ cups whole milk

4 large eggs

1 To make the frosting, combine the butter and chocolate in a small, heavy-bottomed saucepan. Stir constantly over low heat until the mixture is completely melted, 4 to 5 minutes. Remove from the heat and let cool for 5 minutes.

2 In a large bowl, combine the cocoa, powdered sugar, half-and-half, vanilla, and salt. Using a hand mixer on medium speed, beat until smooth.

3 Increase the speed to medium-high and gradually pour in the melted chocolate mixture in a slow, steady stream. Whip until the frosting is light and fluffy, 4 to 5 minutes. Set aside. (The frosting can be made 2 to 3 days in advance. Store in an airtight container in the refrigerator. When ready to use, set out until it returns to room temperature, then beat with a hand mixer until fluffy.)

4 To make the cakes, arrange two oven racks in the bottom third and middle of the oven and preheat the oven to 325°F. Line the bottoms of four 8-inch nonstick round cake pans with parchment paper. Spray the pans and the parchment paper with vegetable cooking spray.

RECIPE CONTINUES 

RECIPE CONTINUED FROM PREVIOUS PAGE

1½ tablespoons pure vanilla extract

¼ pound (1 stick) unsalted butter

1¼ cups hot tap water

Whiskey anglaise

2 cups whole milk

½ cup sugar

Pinch of kosher salt

6 large egg yolks

¼ cup whiskey, such as Jack Daniel's

Chocolate ganache

1 pound dark chocolate, chopped

1 cup heavy cream

2 tablespoons unsalted butter

½ cup whiskey (I prefer Jack Daniel's)

5 In a large bowl, whisk the sugar, flour, cocoa powder, baking powder, baking soda, and salt. In a medium bowl, whisk the milk, eggs, and vanilla. In a saucepan over medium-low heat or in a small bowl in the microwave, melt the butter with the hot water.

6 Add half of the milk mixture to the dry ingredients and beat using a hand mixer on low speed. Beat in half of the butter mixture, then scrape down the bowl. Beat in the remaining milk mixture and then the rest of the butter mixture. Pour the batter evenly among the prepared pans.

7 Place two pans on each of the oven racks and bake until the cakes are springy to the touch, 25 to 30 minutes, rotating the pans halfway through baking. Let the cake layers cool in the pans for 10 minutes, then turn them out onto a rack to cool completely. Peel off the parchment paper.

8 To make the whiskey anglaise, set a medium bowl over a large bowl filled with ice. Place a fine-mesh strainer over the medium bowl.

9 In a medium, heavy-bottomed saucepan, combine the milk, sugar, and salt. Set the pan over medium heat and whisk constantly while gently warming the mixture until scalding; do not boil.

10 Beat the egg yolks in a large bowl. Pour the warmed milk over the eggs while whisking constantly. Pour the egg-milk mixture back into the pan. Cook over medium heat, stirring constantly, until the mixture is thick enough to coat the back of a spatula. Remove from the heat and immediately pour through the strainer into the chilled bowl. Stir in the whiskey. Let stand in the bowl of ice until completely cool, stirring often. Cover and refrigerate until needed.

11 To make the ganache, place the top of a double boiler over simmering water. Add the chocolate, cream, and butter and stir until smooth and warm. Remove from the heat and set aside at room temperature, or for longer storage, refrigerate in an airtight container for up to 1 day.

12 To assemble the cake, cut each cake layer in half through the equator to make 8 thinner layers. (You'll only use 7 of them; set out the top, domed layer of one of the cakes for the crew passing through—they'll eat it!) Lightly brush the cut sides of the 7 cake layers with the whiskey.

13 Place one layer cut side up on a large round cake plate. Spoon ¾ cup of the frosting on top and smooth it to the edge with a pastry knife. Repeat with 5 more cake layers, placing two of the domed layers dome side down. Use the remaining domed layer for the top, placing it right side up. Do not frost the top layer.

14 If necessary, gently warm the ganache in a double boiler. Pour the warm chocolate ganache over the top of the cake. Spread it evenly over the top with a spatula. Let the cake stand for 15 minutes before serving. (The cake will keep for 2 to 3 days . . . if it lasts that long!) Slice and serve with the whiskey anglaise on the side.

Homemade Waffle Cones

The next time the kids are clamoring for ice cream cones and expecting the usual, **blow them away with these monster homemade cones.** You'll need a waffle cone maker and cone roller and these take a little work, but the kind of happiness they bring makes it well worth it.

***MAKES* 8 to 10 waffle cones • *TIME* 35 minutes**

- 3/4 cup all-purpose flour
- 1/2 teaspoon ground cinnamon
- 1/2 teaspoon kosher salt
- 2 large eggs
- 1 large egg white
- 3/4 cup sugar
- 5 tablespoons unsalted butter, melted
- 6 tablespoons whole milk

1 Preheat a waffle cone maker to medium-high (or follow the manufacturer's directions).

2 In a medium bowl, sift together the flour, cinnamon, and salt. In a large bowl, whisk the eggs, egg white, and sugar until light and fluffy, 2 to 3 minutes. Add the flour mixture to the egg mixture and whisk until well incorporated. Add the butter and milk and stir until combined.

3 To make each cone, pour 1/4 cup of the waffle batter onto the waffle cone maker. Using an offset spatula, evenly spread the batter over the surface. Close the lid and cook for 1 minute, then check for doneness; it should be deep golden brown and crispy around the edges.

Just as with pancakes, sometimes the first one will be patchy in color.

4 Remove the cooked waffle from the waffle cone maker and immediately shape it around a cone roller, squeezing the end tightly until it's firmly sealed. Let the cone rest for 5 to 10 seconds to cool and firm up. Remove from the cone roller and place on a wire rack until completely cool and nice and crispy.

5 Serve with your favorite scoops of ice cream piled high!

Note: These are best eaten soon after they are made, but they can be stored in an airtight container at room temperature for 1 day.

One of my favorite pictures in this book.

Flambéed Crepes
with Grand Marnier Caramel Sauce

Sweet crepes are bathed in a butter and Grand Marnier sauce and then set on fire to burn off the alcohol, leaving in its wake a velvety orange sauce and tender crepes. Dessert . . . *Life* doesn't get much better than this.

MAKES **4 to 6 servings** • ***TIME*** **1 hour**

Crepes

1 cup all-purpose flour

2½ tablespoons granulated sugar

1¼ cups whole milk

2 large eggs

6 tablespoons (¾ stick) unsalted butter, melted

1 teaspoon pure vanilla extract

1 orange

Flambé

¼ pound (1 stick) unsalted butter, at room temperature

¼ cup Grand Marnier

¼ cup sugar

Powdered sugar, for garnish

1 To make the crepe batter, in a large bowl, whisk the flour, sugar, milk, eggs, 3 tablespoons of the melted butter, and the vanilla until there are no lumps, 1 to 2 minutes. Cover and refrigerate for 1 hour.

2 Brush a small nonstick pan with some of the remaining melted butter and heat over medium-low heat. Ladle 2 tablespoons of the batter into the center of the pan and swirl to spread out the batter evenly. Cook for 30 seconds, then flip the crepe with a spatula and cook for 10 more seconds. Remove the crepe from the pan and place on a plate to cool. Repeat with the remaining batter and melted butter (you should make about 10 crepes in all). Fold the crepes into triangles (in half to make a half-moon and then in thirds) and set aside.

3 Finely grate the zest from the orange and set it aside. Use a sharp, thin-bladed knife to cut just enough of the top and bottom off the orange to expose the flesh. Set the orange cut side down on a cutting board and slice off the remaining peel and pith, following the curve of the fruit with the knife. Hold the peeled fruit over a small bowl to catch any juice, cut the segments away from the thin membranes holding them together, and let them fall into the bowl. Discard the membrane, peel, and pith. Set the supremes aside.

These are called "supremes" in professional kitchens, and they are supremely fun to eat.

RECIPE CONTINUES

RECIPE CONTINUED FROM PREVIOUS PAGE

4 To flambé the crepes, place the unmelted butter in a large nonstick pan. Cook over medium heat until the butter starts to foam. Away from the flame, add the Grand Marnier, the reserved orange zest, and the sugar. Place the crepe triangles in the sauce in the pan, arranging them evenly in a flat layer. Return the pan to the heat and ignite the alcohol with a stick lighter or the edge of the burner flame. Let the flame continue to burn until the alcohol burns off.

5 Using tongs, carefully turn the crepes in the sauce to coat, then remove them from the pan and layer them on a serving plate in a shingle pattern. Place the reserved orange supremes in the pan and toss to coat in the sauce and warm through, about 1 minute. Spoon some of the sauce and supremes over the top of the crepes. Dust with powdered sugar and serve with extra sauce on the side.

Cinnamon Churros
with Mexican Spiced Chocolate Sauce

Many of us have seen the premade, perfectly formed, previously frozen churros at the gas station . . . Well, these aren't that. *These* churros are inspired by the ones right off the streets of Barra de Navidad, Mexico.

MAKES **4 to 6 servings** • ***TIME*** **1 hour**

Spiced chocolate sauce

Two 2.7-ounce disks Mexican chocolate, chopped

3/4 cup heavy cream

1 teaspoon ancho chile powder

Pinch of kosher salt

Cinnamon sugar

1 tablespoon ground cinnamon

1 cup sugar

Churros

Canola oil, for frying

3 tablespoons unsalted butter

2 tablespoons sugar

1/4 teaspoon kosher salt

1 cup all-purpose flour

3 eggs

1/2 teaspoon ground cinnamon

1 To make the chocolate sauce, fill the bottom of a double boiler with a couple inches of water and set it over medium-low heat. Add the chocolate to the top of the double boiler (or a bowl that fits over the pan) and let it melt gently, 5 to 6 minutes, stirring occasionally with a rubber spatula and taking care not to scorch it. Remove the chocolate from the heat and stir in the cream, ancho powder, and salt. Stir until the sauce is smooth, 1 to 2 minutes. Set aside.

2 To make the cinnamon sugar, combine the cinnamon and sugar in a small bowl and mix well. Set aside.

3 Pour canola oil into a large, heavy pot to a depth of 3 inches and heat it over high heat to 350°F. Line a rimmed baking sheet or platter with paper towels.

4 Meanwhile, to prepare the churro batter, in a heavy-bottomed saucepan, combine 1 cup water, the butter, sugar, and salt. Set the pan over medium heat and heat the mixture gently. When the liquid reaches 155°F, dump in all of the flour at once. Stir vigorously with a wooden spoon, beating the batter against the side of the pot with the spoon for about 1 minute to incorporate it and remove any lumps.

5 Remove the pan from the heat. Add the eggs to the batter one at a time, beating with the wooden spoon after each addition until fully incorporated.

RECIPE CONTINUES 

RECIPE CONTINUED FROM PREVIOUS PAGE

Add the cinnamon and continue to beat until the batter is tight and smooth, 5 to 7 minutes. Spoon the batter into a 1-gallon resealable plastic bag or plastic pastry bag and cut off one tip to create a ½-inch hole.

6 To fry, carefully pipe 6-inch strips directly into the preheated oil, taking care not to overcrowd the pot. Fry the churros until golden brown and crispy, 3 to 4 minutes, turning occasionally with tongs or a slotted spoon to cook evenly. Remove with a slotted spoon and set on the prepared baking sheet to drain. Repeat with the remaining batter.

7 While still hot, dust the churros with the cinnamon sugar. Place them on a large serving platter and serve with the Mexican spiced chocolate sauce on the side.

You can get the "churro" at the Burro.

Universal Conversion Chart

Oven temperature equivalents

250°F = 120°C

275°F = 135°C

300°F = 150°C

325°F = 160°C

350°F = 180°C

375°F = 190°C

400°F = 200°C

425°F = 220°C

450°F = 230°C

475°F = 240°C

500°F = 260°C

Measurement equivalents

Measurements should always be level unless directed otherwise.

1/8 teaspoon = 0.5 mL

1/4 teaspoon = 1 mL

1/2 teaspoon = 2 mL

1 teaspoon = 5 mL

1 tablespoon = 3 teaspoons = 1/2 fluid ounce = 15 mL

2 tablespoons = 1/8 cup = 1 fluid ounce = 30 mL

4 tablespoons = 1/4 cup = 2 fluid ounces = 60 mL

5 1/3 tablespoons = 1/3 cup = 3 fluid ounces = 80 mL

8 tablespoons = 1/2 cup = 4 fluid ounces = 120 mL

10 2/3 tablespoons = 2/3 cup = 5 fluid ounces = 160 mL

12 tablespoons = 3/4 cup = 6 fluid ounces = 180 mL

16 tablespoons = 1 cup = 8 fluid ounces = 240 mL

Guy Thanks

My family: Lori, Hunter, Jules, Ryder, Morgan, Jim, Penny, Bob, Donna. The Langermeier, Price, Cowan, Apel, Bowers, Barrett, Nelson, Garibaldi, Cline, Fieri, Brisson, and Ferry families. Anthony Hoy Fong, Reid Strathearn, Becca Pariser, Marah Stets, Aubrie Pick, Joe Leonard, the Krew, WME, William Morrow, Ron Wargo, James Burleson, James Elliot, Riley Lagesen, Food Network, The Brooks Group, the *Guy's Big Bite* crew, the *DDD* crew, the *GGG* crew, Carnival Cruise Lines, Caesars Entertainment, the Cordish Companies, Legends, Foxwoods, Mera Corp, Big Night Entertainment, Momentum and the teams at Guy's Vegas, El Burro Borrachos, Guy's Baltimore, Guy's Mt. Pocono, Guy's Chophouse, Guy's Foxwoods, Guy's Cancun, Guy's Playa del Carmen, Guy's Bar-B-Que Joints, Guy's Burger Joints, Guy's Smokehouse and Pig & Anchor, Miller Lite, Davis Family Vineyards, Golden West Meats/Completely Fresh Foods, Lifetime Brands, Gia Brands, Single Cup Coffee, Myers Restaurant Supply, Chefworks, Cartronics, Chevrolet, Polaris, NYCWFF, SBWFF, PBFW, Jimmy John's, UNLV, Best Buddies, and Cooking With Kids.

Index

Page references in *italics* indicate photographs.

C

Q

R

S

KNUCKLE
SANDWICH